Changing F

Jeremy Martineau was, until his recent retirement, National Rural Officer of the Church of England, and served as Secretary to the Archbishops' Commission on Rural Areas, which produced *Faith in the Countryside*. He is Honorary Research Fellow with the Welsh National Centre for Religious Education.

Leslie J. Francis is Professor of Practical Theology at the University of Wales, Bangor, and Director of the Welsh National Centre for Religious Education.

Peter Francis is Warden of St Deiniol's Library, Hawarden.

Changing Rural Life

a Christian response to key rural issues

edited by
Jeremy Martineau
Leslie J. Francis
and
Peter Francis

CANTERBURY
PRESS
Norwich

© Jeremy Martineau, Leslie J. Francis and Peter Francis 2004

First published in 2004 by the Canterbury Press Norwich
(a publishing imprint of Hymns Ancient & Modern Limited,
a registered charity)
St Mary's Works, St Mary's Plain,
Norwich, Norfolk, NR3 3BH

www.scm-canterburypress.co.uk

British Library Cataloguing in Publication data

A catalogue record for this book is available
from the British Library

ISBN 1-85311-599-1

Typeset by Regent Typesetting, London
Printed and bound by
William Clowes Ltd

Contents

Foreword

DAVID R. EMISON

This study of 'rural theology and countryside issues' is both timely and welcome.

Rural issues are higher on the popular and political agendas than they have been for many years. A number of factors contribute to this heightened interest. For those living in the urban and suburban areas of Britain hunting is perhaps the most emotive issue, but not far behind are concerns about the planting of genetically modified crops, the guarantee of safe yet cheap food, accessibility to the countryside and farm animal welfare. The emergence of fair trade goods on the shelves of the supermarket is contributing to an increased awareness of the economic plight of primary food producers around the globe.

Within rural areas, the competing claims of agricultural production and landscape management, the growth of part-time farming, the increasing numbers of people migrating into the countryside, the flight of younger people from the land, and an ageing rural community all contribute to a real sense of crisis. This is sharpened when seen within the current context of depressed farm incomes, a low wage economy, soaring house prices, the lack of affordable housing and the long shadow of the Bovine Spongiform Encephalopathy and Foot and Mouth Disease epidemics.

Countless studies and government policy-papers are under discussion. Diverse agencies, both statutory and voluntary, co-operate and sometimes compete to address rural issues. Strategies for rural regeneration abound and millions of pounds are being poured into the rural economy.

In the latter part of the twentieth century the Archbishops' Commission on Rural Areas (1990), involving representatives from a number of Christian denominations, produced its highly acclaimed and influential report, *Faith in the Countryside*. The report recognized that the identity of rural communities was changing and that the churches had an important role in building and sustaining community.

This task is no less important now at the beginning of the twenty-first century but the rural Church also finds itself in crisis. While the Church is still to be found at the heart of most rural communities, congregations are both declining in numbers and increasing in age. Church budgets are soaring and the task of providing ordained rural ministry is becoming more and more challenging.

These studies identify the challenges faced by both Church and society. They demonstrate the ability of the Church to provide a framework of understanding and meaning to support individuals and communities in times of crisis and rapid change. They challenge the Christian community in Britain to understand more deeply, to respond more effectively and, above all else, to grasp the challenge of maintaining an effective Christian presence and exercising an effective ministry in rural areas.

David R. Emison

April 2004

REFERENCE

Archbishops' Commission on Rural Areas (1990), *Faith in the Countryside*, Worthing, Churchman Publishing.

Preface

The Centre for Studies in Rural Ministry was established as a collaborative venture between the Arthur Rank Centre, St Deiniol's Library, Hawarden and University of Wales, Bangor. We were delighted when so many Anglican bishops from England, Ireland, Scotland, and Wales accepted our invitation to contribute to a symposium held at St Deiniol's Library and then after the symposium to shape their contribution for this volume.

In addition to the thirteen bishops who drafted material for discussion at the symposium, the Bishops of Peterborough, Repton and Basingstoke, Dr Jill Hopkinson and Mr John Marks came as discussants to help critique and shape the contributions. The Archbishop of Canterbury contributed to the debate and focused the key theological issues emerging from the discussion. We are now pleased to offer the fruits of this process to a wider readership. The bishops of the Anglican Church in England, Ireland, Scotland and Wales are clearly well informed about and passionately concerned for all that is at stake in the countryside today.

From its outset the Centre for Studies in Rural Ministry was conceived as a fully ecumenical initiative. We are grateful to David R. Emison, Chair of the Cumbria Methodist District, for engaging in this exercise with us and for writing the foreword.

Behind the scenes a number of colleagues have worked with us in shaping this venture. We record our gratitude to Diane Drayson, Mandy Robbins and Susan Thomas who have worked with us on the manuscript, and to the staff of St Deiniol's Library who ensured that the symposium was so sensitively and effectively hosted.

Jeremy Martineau
Leslie J. Francis
Peter Francis

April 2004

The Contributors

Bruce Cameron, Bishop of Aberdeen and Orkney, Primus of the
  Scottish Episcopal Church
Richard Clarke, Bishop of Meath and Kildare
John S. Davies, Bishop of St Asaph
David R. Emison, Chair of the Cumbria Methodist District
Graham R. James, Bishop of Norwich
James Jones, Bishop of Liverpool
Michael L. Langrish, Bishop of Exeter
John Oliver, Bishop of Hereford
Alastair L. J. Redfern, Bishop of Grantham
Anthony J. Russell, Bishop of Ely
John C. Saxbee, Bishop of Lincoln
Alan Smith, Bishop of Shrewsbury
David S. Walker, Bishop of Dudley
John S. Went, Bishop of Tewkesbury
Rowan Williams, Archbishop of Canterbury

Introduction

JEREMY MARTINEAU

This book, by leading Anglican bishops in Britain and Ireland, joins a small but growing literature in which the Christian Church in these islands focuses on rural concerns. While it is addressed primarily to the four nations of the British Isles, urban and rural, secular and religious, policy-makers and those for whom policy is made, the principles examined will resonate throughout the world. While the bishops are writing from the Anglican tradition, we believe that what has been written here will be welcomed as a contribution that all Christians would endorse.

Ever since the industrial revolution of the eighteenth and nineteenth centuries the changes to the once pastoral and agricultural countryside have been the subject of concern, with a generally muted response from government. The myth of the unchanging countryside providing a haven for seekers after peace and beauty is well mirrored in art and poetry, as well as in the characters who have preached and prayed in rural churches and country chapels.

Maybe it was the loss of men from towns and villages across the nation in the Great War of 1914–18 that forced the change in the pastoral scene most suddenly. Or was it the depression of the 1930s, or the near starvation of the 1939–45 war, or the advent of cheap and popular motoring in the 1950s, or the introduction of the Common Agricultural Policy in the 1960s, or the increase in global tourism, or the health scares of BSE or Foot and Mouth Disease, or the use of digital telecommunications in the first decade of this century? The response of the Anglican Church has been to maintain its fundamental structure expressed in the commitment to the parish as the basic building block for impacting on the lives of people.

The report of the Archbishops' Commission on Rural Areas (1990), *Faith in the Countryside*, examined the fundamentals affecting the rural economy, the rural environment and the rural community, as well as the dynamic of the Church in rural areas. This was the first time the Church of England had shown so much interest in what was happening in rural England, although it must be noted that no funds were voted by General Synod to this task, for the attention of that body was still predominantly on internal church matters and the difficulties being experienced in urban priority areas. One recommendation of that report was that the Church of England should have a full-time national rural officer based within the Arthur Rank Centre at Stoneleigh Park, Warwickshire, the home of the Royal Agricultural Society of England. The Arthur Rank Centre is a partnership between the Royal Agriculture Society of England, the Rank Foundation and the churches working in rural England (Arthur Rank Centre, 2004).

The growth in interest in the challenges to and contribution by rural areas is reflected in the work of Rural Community Councils, the Arthur Rank Centre and a growing number of academic institutions as well as government. One university in particular, the University of Wales, Bangor, has done much to study aspects of the work of the rural Church. In partnership with the Arthur Rank Centre and St Deiniol's Library, Hawarden, the University of Wales, Bangor, has stimulated the establishment of the Centre for Studies in Rural Ministry. The three editors of this volume represent these three institutions.

The Conservative Government of the 1980s and 1990s, which might have assumed that the rural area was its heartland, was replaced in 1997 by a Labour Government, which claims over 160 Members of Parliament in rural constituencies. It could be said that Labour was surprised to win the 1997 election and had given little thought to rural policy.

One response to the Foot and Mouth Disease in 2001 was the creation of a Rural Task Force by the then newly formed Department for Environment, Food and Rural Affairs, on which the churches had an active place. Pioneering work was undertaken by the Arthur Rank Centre in establishing a national relief fund for rural businesses affected by Foot and Mouth Disease (the ARC-Addington Fund) through which public donations matched by government channelled over £10 million in a model of efficiency and speed to over 22,000 beneficiaries. The success of this operation, widely admired by government and leaders in rural areas was due, in part, to the structural links between a light-weight national body with the local church system, present in every community and with about 250 dedicated people in the areas of most need. The government system, applying hugely greater resources, in contrast, seemed tortuously slow and bureaucratic.

Having removed the Minister for Agriculture's Cabinet rank and created the Department for Environment, Food and Rural Affairs, government then merged the Countryside Commission and the Rural Development Commission (founded in 1908) into the Countryside Agency. In turn it reduced its range of powers in 2004 so that the overlap of responsibilities between the government department and its own agency was removed. DEFRA's 'Rural Strategy 2004' will result in further dissolution of the rural focus of government agencies. The Regional Development Agencies, now responsible for service delivery, have neither a good record of heeding rural needs, nor of recognizing the vital role of social policies alongside their economic responsibilities. The devolution of rural responsibility to regional systems will not of itself ensure a proper attention to the issues affecting rural areas that are well understood by rural organizations. At present there is no clear mechanism by which their voice will be heard for there has been so much emphasis on the needs of poor urban areas. Although this imbalance had begun to be addressed, rural areas will continue to feel they matter less in a predominantly urban society. The move to regionalization, however welcome, is a fundamental change with huge risks as well as benefits. Rural people need convincing that their concerns will be heard, acted on and responsive policies adequately resourced.

The Rural Affairs Forum, that was established as successor to the Rural Task Force, provided a means, with its several subgroups focused on different themes, for government to listen to and hopefully to hear the voice of rural organizations including Churches Together in England. The abrupt ending of this Forum leaves rural people feeling that their voice will once again be drowned out by more strident urban voices. For the voluntary and community sector to mount the necessary campaign in every region rather than once at a national level puts an unbearable strain on slender resources, both of finance and of key personnel.

The choice of themes for the chapters of this book is the responsibility of the editors alone. Whereas the increasing number of pressure groups with an active interest in rural policy have identified a large

number of high-priority themes, the editors took the view that some of
these themes are fundamental and cross-cutting, with an impact on the
second tier of issues that are being considered by a wide range of organizations and pressure groups. We believe that the treatment in these
chapters will illuminate thinking and practice by everyone engaged in
rural issues for the benefit of rural and urban people alike.

Some themes have an application wider than rural affairs alone. For
example, the potential conflict between private ownership and public
good, an issue not addressed in *Faith in the Countryside* (Archbishops'
Commission on Rural Areas, 1990), suggests how solutions can be
found when they require a change of ownership of a particular asset,
such as land. The attitude of urban people to rural areas is to see them
as places for retreat from the hardness of urban life or work. How
urban people use rural areas has a major impact on what life choices
rural people have. The quality of life in rural communities is an important plank in government policy and it is still not sufficiently recognized that the local churches in rural communities provide part of the
glue that holds people together. The recognition of the contribution
that church buildings can make is welcome, both through tourism (for
instance through the work of the Church Tourism Association and the
Hidden Britain Centre Project) and through provision of space for
community activity (as in the Rural Churches in Community Service).
However, much work remains to be done on the contribution of
people of faith to the social capital that is the subject of so much writing at the present time. Regret at the lack of acknowledgement of the
role of rural churches comes through in at least two chapters, namely
Dynamics of Communities and Parish Governance. The writer of this
latter chapter, being a board member of the Countryside Agency, is
well placed to observe the way policy is shaped without recognition
of one of the main players in rural community life. All local churches
are urged to see the necessity of learning to work in partnership with
other community organizations. The responsibility for this lies with
churches themselves but also in the remainder of the voluntary and
community sector. There may be a tendency either to take the local
church for granted, or to see it with suspicious eyes as being a closed
club. The local church has much to do to change these negative
attitudes.

Rural areas remain, at least to outside eyes, predominantly about
food and farming. Two chapters look at the way these themes are

rapidly changing shape, driven by global forces, the theme of another chapter. The future of the most remote communities is a challenge to those who wish to measure everything by how much it costs. An answer might be, 'How much is it worth?' The contribution from a remote part of Scotland merits serious consideration, for many parts of the UK may have a difficult economic future as the structural funds which help to sustain these areas move to the new members of the European Union.

Does the experience of more than 1,000 years of the Christian Church serving rural areas and contributing to social capital there have anything unique to offer? The following chapters reveal something of this contribution, from an understanding of Scripture, from an Anglican commitment to place and a recognition that the people themselves are making the greatest contribution of all to sustaining rural society.

These essays from thirteen of the Anglican bishops in Britain and Ireland are designed to stimulate further thinking about underlying principles and issues which can help when doing the hard work of devising policy. We offer our text to the people of Britain and Ireland in the expectation that they will not turn their back on the Church which continues to serve them in good times and in bad.

REFERENCES

Archbishops' Commission on Rural Areas (1990), *Faith in the Countryside*, Worthing, Churchman Publishing.

Arthur Rank Centre (2003), *Arthur Rank Centre 2003 Review*, Stoneleigh Park, Warwickshire.

Department for Environment, Food and Rural Affairs (2004), *Rural Strategy 2004*.

Department of Environment, Transport and the Regions (2000), *Our Countryside: The Future, A Fair Deal for Rural England*, London, Stationery Office.

1. A Country Retreat

JOHN C. SAXBEE

Summary

This chapter will explore ways in which the countryside has been accessed by otherwise or erstwhile urban dwellers, as an environment to which retreat can be made in the interests of spiritual growth and refreshment. It will suggest some of the reasons why people with a predominantly urban background choose to live in the countryside, or visit on a regular basis. The impact of these migrations, both on the countryside they access and on the migrants themselves, will be featured together with theological reflections on this urban–rural interchange, in relation to spirituality and the social context of religion.

In Retreat

Retreat might be described as withdrawal with intent to return. Following news of the death of John the Baptist, Jesus withdrew to the countryside, but his compassionate response to the needs of those who came in search of him indicates that he had no intention of abandoning them. The Gospels suggest that Jesus regularly withdrew in this way for spiritual and physical refreshment, and that he found remote and relatively isolated places to be most suited to his needs. Not merely escaping from the town, Jesus was also intent upon benefiting from spiritual refreshment afforded by a rural retreat.

Nowadays people continue to feel the need for such solace and solitude as they can obtain from a rural retreat, and if they come from urban or suburban backgrounds it is likely that they will intend to return to the city on at least an occasional basis. But retreat to the countryside can be for different reasons and take various forms, including the following five examples.

First, retreat to the countryside may attract those looking for a congenial place to live when not at work. This effectively describes commuters who can now undertake round trips of up to 200 miles per day from their homes in the country to city-based jobs. At least one London underground driver lives near Boston, Lincolnshire, and the number of people choosing this option is one reason why the Lincolnshire town of Sleaford is one of the fastest growing towns in Europe. Better quality of life and educational opportunities are commonly cited as reasons for choosing to commute in this way, with high city wages and relatively low rural house prices more than compensating for the cost of travel. As a result, rural house prices in many parts of the country are rising very quickly, but not so fast as to deter this tendency in the near future.

Second, retreat to the countryside may attract those looking for a congenial place to live before they die. Retired people feature prominently in the demography of rural areas, and their influence can significantly affect the socio-economic profile of rural communities. Although no longer linked to the city for employment purposes, those who retire to the country are inclined to retain links with urban family and friends, and are often away from home. Perhaps this group can be divided between those who permanently reside in their country home, and those who might be described as commuters, but for leisure and social purposes rather than in relation to employment. For some, the attraction of retiring to the countryside from the city is that death might be postponed by such a move; after all, Jesus lived in the countryside but died in the city. Of course, this psychology is often characterized by a heavy dose of irony, because in the countryside death is statistically more likely on the roads, and the occasional carcass in the field can be a salutary reminder of our own mortality. Sadly, for far too many people, retirement to the country soon goes sour when a partner dies, and the survivor's sense of being isolated in a remote location simply compounds the bereavement. Here it is worth noting that, as Timothy Gorringe observes:

There is . . . a deep ambivalence toward the city in the Christian tradition . . . On the one hand the city is understood as a focus of violence and human hubris . . . On the other hand the city is the model of what will finally be redeemed, the paradigm of the human home and the focus of human creativity. (Gorringe, 2002: 140)

Furthermore, Christianity began as a mainly urban movement, and for much of its history the countryside has been pagan, a word derived from the Latin for countryside.

Third, for others, the countryside is not seen as *the* place to live but rather as another place to live. They acquire a second home in a rural area, and they will often refer to this as their 'country retreat'. The hurly-burly of day-to-day routine is left behind, and the place in the country takes on an almost spiritual significance, with notions such as renewal and re-creation coming to the fore. The effect of high rates of second home ownership, with occasional and irregular patterns of occupancy, has an inevitable impact on some rural communities. In some places, to talk about 'community' at all is to do so in only a very casual and attenuated sense. Traditional understandings of what it means to 'belong' are stretched to the limit, and for organizations requiring active involvement such as churches, the impact of occasional occupancy can be very significant. Of course, when people so clearly divide their lives into urban–secular and rural–spiritual, there is a reinforcement of stereotyping which can only make it more difficult to promote interdependence between town and country. As we shall see, there is a degree of collusion with idealized fantasies about rurality, which makes the reality hard to believe, let alone to bear.

Fourth, while for most people a second home is not an option, nonetheless they share the same sense of the countryside as a recreational retreat from urban living, if only for two weeks in a year or for the occasional weekend. They are the tourists who are increasingly courted by rural councils to bolster the local economy and to support local amenities which might otherwise prove unsustainable. Sometimes the physical impact of holiday-makers can be extreme, with caravan parks and congested roads threatening the very peace and tranquility which these holiday-makers have travelled so far to enjoy. Yet the feeling among such people of being in some sense on retreat is often very moving, and their spiritual sensitivities are touchingly articulated by entries in church visitors' books or cards pinned to prayer request boards. Of course, this is partly to do with being on holiday and away from home, and so could in theory apply anywhere, including urban cathedrals which evoke the same kind of spiritual responses. However, there is no doubt that time spent in rural locations evokes at least some of those intimations of immortality to which Wordsworth referred, and which are latent in the heart and soul of many a city dweller in search of spiritual as well as physical refreshment, whether in a farmhouse bed and breakfast or in a self-catering country cottage.

Fifth, and by no means least, the countryside is increasingly the destination of choice for day-trippers, with an estimated 18 million people heading for the countryside on summer Sundays (Gorringe, 2002: 78). While many only frequent the 'honey-pot' attractions of beauty-spots rather than venture far into the countryside itself, it remains a fact that walking is the most popular leisure activity and 20 million people were engaged in leisure cycling in Britain in 1995 (Gorringe, 2002: 77–8). First the advent of the suburban railway opened up the countryside to day-trippers, as chronicled by John Betjeman in his bitter-sweet television presentation of 'Metro-land'. Then the motor car provided access to rural areas, with the inevitable consequence that the distinction between national parks and national car parks has become somewhat blurred! Also, alongside the walkers, cyclists and horse-riders we note the increasing number of rally drivers, offroaders and motorcycle packs who come to rural areas not so much in search of peace and quiet, as space to speed and engage in extreme sports. Although there is often a degree of tokenism about these visits, because of their brevity and the exertion of journeying to and from the city, the instincts drawing most day-trippers are the same as those which attract the other urban migrants, and these instincts have a great deal to do with fundamentally theological and spiritual ideas of retreat, revival, re-creation and risk.

Against this background, it is worth reminding ourselves that the Aramaic basis of the name Jesus means 'to bring into an open space', and cognate ideas of freedom and salvation have also become attached to this name. So when urban dwellers embark upon these various kinds of rural retreat and cite the wide-open-spaces as among the chief attractions drawing them there, then they may be in touch with a spiritual truth which goes to the very heart of our Christian faith.

Going to Ground

The factors enticing urban people to live in the countryside may vary, and motives will inevitably be mixed. But what they will all have in

common is a sense that the countryside is different, and this difference
will be something to do with the land, a theme explored by David
Walker in Chapter 5 of the present volume.

As an island people we have a strong sense of our land having
limits, and issues to do with use, access and ownership feature prominently in our social psychology. While those living in continental
Europe are generally content to use public spaces for their recreation,
we place a high premium on privacy and on the need to have our own
outdoor space in the form of an enclosed garden or patio. The fact that
a hedge helpline has been established, to counsel those caught up in
garden boundary disputes, is sufficient testimony to this particular
national characteristic, notwithstanding Robert Frost's dictum, 'Good
fences make good neighbours.' The constant vigilance required to
guard our space can be a major cause of urban stress, and it is no
surprise that a trip to the countryside is taken as an opportunity to
wander at will, resulting in confrontation with farmers and country
landowners, also anxious to protect their property and privacy.

From the point of view of the urban dweller, land has basically been
invaded and colonized by human beings who build a city fashioned
to the requirements of their concrete will. Urbanization could be
described as the subjugation of nature to the needs of a planned
economy predicated upon a built environment. Such aggressive termi-
nology implies a defensive disposition, symbolized by city walls which
protect the occupants as much against the predations of untamed
nature as against the attacks of malevolent rivals.

On the other hand, the countryside is perceived by the city dweller
as being subject not so much to human invasion as to infiltration. The
countryside is believed to retain its natural state and settlers simply
indwell this state of nature. From an urban perspective, the militant
language of subjugation and protection is not appropriate in rural
areas, but rather there is talk of communing with nature and co-
operating with natural forces. This baffles the indigenous inhabitants
of the countryside, who know that the landscape around them is
almost entirely a human creation, and the language of subjugation
applies as much to their land as to urban and suburban development.
Furthermore, in spite of the mythology, incomers often seek to
recreate their erstwhile environment with carefully manicured sub-
urban-style landscaping. Likewise, the apparent conquering of nature
to create a city is no less of a myth, given the speed with which grass

grows through the concrete carapace of a derelict factory or untended inner-city estate.

Yet this underlying psychology of the city persists in relation to the countryside, and it goes a long way towards explaining why rural areas continue to attract those in retreat from urban artifice and aggression. Furthermore, even if such perceptions owe more to fantasy than reality, they are not without theological significance. After all, students of early Israelite history continue to debate whether the pre-settlement tribes invaded or infiltrated the land of promise, and which side we adopt in this debate will significantly influence our account of how they perceived and interpreted their new environment. In the same way, we typically describe the Holy Spirit as invading or indwelling us, and which emphasis we favour will be crucially relevant to our understanding of religious experience. By no means least, if we distinguish between 'human making, which is fashioning' and 'God's making, which is creating' (Oppenheimer, 2001: 81), then it is not difficult to understand why those who inhabit the 'fashioned' world of the city believe they are closer to God in the 'created' countryside.

But the fact remains that going to ground in this way does nothing to overcome the suspicions of rural people that the urban indwellers are, in fact, invaders whose fantasies about the countryside fuel misbegotten attitudes and policies issuing from politicians and planners, in town and city halls. They see people coming to the country to escape industrialization, only to end up living in the middle of a huge factory which does not employ them or most of their neighbours, but the future of which is determined back in the cities from whence they came. (See Anthony Russell in Chapter 8 of the present volume.) It is little wonder that the urban–rural debate becomes a dialogue of the deaf, as urban incomers seem to be signalling 'city bad/country good' by their lifestyle choices but 'city good/country bad' when it comes to their political decisions. It is particularly sad when this is reinforced by a certain kind of spiritual schizophrenia which can't make up its mind between 'holy city/savage countryside' and 'secular city/sacred soil'.

Exodus or Exile?

If perceptions of the relationships between urban and rural cultures are ambiguous, then underlying motives and feelings about coming to the countryside from the city are likely to be just as problematic. Furthermore, it will be intriguing to discover if such ambiguities likewise reflect tensions prevalent in the Bible and in Christian theology.

It is not unusual for people to escape to the countryside but still betray symptoms of homesickness, including spiritual homesickness for urban anonymity or eclecticism. The rhetoric of 'exodus', with its narrative of release from captivity into a new experience of personal freedom, is often qualified by a sense of alienation more appropriate to the rhetoric of 'exile'. These two experiences are central to the history of salvation enacted through the history of Israel and re-enacted through the drama of Jesus' death and resurrection. Insofar as urban migrants to the countryside experience exodus and exile, these may be echoes of key themes in the biblical tradition. For example, it may be significant that four place names feature in the second chapter of the Gospel of Matthew. In addition, each of them is supported by a scriptural citation. So Bethlehem as the place of birth features in verse 1, supported by a citation in verse 6. At the very end of the chapter Nazareth features as the town in which the Holy Family is destined to settle. On the way, Jesus and his family detour to Egypt (verse 15), and the experience of Rachel weeping for her children at Rama is recalled according to the prophecy of Jeremiah (verse 18). In other words, in his narrative of Jesus' very early life, Matthew associates his experience of exodus (Egypt) and exile (Rama) with that of the people of Israel. The new Israel would be founded upon the life, death and resurrection of one who had entered fully into the experiences of the people in order to redeem them. Exodus and exile assume significance as pivotal points in the economy of salvation, and insofar as urban migrants to the countryside identify with these seminal experiences, then to that same extent their experience might be said to assume spiritual significance.

This way of looking at things can be of considerable assistance as rural communities seek to make sense of the incomers' experience and to respond in appropriate ways. It may be a useful interpretative tool to explain why incomers feel the need to belong to local organizations and networks on the one hand, including churches, and yet resent the degree of public scrutiny to which they are thereby subjected. Exodus from the anonymity of the city is accompanied by a sense of being exiled from the privileges of privacy, not least in matters to do with personal faith and morality. Similarly, there can be a tension between buying into the rural idyll of traditional values and lifestyle as an escape from post-modern urban relativism, while grieving as any exile grieves for familiar patterns of behaviour, carefully selected from a disparate range of possibilities. Many a rural parochial church council has found itself torn apart by conflict because often able and articulate incomers seem unable to make up their minds between the traditional form of service or celebration which attracted them to make their exodus from the city to the countryside in the first place, and the some-times freer and more idiosyncratic form of worship for which they grieve in exile.

A visit to a rural churchyard can also highlight this tension between exodus and exile. There we can often see how attempts to manage the churchyard have had to reckon with a felt need to conserve the eco-logy of God's acre on the one hand, and the desire to turn graves and their surroundings into little suburban gardens on the other. The trimly tended grave becomes an icon of the ordered urban plot with its little lawn and prim borders, which have been exchanged for a rural wildness which both attracts and repels.

Above all, the exodus–exile experience impacts upon the different ways in which people living in rural communities belong to those com-munities and participate in their corporate life. It may be observed that in relation to churchgoing, for example, indigenous residents do not need to attend, because they already belong, while in order to belong, incomers must attend. This might explain why urban commuters and people who have retired to the countryside often outnumber the indigenous population in many village church congregations, even though the overall demographic profile might be very different. Whereas Grace Davie's (1994) tag 'believing without belonging' accurately accounts for the attitudes of many born and bred country people toward their local church, the opposite may apply to those who come from the city and for whom what they do or do not believe, is secondary to their need to belong.

Here for a Season

As one who has made the move from urban to rural living, I sense that city dwellers are typically less sensitive to the cycle of the seasons than those more familiar with rural surroundings. The relatively unchanging nature of the built environment, together with the prevalence of street lighting, central heating and air-conditioning, conspires to inure the city dweller against the vagaries of seasonal change. The cycle of the seasons is likely to be signalled more by which sports are being played and what programmes are being shown on television, than by the changing colour of leaves on the trees. Of course, the autumnal leaves blocking the gutters and the first green shoots of spring in the garden will register with the urban population, but the sense of the seasons as a major influence on day-to-day lifestyle will be significantly less than for the rural population.

It is for this reason that some people choose to move from the city to the countryside. They go in search of the seasons, and this is what they can essentially mean by 'getting close to nature'. Yet it can come as something of a shock when the long nights of winter are so dark, spring lambs are so noisy, summer insects are so tiresome, and autumn mists are so impenetrable. Even more disturbing can be the close acquaintance with the cycle of life and death, which is so bound up with the cycle of the seasons, and which cannot be simply controlled and managed. The city seldom knows what it is to experience the dead of winter, and although the first snowdrops appear as harbingers of new life just around the corner, still it is difficult to shake off that profound sense of our own mortality which winter instils and which awareness of another cycle of seasons completed only serves to exacerbate.

This can bring long-suppressed spiritual sensitivities to the fore, as erstwhile urban dwellers come to terms with the fact that they, too, are only here for a season. Whereas the elaborate paraphernalia of death and disposal, majoring on cremation rather than burial, can anaesthetize inhabitants of cities against the profound reality of our mortality, it is almost impossible to escape from death as a fact of life when living in the countryside. Rural clergy are often aware that they are only as good as their last funeral, because their standing and reputation in the community depends to such an extent on the way they manage death and its consequential rituals. This suggests that because the Christian faith has the dynamic of death and resurrection as its essential core, then the Church in the countryside is particularly well placed to proclaim the gospel, so long as it remains pastorally alert to the special needs of urban incomers, whose instinctive acquaintance with death and dying may be less well attuned than those of their rural neighbours.

It is also worth observing at this point that the seasons of the Church's year may be of less significance to country people than the cycle of the natural seasons. It may be the case that, whereas in urban areas we have festivals in search of congregations, in rural areas we have congregations in search of festivals, and some churches in the countryside have been very imaginative in providing for those festivals which rural communities are instinctively drawn to celebrate at seed-time and harvest, Rogation and Lammas. The celebration of Christmas as mid-winter solstice, and Easter as a thinly disguised fertility festival, may be closer to the surface of rural consciousness than we may sometimes like to think, and there is potential here for conflict with urban incomers still wedded to more theologically conventional seasons and to the rituals required to celebrate them.

The Eden Effect

If attitudes to the land, the community and the cycle of the seasons characterize the relationship between city-bred folk and the country-side they come to inhabit, there is also another set of assumptions based on the notion that pre-industrial and pre-urban rurality is therefore prelapsarian, that is, associated with the age of innocence before the fall. People now flock to the Eden Project in Cornwall, and for many it provides an opportunity to be put in touch with that original state of innocence and blessing. This is consistent with the feeling many people have that the city is synonymous with sin, and rurality is equated with righteousness. In spite of the fact that authors like Thomas Hardy, Sue Gee, Mary Webb and Joanna Trollope have made their reputations on exploding this myth of rural innocence, still it persists and can explain why many an exodus from the city in search of the good life, ends in frustration and disillusionment.

To some extent the mythology is founded upon assumptions about noise. To retreat into the countryside is to retreat from urban cacophony into a haven of peace and quiet. As spiritual experience has so often been associated with meditative silence and contemplative quietism, so the assumed absence of noise in the countryside encourages rural retreats as particularly effective ways of experiencing the presence of God. But this begs questions about whether the country-side is actually so noiseless. In reality, the noises are simply different and often no less intrusive. And if it is argued that they are far less destructive of spiritual awareness because they are 'natural' sounds, then we have to ask if this effectively rules out the practice of the presence of God amidst the sounds of the city, which are mainly mediated and manufactured. In recent times there have been moves to promote retreats in the midst of daily life, which includes life lived amidst the noise of machinery, traffic and mobile phones. While most retreat houses are found in rural locations, some are situated in city centres, and courses are provided with an emphasis on spiritual renewal at the heart of urban life. We must beware of colluding with the idea that prayer and contemplation can only be practised where silence comes as standard.

Related to assumptions about noise in relation to spirituality are assumptions about the country life being lived at a slower and more measured pace, with the implication that there must be escape from urban freneticism in the interests of spiritual growth and development. Again questions are being begged here about whether expectations that the money rich/time poor dynamic of urban living will actually be reversed in the countryside are well founded. It is tempting to think that the slow-roasting aga replaces the fast-food burger chain as an icon of rural restfulness, but the reality for most people seldom matches the idyll. Anyway, are we not again running the risk of idealizing stillness in the sense of inactivity, just as we idealize stillness as absence of noise? As R. S. Thomas (1984: 125) famously described in his poem 'Pilgrimage', our God is a fast God, always there before us, so we do not have to slow down in order to allow God to catch up. We may well experience rural places as places to walk slowly, and the opportunities this affords for relaxation and reflection are of inestimable value. But just as it is not the case that urban decadence is directly related to the decibel count, so neither is the daily round of rural living necessarily an echo of Eden!

However, there are important ways in which the countryside can have a particular impact on the spiritual experience of those more familiar with city surroundings. For example, we have already referred to how the deep darkness of the countryside contrasts with the urban experience of light by night as well as by day. The fact that this is called light 'pollution' suggests that it is seen as a negation of what is natural and more desirable. Yet darkness has a sinister reputation in the annals of spiritual experience, with many mystics testifying to a dark night of the soul which may not always be congenial to those in rural retreat. By way of compensation, the big skies of rural Lincolnshire inspire awe and wonder, as the dark nights reveal the heavens in all their splendour, but if to God darkness and light are both alike, this is not so for fallen humanity, and the dark night can seriously unsettle the urban spirit.

Standing on Holy Ground

Finally, we reflect on how religious buildings and sacred sites impact on the spiritual sensibilities of those coming to the countryside from more urban environments. Most city churches were built to meet the needs of an expanding population, and so they post-date the city itself. But many of our great medieval cathedrals and city centre churches hold a fascination precisely because they are 'prehistoric', insofar as modern urban consciousness traces its origins back no further than the industrial revolution. These buildings belong to an age of credulity not far removed from superstition, and while they are 'owned' by the citizens as part of their common heritage, they are also viewed with some suspicion, as sometimes unwelcome challenges to the sceptical ways and mechanistic means of the modern world.

However, in the rural context such buildings and sacred sites are seen by the urban visitor as not so much pre-modern anachronisms in an otherwise post-modern environment, but as symbols of sacredness at ease and at one with the landscape within which they are set, and the soil on which they stand. While the demolition of a church on an urban estate might cause only short-term consternation or controversy, any threat to a country church will meet with a kind of resistance which wells up from deep within the soul, including the soul of the urban incomer. This is partly to do with the sentimental attachment to church visiting shared by such diverse poets as T. S. Eliot, John Betjeman and Philip Larkin, but it actually goes deeper than mere sentiment about places 'where prayer has been valid'. It is something profoundly spiritual associated with sacred sites as central to the presence of God in rural settlements and central to the countryside which sustains them. It has often been remarked upon that guidebooks in rural churches provide detailed architectural and archaeological information sufficient to challenge the digestion of even the

most avid antiquarian, but that little effort is made to nurture those
spiritual instincts which draw visitors there in the first place. Talk of
turning tourists into pilgrims and then into disciples has become somewhat glib these days, but the opportunities are there for us, and church
tourism officers in various parts of the country testify to that latent
spirituality evoked by sacred spaces in rural settings (see Askew, 1997;
Francis and Martineau, 2001; Littler and Francis, 2003).

One of the greatest challenges facing the rural church is how to
accommodate the assumptions and expectations of the modern citizen
in terms of providing even the most basic of amenities, without com-
promising the serious business of sacred space working God's will on
hearts and minds in retreat from urban cynicism and secularization.
Our country churches and churchyards cannot long be sustained at
present levels of care and conservation unless they adapt to contemporary requirements, by recapturing medieval openness to communal
activities and daily use. (For an alternative view see Alastair Redfern
in Chapter 13 of the present volume.) In rural dioceses as many as 50
per cent of the schemes considered by advisory committees for the care
of churches can relate to the provision of toilets and kitchens. Yet in
my experience as an archdeacon I perceived that resistance to such a
return to multi-purpose usage is likely to come most of all from the
urban incomers, who invest so much in the symbolism of the church
building, however ill-attended, as a crucial bastion against perceived
profanity. It is significant that among the fastest growing congregations in Lincolnshire are those which meet in purpose-built low maintenance churches or hired halls. When it comes to places of worship,
the new arrivals on burgeoning housing developments put physical
comfort and modern facilities ahead of medieval splendour or antique
ornamentation. Yet they also fight to preserve the sacred sites which
seem to validate God's presence and special favour toward them. In
some cases, historic churches can be adapted to meet all these aspirations, but where they cannot then consideration must be given to
licensing alternative centres of parish worship, thus releasing the
ancient buildings to do what they do best, witnessing to God's enduring presence at the heart of rural culture and community.

Conclusion

There are many reasons why a country retreat appears attractive to urban dwellers, and these often have spiritual as well as socio-economic significance. All too often such incomers embrace fantasy rather than fact, myth rather than reality, simplistic spirituality rather than systematic theology. At the same time easy assumptions are challenged about where true spiritual experience is to be found, and we must resist collusion with implicit negativity in relation to the city and its potential to reveal God's presence and purposes. Clearly much more needs to be said than has been said here, about the changing face of the countryside and the effect of urbanization on rural economy, landscape and settlements. Yet enough may have been said to show how the countryside as a place of retreat continues to present both challenges and opportunities to rural churches, and to those who have charge of them.

Rural living, and the Church still so often at the centre of rural life, can promote the good news of God in Christ in ways which are not so readily available to those who live, work and worship in urban environments. Enhanced sensibility to the cycle of the seasons, patterns of growth and decay, land use and abuse can have profound theological and spiritual implications for those who retreat permanently or periodically from towns and cities to the countryside. William Cowper (1853: 116) maintained that 'God made the country, and man made the town', and he concluded:

> In cities vice is hidden with most ease,
> Or seen with least reproach; and virtue, taught
> By frequent lapse, can hope no triumph there
> Beyond the achievement of successful flight.

Although we must beware of Cowper's tendency to damn the city in order to extol the countryside, those who make a 'successful flight' into rural retreat may well encounter God in ways which amount to good news for all, whether they be in or out of town.

REFERENCES

Askew, R. (1997), *From Strangers to Pilgrims*, Cambridge, Grove Books.

Cowper, W. (1853), *Poetical Works*, Edinburgh, Gall and Inglis.

Davie, G. (1994), *Religion in Britain since 1945: Believing Without Belonging*, Oxford, Blackwell.

Francis, L. J. and Martineau, J. (2001), *Rural Visitors*, Stoneleigh Park, Acora Publishing.

Gorringe, T. J. (2002), *A Theology of the Built Environment*, Cambridge, Cambridge University Press.

Littler, K. and Francis, L. J. (2003), 'What Rural Churches Say to Non-Church-Goers', *Rural Theology*, 61, pp. 57–62.

Oppenheimer, H. (2001), *Making Good*, London, SCM Press.

Thomas, R. S. (1984), *Later Poems: A Selection*, London, Macmillan.

2. Dynamics of Community

MICHAEL L. LANGRISH

Summary

The purpose in this chapter is to explore the nature of community, together with ways in which the rural Church is able both to contribute to the sense of community and also to model what it is to be 'community' in its own life. The threats to community life are considered, as are the opportunities for the Church to be a major player in responding to the considerable changes that are evident in rural communities today.

Lessons are drawn from my own ministry in rural communities, as a bishop in two very different rural counties, Cheshire and Devon, and as a parish priest in a village in Warwickshire. Reference is made to lessons learned about how a church may grow and change in response to the needs of the community in which it is set, bearing in mind the ministry available to it. This is then related to a broader understanding of the dynamics of community life.

In this chapter an analysis of some of the changes experienced in rural communities within the most recent past is followed by an exploration of the concept of social capital, and the ways in which people have increasingly begun to feel isolated and without a significant sense of community. Consideration is given to some aspects of local governance and the response of the Church to changes in rural life.

The Concept of Community

The promotion of 'community' has become a major feature of rural development programmes in recent years, indeed of social policy more generally. This is for three reasons: 'community' is valued as a 'consumer good', a resource to be tapped into to add value to human life and relationships. Many people long for what they perceive to be a real community. It is valued as a resource, a lot of agencies striving to enhance and exploit it; and for various reasons also at risk. It is also an elusive concept, 'community' is as difficult to define, as 'communities' are difficult to identify and promote (paraphrased from Moseley, 2003: 5).

Yet this sense of 'community' being self-evidently a 'good thing' goes deep. 'The rural community is seen as the essence of the English good life, a collection of people well integrated into their local society and living productive and rewarding lives' (paraphrased from Rogers, 1993: 20–1).

However mythical and romantic this notion may be, it does make the point that community is more than just a group of people who happen to live in proximity to one another. People in 'community' share something in common and, through sharing that something and being conscious that they do so, interact with one another in that context. In fact it is these notions of 'consciously sharing' and of 'interaction' that are at the heart of most useful definitions. They also take us to the heart of a Christian understanding of community expressed in the term *koinonia*, also understood as communion or fellowship. When Christians speak of, for example, 'the fellowship, or community, of the Holy Spirit' they speak consciously of a common participation in the Spirit's life into which they enter through their identification with Christ in baptism.

So, communities are not always or even mostly 'territorial'; they may also be 'communities of interest'. Communities may be particularly strong when a strong sense of territory or locality and a strong sense of common interest or purpose reinforce one another. Indeed the term 'close knit' community describes well such an interweaving texture as this. It suggests a context in which people live in reasonable proximity, feel they belong to a particular place, share something of a common identity, and interact with one another.

However defined, communities are never entirely static. Being composed of living human beings and their relationships, there is an inevitable dynamic of development to their life. Communities are marked by change. To quote the envisioning report on the future of the countryside by the Countryside Agency, *The State of the Countryside 2020*: 'The English countryside occupies a unique place in our affections and lives. We value it as a place to live, to work and to visit. Yet it is undergoing fundamental change' (2003: 4).

Change in the Countryside

Currently such change may be characterized in a number of ways. First, there are *changes in the general outlook*. Rural communities were seen as idylls, in contrast to the cut and thrust of city and suburban life. But rising fuel prices have added huge costs to life in rural areas, the problems of agriculture have spun off to tourism, leisure and a whole range of other rural businesses, and advances in communication technology such as broadband internet access have not reached rural areas as quickly as others. So it can seem as if the countryside is 'second best'.

Second, there are *changes in employment*. Rural areas have generated more jobs in recent years than urban. But rural incomes are typically 10 per cent lower than in town (ACRE, 1994). Many rural jobs are seasonal, casual and part-time. Provision for training and investment is generally not good in rural areas. Further economic development is often hampered by lack of appropriate housing.

Third, there are *changes in housing*. The rented sector has virtually disappeared. Sales of council houses and of former estate houses to private owners have not been sufficiently compensated for by the hard work of housing associations. Reductions in grant levels have pushed up rents. Thus the poverty trap operates. The shortage of affordable housing drives young people into towns, forces them to remain in the parental home (with attendant problems) or makes them homeless.

Fourth, there are *changes in transport*. There has been a reduction in public transport as car ownership has grown, and that makes life very difficult for anyone without access to a car. Women in particular suffer. There are schemes to help communities provide their own transport. This can include car-sharing schemes, but casual lift-giving is not an answer to many journey needs.

Fifth, there are *changes in health services provision*. There are particular strains on single-handed general practitioners. There are financial rewards for general practitioners in rural areas to cover the cost of greater distances, but access to hospital outpatients and for visiting can be very problematic.

Sixth, there are *changes affecting young and old alike*. Both groups can suffer real deprivation. For the young it centres on a lack of provision of transport and poor job prospects. For the elderly, there can be real isolation: 'they are often the ones with few choices in a society motivated by freedom of choice'.

Finally, most of all the rural population itself, those who comprise rural communities, is constantly changing. About 70 per cent of people who live in rural communities today are first-generation villagers who either moved there in their lifetime or are the first of their family to be born in that situation (ACRE, 1994).

The Attraction of Community

We are frequently reminded that we live in an increasingly urban society, and yet it is one in which the attraction of the countryside, and in particular the attraction for many of living in a rural community remains. Why is the whole concept of 'community' itself so attractive?

Community suggests, or is seen to suggest, life on a more 'human scale'. There is a perception of neighbourliness, more opportunity for personal interaction, greater friendliness and the prospect of mutual support, shared identity and commitment, although to what extent reality matches perception, and is true for all, is another matter. Community is also currently valued as an instrument of public policy, with local communities especially being seen to embody attributes valuable to wider society. These include a culture of mutual support, a measure of altruism, the existence of informal networks, a source of local information and means of communication, energy and vitality, and a capacity to reach isolated people. In other words community is increasingly seen as a prime contributor to what is known as social capital.

Social Capital

Social capital is a generic term used to describe a wide variety of quite specific benefits that flow from the trust, reciprocity, information, and cooperation associated with social networks. In the words of the *Faith in the Countryside* report:

> Fundamental to the notion of 'community' is the idea of 'persons-in-relationship', and of shared norms. So a community is one where

people draw together to express their relatedness by focusing on things they have in common . . . any group which shares concerns, norms, patterns of mutual support is a community. They may be said to be rich in social capital. (Archbishops' Commission on Rural Areas, 1990: 23)

Yet social capital may be eroded as well as enriched. Putnam (1995), in his imaginative essay 'Bowling Alone: America's Declining Social Capital', noted the erosion in networks evident in American society. He showed that Americans were less likely to associate together, engage in community affairs and trust one another than in the past. In particular he noted that while more Americans were bowling today than ever before, bowling in organized leagues has plummeted.

> The rise of solo bowling threatens the livelihood of bowling-lane proprietors because those who bowl as members of leagues consume three times as much beer and pizza as solo bowlers, and the money in bowling is in the beer and pizza, not the balls and shoes. The broader social significance, however, lies in the social interaction and even occasionally civic conversations over beer and pizza that solo bowlers forgo. (Putnam, 1995)

So he went on to measure social engagement by looking at the density of formal membership, correlated membership rates with social trust and concluded 'the greater the density of associational membership in its society, the more trusting its citizens. Trust and engagement are two facets of the same underlying factor, social capital'.

Social capital, then, has two key components. The first key component is *networks*, those structural factors that reflect the social relations and interactions among individuals or within groups (whether families, organizations, interest groups, businesses, voluntary societies, churches, or the organs of public life and so on). The second key component is *norms*, those cultural factors relating to the established rules of behaviour or standards of conduct and the shared understandings or values held by any group of people (including practically anything that contributes to the building of trust and reciprocity). Networks and norms are mutually interdependent. While networks and the social interactions associated with them enable shared norms to be developed, shared norms encourage social interaction and reinforce networks.

From a Christian perspective we may speak of all that makes for communities of belonging and mutual dependence opening the way to life in all its fullness. In this we are pointed back to that insight given us in the creation story (Genesis 2:15–24) that human responsibility for the world is set firmly in the context of our being created for community not for autonomy or anonymity. The biblical testimony points steadily to a participation in kingdom living that is meant to be ever increasing in its inclusiveness. There is a resonance here with that understanding of social capital as those social networks and norms that encourage broader identities and solidarity and help translate an 'I' mentality into a 'we' mentality.

Social capital, like other forms of capital, can be drawn on, increased and depleted. It is also both a public and a private good. For example, when a group of parents come together to set up a car sharing scheme to improve the mobility of teenagers in a remote village they both contribute to the balance, sustainability and quality of community life, and at the same time develop friendship and support networks which can be of benefit to them personally as well. This dynamic interaction between the two kinds of good can, though, work both positively and negatively. It can be precisely those who are already 'social capital rich' in terms of existing networks and support systems who can be best placed to derive most from, as well as contribute to, the richness of community life. 'The well-connected are more likely to be housed, healthy, hired, and happy' (Woolcock, 2001), and vice versa.

Positive and negative dynamics can also be at work in the interrelationship between the various types of social capital. First, there is *bonding social capital*. 'Bonding social capital' arises from all those things which serve to unite groups and so is closely related to common identity and interest. It develops with and is sustained by a strong or common identity, a sense of shared values, experience, interests, locality, history and so on. However, it can also be characterized by closed networks, difficult to penetrate by those outside.

Consequently there is also a need for *bridging social capital*. 'Bridging social capital' grows when the interactions and contact between different groups is strong, and is diminished when these are weak. It requires a degree of diversity, and develops, for example, through overlapping networks, and interpenetrating membership, enabling one group or network to access the resources, cultural, intellectual, social and physical, of another. It describes those weaker but nonetheless real ties which foster contact and cross-fertilization between gender, ethnicity, education, socio-economic background, locality and faith.

They are also likely to be helped by access to, and growth in, what has been described as *linking social capital*. By this term is meant those connections between groups and/or individuals in hierarchical or power-based relationships, or as 'the capacity to lever resources, ideas, and information from formal institutions beyond the community' (Woolcock, 2001).

These three different types of social capital impact on one another with different outcomes, not all of them positive. Strong bonding capital may militate against the development of effective bridging capital, through closure to new people or ideas. Some forms of strong linking capital may, through de-skilling local people and an over-dependency on external leadership, for example, undermine the development of effective local bonding capital. Nevertheless, conditions that promote and sustain social capital in all its forms do impact directly on the quality of community life.

Threats to Social Capital and Community

The powerful forces that combine to erode territorial communities, such as mobility afforded by two car ownership, the demise of many village services, the loss of affordable housing and changes to the demographic profile may also erode social capital. But to these specific factors, must be added all the manifestations of an increasingly individualistic culture and worldview that underlies them. As Jürgen Moltmann says:

> We live in free choice societies, for we believe that only in its individual persons can a society become creative . . . Every person must be able to determine everything himself or herself: free choice of school, vocation, partner, domicile, politics, religion and so on . . . 'patchwork families' are emerging in which no one knows or cares anymore just who is descended from whom, but rather only who cohabits with whom or who is living with whom. (Moltmann, 1998: 35–6)

According to Moltmann it is part of the Church's task to question and challenge such trends, not merely for pragmatic reasons, but because those outcomes that affect the stock of important social capital are deeply related to questions about our very nature as human beings.

There is here a strong resonance with the research of the sociologist Grace Davie (2002), who has written of trends in contemporary European society. Almost all indicators that measure firm religious commitment in terms of either participating in (Church) institutional life, or assenting to (Christian) credal formularies indicate steady and continued decline. Yet there are other indicators which suggest that this is not in itself evidence of a more general religious indifference, and that an interest in 'spirituality' for example is very widespread indeed. In almost all European societies, and this is especially the case in rural communities, the Church as an institution is still widely resorted to in time of need. Two points may be noted here. First, this distancing of people from formal structures, beliefs and commitments is not confined to the churches. For example, a study of the decline of traditional free churches in Swansea and the collapse of the trade union movement at the same time, and in the same area, concluded that both were related to the loss of a close-knit, working-class community centred on the docks. 'Both the organizations concerned with religion and those concerned with labour had lost their raison d'être, that is a community to serve whose common interests . . . required institutional articulation' (Davie, 2002: 34). Thus 'believing without belonging is a pervasive dimension of modern European societies'. But second, it would appear that an increasingly observable, and significant, trend which is taking place both inside and outside the historic churches is 'from an understanding of religion as a form of obligation to an increasing emphasis on consumption'.

Moltmann and Davie are making complementary but different points about the nature of our society; one attitudinal/cultural and the other structural, reflecting the two important components of social capital. However, both point not only to the importance of a sense of mutuality, of mutual trust and obligation, in a healthy community, but also to the erosion of this and the implications for the churches.

If they are right about these trends, then there are obvious consequences for community life in terms of the dynamics that underpin both networks and norms, and also for those factors affecting the stock of social capital, particularly those qualities of engagement and trust, both personal and public. These consequences have begun to be explored by Francis (2003: 60–1). His analysis of the 2001 census in England and Wales alongside the British Social Attitudes survey draws attention to 'religious affiliation as a . . . significant predictor of variations in levels of social capital', as manifested most clearly in both levels of volunteering in local communities and degrees of trust. He also suggests that 'if the affiliation to the Christian tradition is in decline . . . the government might well be wise to anticipate some consequent erosion in social capital'.

Principles of Local Governance

The challenge to deal with the erosion of social capital is a significant issue for urban and rural communities alike. What patterns and principles might inform patterns of governance designed to protect and enhance social capital, and so strengthen and support the networks and norms that constitute the warp and weft of community? A key writer in this field, Malcolm Moseley (2003), suggests three fundamentals.

The first fundamental is *local identification and mobilization*. Local people, both as individuals and collectively in groups, organizations, and firms, are key resources in local development, as sources of information, ideas, energy and enterprise. People will, however, only be enthused to participate if they feel that a particular venture or issue is clearly relevant to their concerns and that any contribution they make is likely to produce beneficial change. Thus the government's Rural White Paper emphasized the following point: 'We want to see . . . people living in rural areas being fully involved in developing their community, safeguarding its valued features, and shaping the decisions that affect them' (Department of Environment, Transport and the Regions, 2000: 145).

The second fundamental is what is termed *valorization*. This is a French concept which, understood narrowly, means 'adding value to a product'. In the context of writing about social capital it is used more broadly to describe any process or action which enhances the value of any local resource whether 'marketed' (in the usually accepted way) or not. So a redundant parish hall may be valorized by restoration for community use, through making opportunities for the employment of redundant labour or the development of employment skills, or by a developing programme of participation and empowerment of the local community.

Third, there is the importance of building and nurturing *partnership*. A recent report on rural regeneration partnerships in Mid-Wales and Shropshire makes the following observation:

> Partnerships have emerged over the course of the past 15 years as an increasingly commonplace feature in the landscape of . . . rural regeneration in Britain. Partnership working was developed in the 1980s by the British Government as a means of loosening local government's hold over urban economic development and by the European Union as a mechanism for redirecting its structural Funds from large-scale state-led projects to small-scale bottom-up initiatives, [but] the 'partnership principle' has now become established as a preferential mode for management across a diverse raft of policy arenas. (Edwards, Goodwin, Pemberton and Woods, 2000: 3)

Partnership in this context means an arrangement that deliberately draws together the resources of specified partners from at least two societal sectors (for example, state, public, voluntary, commercial, faith, civic) with a clear organizational structure, for the development of a particular locality and its population.

Government or Governance?

Taken together these three principles, stressing the importance of local identification and mobilization, valorization and partnership, suggest a fundamental shift away from the notion of *government*, with the state and elected local authorities as unequivocally centre stage, to one of *governance* which acknowledges the interrelated roles played in communities by a host of actors, including the state and local authorities, but also embracing private businesses, voluntary organizations and community groups, as well as regional, sub-regional and supranational institutions whose activities and decisions impact on those communities. So locally focused partnerships, which add value to the lives of people and the communities they comprise, are seen to be key to emerging patterns of governance in both rural and urban areas alike. They are seen as helping to achieve the desired goals of participation and ownership through the following three factors: their 'process' (for example, groups having the ability to sort out their own problems, consider options for action and develop mechanisms for evaluating achievement); their 'outputs' (for example, the existence of new groups and activities; the establishment of programmes and projects which address community need); and their 'outcomes' (for example, individuals and participating groups becoming more enthusiastic and self-confident; a sense of a greater influence on the decision-making process; greater engagement with the structures of governance and government alike).

However, in practice many such partnerships encounter real problems. It can be much easier for such partnerships to focus on physical, financial and environmental capital, rather than human and social capital, and to become very project based.

Local partnerships can be dominated by the public sector, especially local authorities and local and regional agencies of central government, to the detriment of genuine community participation. Funding streams for community regeneration programmes are often complex and some grants are given as loans. Some poor communities end up paying back money so that other poor neighbourhoods can then be granted it. Regional development agencies often work in this way.

Too often the value of existing and developing supportive but informal networks is insufficiently recognized and affirmed. Also a disparity in access to information may mean that local people and small groups are not as well informed as relatively powerful local authority officers and community/voluntary organizations that have a broad remit and most closely resemble the statutory sector. This has implications for the notion of 'partnership' in determining who are the junior and senior partners. Sometimes people feel that they are part of a 'box-ticking' exercise or an 'output' to substantiate another agency.

The Local Church

In the task of building and supporting community what is the role of the Church? *Faith in the Countryside* argued as follows:

It is part of our response to God to create conditions where others in community can experience care and well-being. For the Church to be truly committed to enabling persons to grow will involve the task of ensuring that society is organised in such a way that human beings can enter freely into these relationships of spiritual and material exchange that we call loving relationships. (Archbishops' Commission on Rural Areas, 1990: 22)

There is an important reminder here that for Christians questions about the nature of community and the dynamics that shape and govern them need to be addressed as a theological as well as a practical imperative. They bring a distinctive contribution to these concerns.

Social analysis does not and cannot ask or answer theological questions. Christians must ask theological questions: at their simplest, about what God is saying and doing, what words of judgement and hope there are in the present . . . otherwise we easily get locked into some kind of deterministic bondage to statistical trends or psychological processes, with little place for grace, newness, forgiveness or freedom. (Forrester, 2000: 63)

To grapple with questions of what God is saying and doing in the life of communities today, requires us to focus first on what God is, and what that might say to us about the nature of community itself, in a world which God has created and in which men and women are made to be in God's image. For Christians a key to that understanding is to be found in our speaking of God as Trinity. As Elizabeth Johnson puts it:

The symbol of the Trinity expresses that the very essence of God – at the heart of all reality and shown to us particularly in the dynamic of Christian community and the Eucharist, is relatedness rather than partiality or solitary ego. This particular kind of relatedness . . . is not one of hierarchy involving domination and subordination, but rather one of genuine mutuality in which there is radical equality, while distinctions are respected. (Johnson, 1998: 201)

God the Trinity is a community of persons pouring out a liberating love and compassion in a real and historically located human context, and empowering human beings to be drawn into and participate in such concrete community too.

Questions about our communities and community life are therefore, at root, also profoundly spiritual questions, touching our deepest nature as human beings and our relationship with God. A failure to engage properly in community is a failure to engage properly with God in whom we encounter a mutuality of loving communion, into which we are drawn in the person and work of Christ in the Spirit.

> Those who do not love a brother or sister whom they have seen cannot love God whom they have not seen. The commandment we have from him is this: those who love God must love their brothers and sisters also. (1 John 4.20–21)

The Church and Social Capital

The Church, when it is true to its nature as expression, agent and advocate of community *koinonia*, has an important role to play in sustaining and developing all three types of social capital: bonding, bridging and linking. Especially where a church operates through a traditional parish structure, its embedding in so many local communities, its opportunities of continuing contact with the lives of a still considerable number of people through, for instance, baptisms, marriages and funerals, and its historic means of engagement with government and the structures of society, may give it a particular role in helping to build bridging and linking, as well as bonding capital.

Throughout the United Kingdom and Ireland the Church continues to have a very considerable presence, and is both a considerable stakeholder and key player in the communities of which it is a part. Taking my own diocese of Exeter: in 620 communities throughout Devon, the Church of England alone has a visible presence in terms of both buildings and people. As represented by all its denominations, the Christian Church is, even now, more strongly represented and involved in community life than almost any other organization in the country.

In terms of buildings, the Church also has a wonderful community resource in its places of worship, its halls, schools and houses. Probably better maintained than ever before, they are already contributing hugely to the life of local communities and offer considerable

potential for further development and use. Through creative co-operation with agencies such as police, post office, health and social
services, banks and so on, and with the support of government, both
local and national, there is real scope for rural churches to become
even more effective centres for community life. Church schools also
have a particular role to play. Church of England schools generally
reflect a twin commitment both to providing education within a distinctive Christian ethos and also to serving the communities in which
they are set. As institutions that are open to diversity, but embedded in
the life of the local parish, and with a clear, underlying Christian
rationale, they can contribute richly to the quality of community in a
whole variety of the different networks that constitute the wider community they serve.

Turning to people, the Church is a major source of local community
leadership. Again, within the Church of England in Devon alone
there are over 4,000 churchwardens and office holders, many of
whom, together with clergy (in post and retired), licensed readers, and
many thousands of lay Christians, are deeply involved in the myriad
of voluntary organizations, statutory agencies, public bodies and
informal groups that constitute the fabric of civil society.

An analysis of information from the British Social Attitudes Survey,
and the most recent census, has shown that the third strongest predictor of social engagement and contribution to the building of social
capital, after age and class, is faith affiliation (Francis, 2003). Older
people are more likely to contribute to the relationship and bonds of
trust that build community than the young. Class and education can
be predictors of this too, but the next key indicator is to be found in a
person's faith. A breakdown of the statistical information shows that
the contribution of the different faith communities and the different
churches to the building up of the quality of social life does in fact vary
between them in quite significant ways. Christian affiliation in particular seems to be a significant predictor of engagement in the democratic process, and of the likelihood of people contributing to such
groups as tenants' or residents' associations, becoming school
governors, joining political parties or parent-teacher associations,
standing for the parish or town council, getting involved in things like
neighbourhood watch, local conservation or environment groups,
other local community or voluntary associations or schemes to help
the sick, elderly, children or other vulnerable people. Similarly, there

is a much higher relation between those who show a Christian affiliation with local cultural groups such as arts or drama clubs, or who are committed to other volunteer work than tends to be found among non-Christian categories. The fact is that faith-based groups in general, and churches in particular, are major contributors to the building of healthy and stable community life. The Rural White Paper made the following point:

> Churches continue to be a central focus of spiritual and community life in many small rural communities. They form the major voluntary organizations in much of the countryside . . . The Churches can help to build bridges between different sections of the rural community and between town and country, and they can give a lead on the traditional values associated with rural life, such as good neighbourliness and stewardship of the land. (Department of Environment, Transport and the Regions, 2000: 26)

However, although much contemporary government rhetoric seems to recognize this, when it comes to being allowed to build on this potential by applying for community funding or joining partnerships for local renewal and regeneration, they are often discriminated against through prejudice or sheer ignorance of the role they can and do play. One of the challenges for the rural Church is to be more upfront and confident about what even a small congregation can and does contribute to community life.

Because of their widespread presence and key stakeholding role, churches can play a pivotal role in improving the quality of life for people in their area, and redressing some of the problems of social exclusion that concern them. Many rural congregations are at the core of the local social fabric, truly salt and light in their neighbourhood. They can speak up clearly for the needs of the most vulnerable. For instance, their links with long-term sick, elderly, and housebound people, who are easily overlooked in community initiatives, can be the best of any local group. There are many opportunities for them to do so on a formal basis as well. For example, churches can and do play a key role in helping the communities they serve to develop a representative, far-sighted parish plan. While ultimate responsibility for preparing a parish plan rests with the parish/town council, these bodies are expected to work with other local organizations. This can offer a real opportunity for a church to take initiatives to foster local partnership working as an important part of that transforming mission to which we are called.

The Church as an Expression of Community

Dietrich Bonhoeffer (1954) reminds us that Christianity is synony-mous with community: 'Christianity means community through Jesus Christ and in Jesus Christ.' The centrality of the covenant community is at the heart of biblical faith. This central aspect of the gospel is often lost in our culture with its overemphasis on individuality. Recovering a profound sense of community is one of the major tasks of mission anywhere. The crisis in small rural congregations today may be the situation through which God's gift of grace enables these congrega-tions to be on the leading edge of changing values, models and behaviour in such a way as enables the gospel to become available to our world. In responding to this, the challenges of working for the renewal of community and working to be renewed as community are inextricably intertwined.

What this might mean in practice may be illustrated from my own experience of being a rural parish priest in Warwickshire. A small church in the context of a small village which had lost almost all its other significant institutions and organizations, had to grapple with precisely this question of what it means to be community *koinonia* in such a way that enables community *koinonia* and witnesses to that wider community *koinonia* for which we have been made, as it experi-mented with ways to live out what it meant to be the body of Christ in a community in which so many other manifestations of community, and thus the stock of social capital, had been eroded. As that small rural church learned to reflect on its experience and that of the village community in the light of the gospel, it was led to act and experiment in different ways. This in turn led, in time, to the articulation of a number of principles as being central to its life and mission. The local church, it discovered, should display the following characteristics.

First, it should be *incarnational*. The gospel begins with the word that became flesh and dwelt among us. A church that was not seriously involved in its local community, listening to people, and responding to their real concerns was not worthy of the name.

Second, it should be *unifying*. The word become flesh was also the Christ who took down the barriers that divide. So a church cannot be content to be just another organization and interest group among many. The task is to find ways in which old villager and new incomer can both feel that they belong. This also involves a recognition that many of those moving into a village are from different Christian traditions and from none. Ecumenism in a rural setting has to be taken very seriously and has its own distinctive character. There are many ways in which a church may function truly as *parish* church open to Christians of all denominations, while enabling the denominational allegiance and spiritual integrity of each to be properly preserved.

Third, it should be *fuzzy edged* or *open-doored*. Nothing destroys any body more than the feeling that it is just a private club, which cannot adapt to the fresh and the new. People need help to feel that it is natural to come in and to belong.

Fourth, it should be *celebratory*. It should provide appropriate opportunities for people to give thanks, and to shed tears, at the most important moments of both personal and community life. Family occasions such as baptisms, marriages and funerals; as well as celebrations related to the important memories and rhythms of the village as a whole, and of its inhabitants wherever the main focus of their lives, have an important role to play in building those networks of relationships and trust by which the social capital of community life is developed and maintained.

Fifth, it should be *light on structures*. It should attempt to take seriously the challenge of the liberation theologian Leonardo Boff (1992) for the Church to strive towards structures that 'model immediacy, face to face presence and reciprocity as advance signs of God's new society'. That means not having to be like town churches. Is there a need for many parochial church council meetings when most business can be done by the whole congregation over coffee after the Eucharist? Why worry if activities and events come and go according to who is available at any one time: one year a choir, another a music group, a couple of years later bell-ringers or a Sunday school and so on. It is not possible to do everything, so at any one time do the most important things with the resources that are there.

Sixth, it should have *buildings that are to be taken seriously, but as a means not an end*. A well looked after and welcoming building is a great witness to faith, but let it become the most important thing in parish life and it becomes a millstone around everyone's neck. By contrast though, it is equally important to take all people seriously, young and old alike – as an end not a means.

Seventh, it should have a culture of *nurture and growth* providing opportunities for people to grow and develop in understanding and in skill, again based on mutual responsibility and support, and driven by people's own needs.

Eighth, it should have *spiritually growing people*, with prayer and worship of the triune God at their heart, striving to enter into, know and celebrate that 'interchange of divine love' at the core of the good news we have to share.

These eight 'principles' were then augmented by a further one that was discovered on the way. This was the conviction that, especially in the countryside, *small really can be beautiful*. In a big world, the small church can remain intimate. In a fast world, the small church can remain steady. In a smart world, the small church can remain plain. In a complex world the small church can remain simple. In a noisy world, the small church can be a place for listening. In an anonymous world, the small church should be able to call us by name. This is key for the future of the rural church and the community it serves.

So the Church is called to 'be community'. But community by definition is never exclusive, and part of the living out of the 'being of community' today will recognize, and affirm, the reality that in the mobile society in which we live today the vast majority of people will draw their identity and sense of community from belonging to a number of different 'localities'. For example, there will be those worshipping in one place on Sunday, working elsewhere, living in a third locality and pursuing their main recreation in some other place still. Their experienced reality of networks and norms is multifocused with potentially conflicting allegiances, and forms of discourse, for example, when sports events for young people clash with church services. This complex situation not infrequently leads to a compartmentalizing of life, and possibly also stress and an unwillingness or inability to make connections between these core 'centres of being'. In response to this, part of the subversive character of the Church is to continue reshaping itself in order to show society its true life, through making creative connections between the worlds of work, home, recreation and faith. This has implications for the ways in which the Church develops both as community and as a true community of communities, and thus also for the way in which it structures its life, its ministry and its patterns of organization.

The Church and a Prophetic Voice

Davie links her perception of a movement from a culture of obligation to one of consumption in European societies to a parallel and inter-related trend towards what she terms vicariousness. In spite of a decline in institutional membership and credal assent, 'European populations continue to see . . . churches as public utilities maintained for the public good' (Davie, 2002). While the negative consequences for community and social capital of 'believing without belonging' or 'consumption without obligation' have been noted, this concept of vicariousness does have other implications, with attending possibilities, too. There can still be an expectation that the Church can and will articulate and champion the concerns of those who are not simply its own members. It can do this in various ways, through engagement in the life of the wider community, through offering its structures, buildings, contacts and ministry to support and facilitate communication, to articulate concerns, and through becoming a partner in action to build social capital and enrich community life. In so doing it is obedient to its call to be salt and yeast.

But Christians are also called to be light, and sometimes this will involve a prophetic role, challenging those things that actually, or potentially, damage or undermine what community is about. Much human experience reminds us that one of the most pernicious cultural mechanisms for creating or sustaining so-called community is the isolation or marginalization of groups or individuals who do not fit. Roger Hooker, commenting on his own experience in rural India and urban Birmingham wrote that:

> no matter who we are, the abolition of distance disturbs us . . . we do not like it when people who are different get too close . . . People who used to feel reasonably secure in their own place . . . now feel threatened by the presence of strangers. (Hooker, 1986: 1–2)

We see many examples of established 'communities' doing this with incomers, new arrivals seeking to preserve or recreate their own cultural or 'tribal' identities, failing to engage with the host community and culture, or even attempting to displace it. In many villages it is not unusual to find that while some such groupings become or remain dominant in the life of a church or village, others are marginalized, or even not noticed at all.

The Church is called to be catalyst, facilitator, learner, participant, advocate and prophet of true community at every level of community with which it is involved, large and small. This is why the currently fashionable emphasis, but overconcentration, on seeing the local church in purely parochial terms, can be so very unhelpful. The Church in its work of building community needs to engage, and be equipped to engage, in a variety of different forums, parochial, diocesan, county, and national, if to be faithful to its calling and effective in its mission task. We do well to heed an observation of Greenwood's on the role of institutions: 'Institution and community are easily set up as falsely irreconcilable opposites, institutions 'bad' and community 'good'. In fact the formation of an intimate church requires routines and organizations that make it so' (Greenwood, 2002: 13).

Responding to the Challenge

It is very easy for small communities, and perhaps especially the rural churches that serve them, to respond to the pressures on rural life and the kind of erosion of community and social capital negatively rather than positively. Often the trends outlined at the start of this paper combine to create what has been called 'survival thinking', in which people become increasingly trapped in attitudes that limit vision and potential. One manifestation of this is what Newby (1985) describes as 'rural retrospective regret', a hankering back to, and seeking to recreate, some perceived idyll of former years. It is one of the greatest threats to healthy communities today.

Such attitudes often lead to the inability to grasp new opportunities not only in the economic and social areas, but in every aspect of life, including the religious. Added to other pressures on rural churches (such as increasing stipends and pension costs, the burden of ancient historic buildings, and the demands of new legislation affecting everything from the keeping of records to the use of volunteers) this survival attitude can make it more difficult for the Church to function in healthy ways within the community. In *Leadership Without Easy Answers*, Ronald Heifetz (1994: 37) points out that communities may then fail to adapt as they need to for several reasons: they may mis-perceive the nature of the threat and make no response at all; they may see the challenge but believe that it exceeds their ability to adapt; or in the face of the distress created by the changes demanded of them, people resist the pain, anxiety and conflict. They hold on to past assumptions, blaming, scapegoating, and externalizing the challenge, denying the problem or they find a distracting issue on which to focus instead.

Like the culture around them, churches develop survival attitudes focusing on the maintenance of the institution rather than on mission and ministry and the development of true community. In so doing they ignore the purpose for which they exist, and so sign their own death warrants (made worse because the death is often painful and drawn out). This in turn may lead to a downward spiral of shame, guilt and even despair that negates the gospel and the kingdom.

This survival culture has to be taken seriously and an attempt made to understand it. To ignore the social, economic and financial factors that shape such attitudes is to weaken the effect of any creative ministry. The discomfort and pain involved need to be sensitively named and respected. It is also important to recognize that many of the dynamics involved within these communities are deep and unconscious.

Yet the positives of the Church's continuing presence and potential must also not be forgotten. Rural churches need to be helped to describe and evaluate themselves in terms of their own context (and using criteria that reflect that context) rather than using inappropriate models drawn from elsewhere. It should be a self-evident truism that rural churches are not at all the same as their large suburban counter-parts. Urban churches, suburban churches and rural churches each need to discover and develop a style that is appropriate to them, and it is not likely to be a 'one size fits all'.

The key to the future of all our churches is in continuing to discover what it means to live and work for, and in, community. This involves a reconnecting with that consciousness of a common participation in the Spirit's life into which we enter through our identification with Christ in baptism, leading to a recognition of the contribution to the life of the Church of all the baptized, not simply as a biblical truth, but as an imperative for mission and the pattern of our common life. One American writer, D. R. Ray, puts it as follows:

The small church, like small communities, must be seen as relational by nature, rather than programmatic. The failure of many well-intentioned initiatives by both church and government in small communities lies in the insufficient grounding of such efforts in the relational nature of small communities. Continuity of leadership and commitment to the long-term development of relationships within the church community and with the wider community are essential for effective ministry and mission. (Ray, 1992: 14)

The essential trust and engagement needed for mission in community will only occur as the church develops patterns and strategies for mission within the context of this relational nature of the small church. As Ray concludes:

That relational nature is both key to effective ministry and mission, and an essential gift of Gospel life. It is a gift that the small church might offer our hungry world. (Ray, 1992)

REFERENCES

Archbishops' Commission on Rural Areas (1990), *Faith in the Countryside,* Worthing, Churchman Publishing.

ACRE (1994), *Rural Life: Facts and Figures,* Cirencester, Action with Communities in Rural England.

Boff, L. (1992), *Trinity and Society,* London, Burnes and Oates.

Bonhoeffer, D. (1954), *Life Together,* London, SCM Press.

Countryside Agency (2003), *The State of the Countryside 2020,* Cheltenham, Countryside Agency.

Davie, G. (2002), *Europe: The Exceptional Case. Parameters of Faith in the Modern World,* London, Darton, Longman and Todd.

Department of Environment, Transport and the Regions (2000), *Our Countryside: The Future,* London, Stationery Office.

Edwards, W., Goodwin, M., Pemberton, S. and Woods, M. (2000), *Partnership Working in Rural Regeneration,* Bristol, The Policy Press and Joseph Rowntree Foundation.

Forrester, D. B. (2000), *Truthful Action: Explorations in Practical Theology,* Edinburgh, T & T Clark.

Francis, L. J. (2003), 'Religion and Social Capital: The Flaw in the 2001 Census in England and Wales', in P. Avis (ed.), *Public Faith: The State of Religious Belief and Practice in Britain,* London, SPCK, pp. 45–64.

Greenwood, R. (2002), *Transforming Church: Liberating Structures for Ministry,* London, SPCK.

Heifetz, R. (1994), *Leadership Without Easy Answers*, Cambridge, Massachusetts, Harvard University Press

Hooker, R. (1986), *Re-Inventing Distance?* Occasional Paper 3, London, Church Missionary Society.

Johnson, E. (1998), *She Who Is: The Mystery of God in Feminist Discourse*, New York, Crossroad Herder.

Moltmann, J. (1998), 'Christianity and the Revaluation of the Values of Modernity and the Western World', in Miroslav Volf (ed.), *A Passion for God's Reign*, Grand Rapids, Michigan, Eerdmans, pp. 23–44.

Moseley, M. (2003), *Rural Development: Principles and Practice*, London, Sage Publications.

Newby, H. (1985), *Green and Pleasant Land?* Harmondsworth, Penguin.

Putnam, R. (1995), 'Bowling Alone: America's Declining Social Capital', *Journal of Democracy*, 6(1): 65–78.

Ray, D. R. (1992), *The Big Small Church Book*, Cleveland, Ohio, The Pilgrim Press.

Rogers, A. W. (1993), *English Rural Communities: An Assessment and Prospects for the 1990s*, Salisbury, Rural Development Commission.

Woolcock, M. (2001), 'The Place of Social Capital in Understanding Social and Economic Outcomes', *Isuma*, 2(1): 11–17.

3. Isolated Communities

BRUCE CAMERON

Summary

This chapter seeks to explore the experience of isolated communities primarily from the insights and experience of the Scottish context, though its themes are of wider application. It begins by describing two situations, one historical and fictional, the other contemporary and factual, which illustrate the effects of social and economic change on the lives of isolated and remote communities, and the responses of those who live there. Both positive and negative elements are highlighted, recognizing the enriching elements of isolation as well as the sense of marginalization.

The next section focuses on more recent research indicating some of the practical issues which such communities face and the sense of 'powerlessness' that some can feel. The lack of resources and the consequent social deprivation and exodus of young people are regarded as significant.

An exploration of Old Testament themes of 'wilderness' and 'exile', and the upbringing of Jesus in Nazareth, offer 'biblical pointers' within which the struggles and achievements of those in isolated communities can be perceived, and through which a message of hope and. transformation can be heard.

The chapter ends by recognizing the paradoxical challenge that lies at the heart of many rural communities. In particular, it considers the challenge to the Church and how, as an example, the Scottish Episcopal Church has sought to respond through its recent Rural Commission report and review.

The Experience of Isolation

Kinraddie

Lewis Grassic Gibbon's novel *Sunset Song*, first published in 1932, is set in north-east Scotland at the beginning of the twentieth century. It presents a powerful picture of Scottish rural life in a period of significant change. Set in the Mearns district, just south of the city of Aberdeen, it relates the story of rural community life and its people through the life of a young woman, Chris Guthrie, in the fictional village of Kinraddie. Gibbon begins with a picture of this village as a close-knit community defined very much by its crofting and farming roots, still reflective of an hierarchical class system. At the centre of community life is the local church, at times revered, at times feared, and sometimes mocked! Gibbon describes the villagers' thoughts on visiting preachers:

> But on that December in 1911 the Manse was empty, the old minister dead and the new one not yet voted on; and the ministers from Drumlithie and Laurencekirk would come time about in the Sunday forenoons and take the service here at Kinraddie; and God knows for all they had to say they might well have bidden at home. (Gibbon, 1988: 9)

It is to be as a result of the events of the First World War that the village of Kinraddie's sense of self-sufficiency begins to fragment. Initially Chris Guthrie seeks to hide from the sound of war beating on the continent. Gibbon describes her retreat into the isolation and isolationism of her life at Kinraddie:

> But Chris didn't care, sitting there with her young Ewan at her breast, her man beside her. Maybe there was war and bloodshed and that was awful, but far off also. You'd hear it like the North Sea cry in the morning, a crying and a thunder that became unending as the weeks went by, part of life's pain, fringing the horizon of your days with its pelt and uproar. (Gibbon, 1988: 199)

But soon the men leave to join the war, some never to return as with Chris's husband. Those who do return now view their life and that of the village in a less defined and committed way. The old ways of doing things no longer suffice, and many of the younger men are attracted to the city of Aberdeen to discover work other than on the land, with its less harsh lifestyle. The church, too, loses its authority even though the minister and some elders attempt to cling to it; and the vestiges of the old feudal system are further dismantled. For those who remain in Kinraddie it is a painful time as they become more isolated not so much in terms of geography, for travel was becoming more accessible, but in their distance from a new generation's lifestyle, changing attitudes, and, for them, its lost values.

> Divided between her love of the land and the brutal harshness of farming life, young Chris Guthrie finally chooses to stay in the rural community of her childhood. Yet the First World War and the economic and social changes that follow make her a widow and mock the efforts of her youth. But although the days of the small crofter are over, Chris symbolises an intuitive strength which, like the land itself, endures despite everything. (Gibbon, 1988: cover description)

It is that 'enduring' quality that remains one of the strengths of many rural and isolated communities at the beginning of the twenty-first century. In Gibbon's time it was the war and social and economic development that changed and challenged the village people of Kinraddie. Today similar communities struggle to perceive their future amid new difficulties, fish quotas, farming subsidies and so on. The nature of the changes facing rural community life may be very different from those of the early twentieth century, but the challenge of creating vibrant and meaningful community, as old ways of doing things are dismantled and the way ahead is still unclear, remains the same. The Church is also part of that challenge, no longer, thank God, to preserve some autocratic institution demanding obedience, but to explore new ways of being a significant and meaningful presence in these communities.

Burravoe

Let me now take you to another part of the north-east of Scotland which in terms of geography cannot be more remote, to the village of Burravoe on the island of Yell, one of the Shetland Islands. The small episcopalian congregation gathers in the church dedicated to St

Colman and is the most northerly Anglican parish in the United Kingdom. The Shetland Islands as a whole have a population of about 24,000 but are a 12-hour ferry journey from Aberdeen, or an hour by plane. Indeed, to get an accurate picture of how isolated these islands are from the mainland of Britain is to imagine you are travelling from Aberdeen southwards and the same distance would take you to the middle of Lincolnshire. This was illustrated some years ago when a priest in Shetland was asked to fill in a form from the former British Rail. One of the questions was to indicate the nearest main railway station to his home. He answered, quite correctly, 'Bergen in Norway'.

Burravoe, however, can even feel isolated from the rest of Shetland, given that it is a further ferry trip and a total of about 40 miles from the capital of Shetland, Lerwick. The village takes its name from the harbour inlet, Burra Voe, and this harbour has been in use since the 1500s. It was the link between the island of Yell and the Shetland mainland for many years until 1973 when the new ferry terminal was built four miles along the coast. Today it has become a small marina for those leisure sailors who are ready to brave the North Sea waters.

At a crossroads stand two buildings that are important to the life of the village, the small primary school and St Colman's episcopal church. The church was built in 1900 and had its own priest living in the nearby parsonage until 1950 when it was, as now, linked with St Magnus congregation at Lerwick on the mainland of Shetland. Regular services are held fortnightly on a Sunday afternoon and during the week. Recently on one of my twice yearly visits, two members of that congregation shared with me their reflections on what it meant to live in this small isolated community.

Barbara has lived in Burravoe most of her life. She remembers the days when there were only five cars on the whole island. From her young days she was aware of the 'peace all around'. In her adult life she became a teacher, eventually becoming headteacher of the Burravoe primary school. Alma is also a teacher and indeed followed Barbara as headteacher of Burravoe primary school. She has now retired, and living on this island gives her the experience of belonging to a real community which has encouraged her to make Burravoe very much her home. The three of us sat in the front room of the former parsonage, now Alma's home. What of the isolation on this island? How did, and does, that impact the life of community? These were questions to which I sought answers in my conversation with them.

Our two residents of Burravoe initially surprised me by bemoaning the fact that modern communication had resulted in people in Burravoe feeling less isolated. A daily half-hour ferry service to the mainland of Shetland was very different from Barbara's younger days when the steamer would arrive from Lerwick three times a week. In contrast, therefore, to a community whose isolation had created a sense of self-sufficiency and cohesion, there was now greater fragmentation as people left the island for work and for social life. While this had been good economically for many, that sense of community and dependency on each other had lessened.

The ease of travel had also meant a loss of some shops and services, although as yet the post office remains. Responsibility for caring had shifted from the local community to the local authority, and the 'watching eye' over the young and the vulnerable, so important to community life 50 years ago, was now sometimes interpreted as interference. Thus the greater mobility and communication which had improved the economic base of a community like Burravoe had paradoxically created an isolation within, people becoming less dependent on each other, and, as a result, community life was not as cohesive as in the past.

There remained, however, for Barbara and Alma and for many others, elements of community life that were being sustained in Burravoe and precious to them. There was space to be yourself, a lack of stress, and still an element of caring for others. In the school every child was important, and the teachers had the time to make that real. It is true that young people moved away for schooling and further education, but some came back discovering that quality of life for their families was more important than the accumulation of wealth in the city. Our two residents of Burravoe found in the isolation of their community a sense of peace, identity, security and belonging. They feared the loss of that if the attraction of a town or city took too many people away; yet others had come to the island communities attracted by a quality of life which their very isolation enabled.

These two scenarios serve to illustrate the multifaceted nature of isolation. Geographical remoteness is one feature, yet people's experience of it varies from frustration at the lack of resources and services to contentment at the greater degree of interdependence. Isolation is also to do with power or the lack of it, reflected on the one hand in the independent spirit of country folk, and on the other hand in the experience of what some see as the creeping control of bureaucracy. Lastly there is what might be described as an 'isolation within' which some experience as the loneliness of separation, and which others encompass as an enriching solitude, bringing with it a greater sense of peace. To understand and recognize the challenge of and for our more remote communities, those concerned need to take cognizance of this paradox of experience which lies at the heart of their isolation.

Issues Facing Isolated Communities

Those who live in remote rural areas are, in one sense, no different from the people who populate our larger towns and cities when it comes to coping with the reality of living. Adequate resources and services are required if such communities are to survive and no nostalgic or romantic view can remove the need, for example, of services concerned with transport, health and education.

Professor Mark Shucksmith from the Centre for Rural Development and Research at Aberdeen University has recently commented that, when viewed through a car window or a television screen, it is easy to see the countryside as idyllic and changeless. The reality, however, is of rapid and uneven change, including economic and social pressures that create growing social exclusion for people on low incomes (Shucksmith, 2000).

Recent research has indicated that as 'economic and social pressures' bite they can potentially sap the lifeblood of these rural communities.

Loss of values

One characteristic that the modern isolated community can often reflect is a sense of powerlessness, which comes as a consequence of policies, decisions and events that are not of their own making. This has been expressed nationally in the growth of the Countryside Alliance and the various campaigns which they have organized. We would, I believe, fail to understand the motivation of these actions if we restrict it to the issue of fox hunting. At its heart there lies a belief that political control has shifted to what the Countryside Alliance sees as an urban and more liberal agenda which attacks some of the values which are held dear. The consequence has been to create potential confrontation between two sets of values, urban and rural.

The Scottish Episcopal Church, in a report on the Church in rural areas, used some research into Scottish rural communities carried out by Professor Mark Shucksmith and Ms Polly Chapman of the Centre for Rural Development Research at Aberdeen University. They confirmed that: 'rural people were perceived to have a completely different way of looking at things compared with urban dwellers' (Scottish Episcopal Church, 1995: 4). Rural people were said to be less materialistic, placing more importance on the family and community, and less on material possessions and wealth. However, this same research seemed to reflect a fear of change, as in the twentieth-century Mearns community of *Sunset Song*. 'Many', said the researchers, 'feared the impact of social change in rural areas as the volume of commuters increased.' The fear was that they would bring with them urban values which would ultimately begin to change the indigenous values of rural life (Scottish Episcopal Church, 1995: 4).

There is, of course, a danger in overstating this polarization between urban and rural. That same sense of powerlessness can equally be felt in the housing estates of our towns and cities. Geographical distance is not a prerequisite to feeling isolated from policies and decisions that determine the life of a community.

Lack of resources

A primary concern, however, is the lack of resources and reduction of services from which many rural areas suffer. The infrequency of transport, which in turn creates difficulties in making use of more centralized medical services and educational provision, is just one of the problems that confront isolated communities. In addition, the disappearance of the local post office or even grocery shop forces people to move out of the village to find these services.

In its report to the General Assembly of the Church of Scotland in 2003, the Church and Nation Committee highlighted some of these issues which faced the rural economy and lifestyle. It pointed out, for example, that of the 1,933 post offices in Scotland, 1,878 were sub-post offices, often an essential lifeline for many isolated communities. The committee commented that: 'most affected by post office closures in both rural and urban deprived communities are the elderly, the poorest and the least mobile' (Church of Scotland, 2003, section 1: 2). And such pressures and stresses on isolated communities was, said the report, further exacerbated by poor transport services: 'Those without transport are more significantly isolated and former focal points of community life have withered away' (Church of Scotland, 2003, section 2: 2).

In such a context the Church may well have a significant and practical witness to make. This same report highlights an initiative in the Orkney Islands, where congregations have offered their church hall as a new home for the local post office. There are similar ventures in other parts of the country, like a project run by a Baptist church in Norfolk which provides a care facility for the elderly. A semi-derelict building has been transformed to become a day care centre for about 20 elderly folk in the rural community of Meeting Hill in Norfolk (Fox and Fox, 2003).

Recent research has also highlighted the effect that central government policies, though motivated by genuine environmental concerns, have had on more rural areas which are dependent on public or private transport. Professor Shucksmith (2000), commenting on various studies done on this issue, draws the conclusion that transport is a problem that all the research studies identified as a major barrier to social inclusion in rural areas. According to his analysis, there is a fundamental contradiction at the heart of government thinking when fuel taxation and other policies designed to reduce car use and ownership serve to exacerbate rural exclusion and intensify barriers to employment.

Therefore the view of the Countryside Alliance that 'a sustainable rural community requires many things from the supply of affordable housing and jobs for everyone to provision of goods and services such as adequate public transport' (Countryside Alliance, 2002) does find resonance among many inhabitants of rural Britain.

Exodus of the young

Probably one of the more significant and concerning issues facing small isolated communities is the exodus of its young people. One of the very values which the rural community cherishes and seeks to preserve, the closeness of community life, may be the very thing which younger folk find claustrophobic and restrictive; and so they escape to the towns and cities.

In a research study surveying 700 young people aged 15 to 24 in Somerset and Dorset, Pamela Storey and Julia Brannen of the Thomas Coram Research Unit found that 'learning to drive and getting a car were major priorities' for these young people. However, since many were working in local manual jobs or were unemployed the 'lack of access to a car reinforced their feelings of exclusion'. As to public transport, 'high fares and limited availability' were a barrier to using it. Reflecting on their study, Storey and Brannen gave the following warning: 'If the only households that can survive are those without children or with substantial funds, then the social mix of villages and small towns is bound to alter' (Storey and Brannen, 2000).

At the other end of the country, research into job opportunities for young people in the Highlands reflected a more complex picture. In their publication *'Quality Jobs' and 'Real Choice' for Rural Youth*, Dr Ian Dey and Dr Brigit Jentsch point out that finding ways of retaining young people in their rural communities can not only be costly but can also restrict the choices available to them. So they argue that 'separating the problems of rural youth from those of rural communities allows a more positive agenda to emerge regarding the latter, as a more broadly-based approach can be pursued' (Dey and Jentsch, 2000: 24).

In a world where opportunities for young people are greater, and their horizons are wider, it would seem that the exodus of the young may well be the norm. Yet the rural community also has the opportunity to be part of that horizon for others. So comment Dey and Jentsch: 'this could involve a much more positive perspective on inward migration of "newcomers" and their capacity to sustain rural economies and services' (2000: 24).

Self-sustaining community

The solution, therefore, does not lie in trying to 'turn the clock back' for this is not feasible. The Scottish Rural Forum believes it is essential that authorities affirm and support the people within their own communities. Rural development will depend on effective, workable policies and adequate financial resources. But in the final analysis, these policies should be implemented at local level. This is reflected in the

Cork Declaration that stated: 'The emphasis must be on the participation and solidarity of rural communities. Rural development must be local and community-driven within a coherent European framework' (1996: point 5).

The role, therefore, of local people, individually and collectively, is vitally important, for there still remain, as my friends in Shetland highlighted, enduring characteristics of community in these areas. As Gillian Munro has written in her Arkleton Research Paper:

> While many people have rushed to predict the disappearance of community others have been keen to assert its reinvention or continuation. Industrialisation and urbanisation have long been thought to lead to the demise of community . . . with an added emphasis on the individual and individual gain. Community was thus to be found in non-industrialised, rural places which represented an earlier-evolutionary stage in modern society. Rural places are still perhaps thought about in this way, as places where social and economic interaction is mainly with kinsfolk and neighbours, defined by sharing not only a community of place but also a community of interest. (Munro, 2000: 7)

And she concludes that: 'The meanings and forms of community do change, but community certainly is still and always was, highly relevant' (Munro, 2000: 23).

Biblical Pointers

The Christian Church has to face up to change in its response to the social and economic evolution in rural communities. Holding together in tension the sense of isolation and exclusion in a time of social change, while finding inner resources to sustain and develop community, is a theme that resonates with aspects of the biblical witness in both the Old Testament and the New Testament.

Wilderness

The wilderness experience of the children of Israel in the desert of Sinai reflects how a community isolated from the mainstream of life's resources had to discover new ways of not only surviving but also rediscovering its own self-identity. The return to a former time in Egypt's 'modern' civilization was no longer an option, while the possibilities of a 'promised land flowing with milk and honey' remained a dream. The reality of the present lay in responding to the context of a desert nomadic existence. Through this they began to discern the call of God to sustain and develop their life of community.

It is interesting to reflect on how the children of Israel responded to a nomadic and isolated life as recorded in the book of Exodus. It clearly was not an idyllic existence for many of them, and led at times to unrest and unhappiness. There are a number of instances recorded when their lack of material resources was a major problem. And so, in common with humanity throughout the ages, they complain about their leaders, both human and divine:

> The whole congregation of the Israelites complained against Moses and Aaron in the wilderness. The Israelites said to them, 'If only we had died by the hand of the Lord in the land of Egypt, when we sat by the flesh-pots and ate our fill of bread; for you have brought us out into this wilderness to kill this whole assembly with hunger'. (Exodus 16.2–3)

> When the people saw that Moses delayed to come down from the mountain, the people gathered around Aaron and said to him, 'Come, make gods for us, who shall go before us; as for this Moses, the man who brought us up out of the land of Egypt, we do not know what has become of him.' (Exodus 32.1).

At the heart of the whole nomadic experience in the desert there lies the more significant and more enduring building up of community. This is the task to which Moses' leadership is committed. So throughout the wilderness experience community rules are developed, above all as reflected in the ten commandments. Tasks are shared in a more collaborative style as described in the encounter between Moses and his father-in-law Jethro:

> You should also look for able men among all the people, men who fear God, are trustworthy, and hate dishonest gain; set such men over them as officers over thousands, hundreds, fifties and tens. Let them sit as judges for the people at all times; let them bring every

important case to you, but decide every minor case themselves. So it will be easier for you, and they will bear the burden with you. (Exodus 18.21–22)

So the children of Israel come through their wilderness experience stronger in their sense of identity, their understanding of community, and in the foundations of their faith. The desert, as Hugh Pyper points out, is 'a liminal space where the constraints of social life are stripped away and both destruction and transformation are possible' (2000: 161). It is through this experience that the children of Israel 'are faced with the refiguring of their existence and of their relationship to God' (2000: 161).

Exile

A similar theme emerges at the time of exile in the sixth century BC when the Jewish people once more became an isolated and dispersed people, from each other and from the focus of their faith, Jerusalem. Jerusalem and the temple had been destroyed and this once great nation that emerged out of the wilderness experience in the desert under Moses was now in exile, subject to another great empire of Babylon. The prophets speak to a people now dispersed, struggling to hold on to their identity, their faith, and their worship. For those exiled it must have seemed that their life as a nation was at an end. The prophets, too, would sometimes reflect this in their writings as they identified with the experience of isolation and separation, and alienation. As David Reimer has commented, 'The symbol of alienation is at the forefront of the Christian usage of the metaphor of exile' (2000: 227). But Reimer goes on to argue that the 'use of the language of exile commonly neglects the aspect of restoration'.

The prophets, however, were also those who spoke of hope. Isaiah offers words of hope in response to his people's experience of isolation and weakness: 'For even although mountains depart and hills move, my grace shall not depart from you. My Covenant of Peace shall not be removed' (Isaiah 54.10). So the nature and experience of exile is one not of faith's weakness, but of space within which God can truly speak. The very experience of alienation becomes a means through which a new future is discovered.

Nazareth

Nazareth today is a lively, bustling town in the north of Israel. But the town of today is very different from the Nazareth of Jesus' boyhood. On a pilgrimage to the Holy Land a few years ago I was shown the results of excavations under the present Convent of the Sisters of Nazareth. Here as pilgrims we were able to walk along part of what was a first-century road and bend low to enter a cave-like dwelling of first-century inhabitants of Nazareth. It is here that you are able to touch and sense the environment in which the childhood of Jesus of Nazareth was lived.

The Nazareth of first-century Palestine was not a place of any previous significance. It was a small peasant village in Galilee, four miles, though, from the city of Sepphoris. The contrast between the two places would have been great. 'There (Sepphoris),' remarks Professor Marcus Borg, 'Jesus would have encountered levels of wealth and cultural sophistication unknown in Nazareth' (Wright and Borg, 1999: 182). As Borg goes on to point out, the remarkable story is that this Jesus 'born into a marginalised peasant class' should then engage in a religious quest that led him to be crucified by the empire that ruled the world, and 300 years later he would become the 'Lord of that empire that had executed him'.

The message he brought might well have been influenced by his upbringing. As Professor Adrian Hastings recounts:

Jesus was a Palestinian Jew living entirely within a Jewish society . . . He was identified with ordinary people, particularly the poor and marginal, starting where they started . . . He was an itinerant teacher and controversialist, wandering almost ceaselessly from place to place, calling a group of people to follow him, and usually, they did. (Hastings, 2000: 341)

It is from this Jesus, whose formative years were in a deprived and isolated Palestinian community, that we hear proclaimed the message of God's kingdom. It is encapsulated in the words of his sermon, preached at the synagogue in Nazareth.

> The Spirit of the Lord is upon me,
> because he has anointed me
> to bring good news to the poor.

He has sent me to proclaim release to the captives
and recovery of sight to the blind;
to let the oppressed go free,
to proclaim the year of the Lord's favour. (Luke 4.18–19)

In following this mandate, Jesus creates a new movement which was set to transform human lives, and offer hope to those who were powerless. Thus we discern in Jesus of Nazareth this powerful image of God revealing his nature through the isolation of human experience.

Rural communities today may often feel that their isolation reflects a first-century Nazareth; they may experience that sense of 'wilderness' in their alienation, and of 'exile' from the decisions taken by political and other power bases. They might also nostalgically or enviously look back to the 'Egypts' and 'Jerusalems' of their past and wish to turn the clock back to the time when their communities played a more central part in the life of the British economy. They may complain about the lack of resources (who doesn't!) and of traditional values that have been lost. Like those children of Israel in the desert, it is tempting for today's rural communities to retreat into despondency. The biblical message, however, is essentially one of hope and of transformation.

The Challenge Ahead

So what has this to say of our vision for the future of isolated communities and the Church's task in articulating that vision? We have discerned in their present experience a paradox that seeks to hold diverse truths in balance.

They are communities which on the one hand feel powerless in determining their own futures, and yet can be powerful in reflecting the qualities of interdependence and self-resourcing. They are also communities which certainly lack vital material resources and services, yet they would not wish to be so well resourced that the peace and space of isolation is destroyed. While there is a place for rural people to engage in legitimate protest to ensure authorities hear their complaints, this should not deflect from them using their creative energy in partnership and self-responsibility to determine their own future. And finally, those values of rural life should be seen as 'gifts' to be shared with urban dwellers, rather than regarded as 'precious jewels' to be locked away, and inevitably lost.

The challenge to those 'in power'

It may not always, of course, be a matter of pouring more financial resources into the rural economy, but of how such resources are distributed in order not to disadvantage those in more remote areas. For example, in the sphere of health, different health boards can sometimes approach this issue in different ways. While many small cottage hospitals have closed, some boards still see the importance of maintaining a network of local hospitals and medical centres. Others seem to favour a more centralized policy focusing the facilities in a smaller number of more updated hospitals, usually in areas of large populations. Recently local unrest was created in the west coast of Scotland when the future provision of services in hospitals at Oban and Fort William was threatened. The campaign gained massive support in the rural villages and towns of the west coast. It would, they claimed, give little incentive to families to remain in or to move to these more remote communities. The challenge to those with power is to act creatively in improving the standard of service while ensuring accessibility to all.

Indeed, the challenge for all of us, government, local authorities, churches, urban and rural dwellers, is not to create a battleground for different self-interests to fight for their 'rights', but to encourage the diversity of insights and experiences that all can bring to our global village.

The challenge for the Church

The Church has a significant role to play in this vision. It is present, and needs to remain a presence, within many of our small and isolated communities. That 'presence', of course, is no longer symbolized by the priest in a vicarage or rectory. It is, however, represented in many villages and small communities by people, and often by a building.

I have already referred to the simple but practical ways in which churches in rural communities have taken initiatives to sustain some of the services which people require. In this way the Church can contribute to the social and economic viability of such communities. Another example of this is how the Church is seeking to pioneer a community-based tourism project called 'Hidden Britain Centres' the purpose of which is to attract visitors to the countryside. At present it is at an early stage with the support and encouragement of the Arthur Rank Centre, but it offers real possibilities of a local church and community partnership. The word 'centre' does not refer to a building as such but to an area where tourists and the local community interact. It will offer a collage of experience of rural life and will be very much owned by the local community itself.

But what of the future of the Church itself in rural communities? I cannot speak at first hand for other parts of the United Kingdom, nor indeed for other denominations, but the statistics of the Scottish Episcopal Church show that almost 60 per cent of congregations are rural charges served at present by 40 per cent of the stipendiary clergy and an equal number of non-stipendiary ministry, lay and ordained (Scottish Episcopal Church, 1995: 37–8). Many of these have congregations on a regular Sunday of 25 or fewer people. The danger we face is that the Church could turn itself into a 'chaplaincy to the faithful' whose main concern was one of survival and maintenance.

A few years ago the Scottish Episcopal Church realized it had to change or die in many of these rural areas. A Rural Commission was set up and its Report (1995) and Review (1996) argued strongly that:

> mission can be integrated into the life of the rural congregation as members grow in their own ministry which extends beyond the bounds of the worshipping unit out to a wider service in the community. (Scottish Episcopal Church, 1995: 16)

In particular it identified the need to use all the gifts of its members if the Church was ever to get beyond simply ministering to its own.

> If we believe God has given ministry to each local unit of his Church, then we must have an agreed stated policy to identify, train, and utilise such gifts. Local congregations need to be helped to see that within their own membership there are the resources adequately to run a church and promote its life, work and mission. (Scottish Episcopal Church, 1995: 16)

> The future for the Church in rural areas lies in focusing outwards on the needs of the community and allowing that focus to lead the

development of appropriate styles of worship and ministry. (Scottish Episcopal Church, 1995: 17)

Since then we have made practical efforts to respond to this challenge, in particular, in the development of local collaborative ministry projects involving whole congregations, and the discerning of a diversity of ministry gifts within a local church. It is early days yet, but there are signs of new life and vitality in small rural congregations in different parts of Scotland.

Isolated villages and communities, whether in rural or urban settings, should not be at the periphery of the Church's concerns but at the heart of its vision. The promises of God were what sustained and developed the children of Israel through their desert sojourn; the hope of the prophets were what encouraged the exiles in Babylon; but above all, it was out of an isolated backwater of a Palestinian village that the vision of God's kingdom came in the life and ministry of Jesus of Nazareth.

To earth this challenge I return to the Shetland Islands, this time to the church in Lerwick, St Magnus, who are engaged in a local collaborative ministry project. Previously the provision of ministry to the Shetland Islands was primarily seen as a full-time ordained ministry with congregation and any non-stipendiary clergy existing as the rector's 'helpers'. Two years ago St Magnus's congregation embarked on a local collaborative ministry project where the focus of theological education moves from the individual to the congregation. Thus 'being church' is transformed from a community gathered round its priest to being 'ministering' communities exploring and putting into practice the ministry of the baptized. Over this period the congregation has been engaged in asking of themselves, 'What is the mission of the Church in this place?'; 'What ministries does that mission require?'; and 'How do we enable as many people as possible to participate to the maximum of their potential?'

Let one of the members, Joan Sandison, take up the story.

We are happy to be where we are now. No-one said growing up was easy! It is difficult to articulate how we have changed. We could say that we now undertake certain duties we didn't formally have, but that would not adequately express what has happened to us. We have grown both in size and within ourselves. We think differently and have become more confident. Perhaps most importantly, we feel like a family rather than isolated individuals. (*Scottish Episcopalian*, 2003: 8)

In the harbour at Lerwick lie two large boats. One is the ferry that sails to Aberdeen, the other the trawler which, with others, will brave the North Sea to gather in the harvest of the sea. The ferry is by far the more comfortable way to travel, since the majority of people on board are passengers who have little to do but be served by the crew. The trawler is very different. There are no passengers, only crew, each with their own responsibility, each one important and significant to the task. The challenge to local churches, in isolated or any other kind of community, is to become 'trawler' churches, competent and effective for that mission and witness which is their calling.

REFERENCES

Church of Scotland (2003), *Church and Nation Report: Post Office*, Edinburgh, Church of Scotland.

Cork Declaration (1996), *A Living Countryside*, European Conference on Rural Development, Cork, Ireland, 7–9 November 1996.

Countryside Alliance (2002), Letter from Richard Burge, Chief Executive, to the Right Honourable Tessa Jowell MP, 10 December 2002.

Dey, I. and Jentsch, B. (2000), *'Quality Jobs' and 'Real Choice' for Rural Youth: A Reassessment*, Aberdeen, Arkleton Research Paper.

Fox, D. and Fox, M. (2003), 'Meeting Rural Needs', *Country Way*, 32, 14.

Gibbon, L.G. (1988), *Sunset Song*, Edinburgh, Canongate.

Hastings, A. (2000), 'Jesus', in A. Hastings, A. Mason and H. S. Pyper (eds), *Oxford Companion to Christian Thought*, Oxford, Oxford University Press, pp. 340–2.

Munro, G. (2000), *How Do Individuals Relate to their Local Communities through Work and Family Life*, Aberdeen, Arkleton Research Paper.

Pyper, H. S. (2000), 'Desert', in A. Hastings, A. Mason and H. S. Pyper (eds), *Oxford Companion to Christian Thought*, Oxford, Oxford University Press, pp. 161–2.

Reimer, D. J. (2000), 'Exile', in A. Hastings, A. Mason and H .S. Pyper (eds), *Oxford Companion to Christian Thought*, Oxford, Oxford University Press, pp. 226–7

Scottish Episcopal Church (1995), *Rural Commission Report*, Edinburgh, General Synod Office.

Scottish Episcopal Church (1996), *Rural Commission Review*, Edinburgh, General Synod Office.

Scottish Episcopalian (2003), 'Local Collaborative Ministry in the Scottish

Episcopal Church', November, pp. 5–8.
Shucksmith, M. (2000), *Exclusive Countryside? Social Inclusion and Regenera-tion in Rural Areas*, York, Joseph Rowntree Foundation.
Storey, P. and Brannen, J. (2000), *Young People and Transport in Rural Areas*, Leicester, National Youth Agency.
Wright, N. T. and Borg, M. (1999), *The Meaning of Jesus*, London, SPCK.

4. Parish Governance: Has Dibley a Future?

GRAHAM R. JAMES

Summary

Nearly a quarter of a million people are members of parish councils and parochial church councils, yet they sometimes feel frustrated and powerless. The Quality Parish Council Scheme is intended to bring new vitality to civil parish councils. A new professionalism and more competitive elections at parish level are keystones of the scheme. Are these the best means of regenerating parish governance? What lessons may be learned from the (largely disappointed) expectations at the time of the creation of parochial church councils? And what has the rural Church to offer in wider community governance? The organic character of rural community life suggests that belonging and vision have deeper roots than transient connectedness with those among whom we may happen to live. Building community is more complex than many secular initiatives recognize, and has historical and spiritual characteristics which cannot be ignored.

Introduction

The Diocese of Norwich is linked with the Diocese of Luleå in northern Sweden, a diocese that stretches into the Arctic Circle. When I was there in February 2002 someone told me that his favourite television programme was *The Vicar of Dibley*. I confessed that I was rather surprised. He then said, 'Is the Church of England really like that?' I had to admit that it caught certain features of our Church with strange accuracy, even though it got some basic things wrong.

Anyone watching *The Vicar of Dibley* would soon become confused about the distinction between the parish council and the parochial church council in an English village. The two are amalgamated into a rather extraordinary hybrid body in the programme, though one that is curiously recognizable to those who participate in either ecclesiastical or civil parish government.

Participation in Parish Governance

There are around 8,350 parish councils in England and over 10,000 more parochial church councils. Parochial church councils are found everywhere, but the whole of England is not 'parished'. London and many other metropolitan districts do not have civil parishes. Many civil parishes were established in 1894 through an Act of Parliament. This separated them from any formal connection with the Church of England. Geographical boundaries sometimes continued to coincide, but, for the first time, the civil parish became a unit which no longer necessarily had any ecclesiastical significance.

There are around 70,000 parish and town councillors presently serving in England. Figures are not easy to come by for members of parochial church councils, but there are bound to be well in excess of 100,000 people. There is plenty of overlap especially in rural areas. As far as I am aware no statistics exist to illustrate the extent of this common membership. What is noticeable in the Diocese of Norwich is that the advent of ordained local ministry has meant that a small, but increasing, number of parish (and district) councillors are not simply members of the local church and on the parochial church council, but are also ordained. Alongside this development it is noticeable that fewer and fewer stipendiary parochial clergy serve as parish councillors. The reluctance is partly a result of increasing workloads in multi-parish benefices. It also derives from a belief among some clergy that there is an adverse effect on pastoral ministry if the parish priest is involved in making local decisions that could be controversial. Equally, contemporary stipendiary clergy do not regard themselves as part of a natural governing class, in the same way as their predecessors would have done, for example, in the eighteenth century when so many clergy were magistrates. This reflects a significant social shift, but it is a theological shift too. The motif of the servant Church has been a consistent model by which the Church has understood itself since the 1960s (partly the result of the Second Vatican Council). This is one of the outworkings of that understanding. Service is not equated

with being in authority, even though the *raison d'être* of all ecclesiastical hierarchies has been service of the people of God. What is intriguing is that the advent of ordained local ministry is beginning to
reintroduce clergy to parish councils, the magistracy and other areas
of local governance and justice. This may help to recover the link
between civil authority and Christian service, weakened over the past
century in relation to parish governance as an inevitable consequence
of the 1894 Act of Parliament.

Since somewhere approaching a quarter of a million people in
England serve on parish councils and parochial church councils (and
the figures would be much higher if all those who have served in the
past but do not do so now are included) these would seem to be deeply
worthwhile activities. Yet many members of both bodies speak of their
membership with an air of heavy resignation. There is a widespread
feeling both in civil and ecclesiastical life that power does not belong
at the really local level but is exercised elsewhere. (There is no agreement where this location is to be found, but it is definitely 'elsewhere'.)

The newly appointed civil parish councillor soon discovers that the
council has responsibility for street lighting, allotments, cemeteries,
playing fields, war memorials, seats and shelters, and the like. These
things are important, but they do not send a thrill down the spine
when you think of them. The excitement of political power seems to
rest elsewhere. Certainly the parish council has a contribution to make
on planning, highways and traffic management, but it is not often a
decisive one. Most of the things for which direct responsibility is exercised are static structures in village life. Little wonder then that parish
councils are often regarded as conservative in outlook whatever political make-up they may possess.

Mr Nigel Holmes, a parish councillor in Cumbria, wrote to *The
Times* as follows.

As a member of one of the larger parish councils for seven years
(and chairman for two, until May 2003), I have yet to discover
where our raison d'être really lies. We have little influence and less
power. We can paint signposts, maintain footpaths and run a cemetery but in key areas like transport and planning we can but advise.
(letter to *The Times*, 2 January 2003)

Quality Parishes

The Quality Parish Council Scheme, which the government launched in 2003, originated in the process that led up to the publication of the Rural White Paper (Department of the Environment, Transport and the Regions, 2000). The Countryside Agency, as the main rural policy advisor to government, developed the proposals for quality parishes. Many new opportunities for parish and town councils derived from recommendations in the Rural White Paper. Many councils received grants under the Vital Villages programme for parish plans, and used community service grants for village amenities such as ensuring the continuation of a village shop and post office. Fewer parish councils sought parish transport grants, though there have been some notable and innovative schemes to reduce isolation and increase mobility for rural residents, especially the young and the elderly poor. Some councils worked with the network of rural housing enablers across the country to increase the provision of affordable housing in their areas. But the response has been patchy. When the Countryside Agency reviewed the effectiveness of parish councils in 2001, it described a significant number as 'sleeping'. That description certainly acted as a wake-up call in some places since the screams of protest were loud. What it revealed, however, was that some parish councils prided themselves on their tiny budgets, and sought to avoid more than a minimal 'precept'.

In 2003 a national training strategy was introduced for parish and town councils. The steering group for this training strategy embraced a broad constituency. It included the Countryside Agency, the Society of Local Council Clerks, the Department of the Environment, Food and Rural Affairs, the Office of the Deputy Prime Minister, the Local Government Association, and the University of Gloucestershire, as well as representatives from Rural Community Councils. The strategy established a new professional qualification for parish clerks (the AQA Certificate in Local Council Administration). It was the first time a core qualification had been designed specifically for parish council clerks. It was claimed that this would raise the profile of the first tier of local government. For a parish council to gain quality parish status the clerk would have to be professionally qualified. Long experience would not be sufficient on its own. The training was intended to help parish clerks realize the potential of the councils they served. It was argued that it would also give them professional standing and enhance their career prospects.

All this formed part of a wider strategy to commend training to parish councillors themselves. The training of democratically elected representatives of the people in their roles as councillors is not without its complications. Who is being trained for what? There has never been a qualification for democratically elected representatives other than securing sufficient votes from the electorate. Members of Parliament are not trained for their work. Nor are cabinet ministers. When he became Prime Minister in 1997, Tony Blair had not previously served even in a junior post in government. In this context it may seem surprising that it is at the first level of local government where responsibilities are least far reaching that a national training strategy has been put in place. It could be argued that it may set a template for further extension elsewhere. It does raise questions. What is the effectiveness of training? And will a new professionalism in parish clerks, let alone parish councillors themselves, necessarily reap benefits? The professionalization of the first tier of local government could be regarded as distancing it from the people it serves, even though the rhetoric is one of service and best value.

One of the consequences of professionalization is to create detachment. The development of expertise can undermine common identity and solidarity within an organization, community or society. The work that Anthony Russell has done on the professionalization of the clergy in the nineteenth and twentieth centuries (Russell, 1980) has shown how this created a growing distinction between clerical and lay roles. This did not necessarily serve to strengthen the corporate fabric of Christian life and witness. It also rendered the clergy as specialists within a much narrower frame of reference.

A further feature of the Quality Parishes Scheme was that such benefits as would accrue from it were dependent on the parish council being predominantly or wholly elected. A parish council where there was no competitive election or where unfilled places were filled by co-option was assumed to be less desirable than the elected variety. Targets were set whereby a parish council would accrue the greatest benefits only if it was predominately or wholly elected. It remains true that a significant proportion of parish councillors continue to be co-opted. Some councils even find it impossible to fill the vacant seats by co-option. By definition, co-opted councillors have not stood for election. The prevalence of co-option and continuing vacancies is a weakness in local government which the Quality Parishes Scheme seeks to eliminate.

Distinctions are beginning to be drawn between two types of parish councillor, the elected and the co-opted, not least in terms of payments and expenses. Mr Colin Stevenson, a parish clerk, writing to *The Times*, welcomed many of the features of the Quality Parish Council Scheme but went on to ask the following question.

> Recent regulations allow elected parish councillors to draw a stipend (no-one around here proposes to do so) and allowances for necessary travel and similar expenses. However, the regulations do not extend to co-opted councillors, who may not receive any funding. May we assume that those nominated, rather than elected, to the House of Lords will be subjected to similar rules? (letter to *The Times*, 2 January 2003)

Parishes, both civil and ecclesiastical, are the units that come closest to notions of neighbourhood, family and community. For the Church of England the parish system is often at its weakest in metropolitan England where parish boundaries seem arbitrary and various diverse neighbourhoods may be included within a single parish with a very large population. Yet in the rural Church parish identity often remains strong because it possesses a human scale and seems directly related to neighbourhood and community.

I have already drawn attention to the way in which the professionalization of the parish clerk (and indeed the parish councillor, though training is not compulsory) is a new feature of the government's plan to renew the life of parish councils. The other is to ensure that competitive elections at parochial level will produce an interest in the first tier of local government, and create a properly representative parish democracy. It is these two assumed virtues, professionalization and democratic election, that I wish to examine in relation to healthy rural governance at parish level.

Changing Patterns of Local and Regional Governance

The government's desire for active, more representative and better resourced parish councils is commendable. Since central government has often shown little interest in parish governance, any renewed attention inevitably arouses suspicions as well as appreciation. I see no evidence of some sort of hidden plan to do them down. Governments are much less subtle than we often imagine. But there does seem to be a lack of integration in some of the government's aims for regional, county and local governance, given the various possibilities now being unleashed. Mr Nigel Holmes writing to *The Times* again expressed the problem well:

> Here in Cumbria the Boundary Commission has just announced its options for unitary authorities, were the coming referendum to support a regional assembly. The smaller of the two would, amazingly, cover half a million hectares and be larger than all but five existing counties in England. They, of course, have a district council tier of government. The population would be 313,000.
>
> This is larger than the pre-1974 county of Cumberland. Its population was 225,000 and then there was a lower tier of urban and rural district councils as well as county boroughs.
>
> Parish and town councils, adequately resourced, would be well placed to fulfil additional responsibilities and so avert the democratic deficit which would be the inevitable consequence of the imposition of such a unitary authority. (letter to *The Times*, 2 January, 2003)

What the writer ignores, however, is that there is something about the conventional wisdom on professionalism and democratic election that can make an uneasy fit with the dynamics of community at local level. The Church of England has suffered itself from this uneasy fit. A history of the creation of parochial church councils may be instructive.

Parochial Church Councils: Expectation and Disappointment

The Church of England has long been a lay Church with varying degrees of clerical control. As patrons and local landowners, some sections of the laity had enormous influence over the life of the Church of England in the eighteenth century. Read Parson Woodforde's diary and it is quite clear that the parson is very keen to keep on the right side of Mr Custance, his local squire (see, for example, Beresford, 1978).

In the nineteenth century the increased numbers of parochial clergy and the introduction of specialist training in theological colleges produced several generations of parish priests able to dictate what should happen in worship and church life, while gradually losing authority in society more widely. In 1919 the Enabling Act was passed, soon to be followed by the Parochial Church Councils Measure two years later. It might be imagined that many clergy at the time would have resented consulting elected laity on matters related to the mission and ministry of the Church. This was generally not so. Many expected this to herald a revival of interest among parishioners in the life of their parish church. For those who had returned from the First World War, conscious of the need for radical changes in the organization of society, this was just the sort of democratic development that would bring renewal. It did not. One of those who was disappointed was Canon Walter Hubert Marcon, the rector of Edgefield in Norfolk. He was born in Edgefield rectory in 1850 and died in the same rectory in 1937, having succeeded his father as rector in 1875. He was a symbol of a passing world and yet in his final years he implemented new forms of parochial government. He did so hopefully. He had rebuilt the parish church in Edgefield, moving it stone by stone to a new location nearer to the heart of the community. He farmed his glebe, identifying with the agricultural life of his parishioners. Yet in 1934 he wrote to a neighbouring incumbent:

> What do you think of the average Norfolk labourer? I have worked and worked hard for nearly sixty years among them and I am no nearer to them – generally speaking – than I ever was. We are good friends but oh! the gulf between us makes my heart shrivel up. The conversation is generally my own ideas, just altered a bit and handed back. (Linnell, 1961: 175)

The building of the church was his 'great effort for the souls of my people'. But, he went on to lament that:

> My choir is now reduced from five men to three, of whom one is occupied on Sunday mornings with horses and bullocks (I as a

farmer for 40 years know it all). And the other two that are left are mightily afraid of being left alone. And if the church is likely to be nearly empty the few won't come. The herd instinct is always on top. (Linnell, 1961: 175)

This rather sad reflection at the end of a long ministry indicates the minimal impact of the introduction of an elected parochial church council in a traditional Norfolk village. The social network, 'the herd instinct' had a certain cohesion, even if rural decline was unmistakable. But somehow a participative democracy, while introduced in theory, did not fit the social fabric of rural life in relation to the parish church in ways that it fitted the flourishing eclectic suburban church. Is the fit any better now, years on? The social fabric has certainly altered in and around Edgefield nowadays (and in similar places) there is a mix of village people born and bred in the area, a few second home owners arriving for weekends, the active retired, those now too elderly to do much, a handful of farmers though employing few others themselves, some self-employed people, and a surprising mixture of working people, many of them professional, commuting to the nearest towns or into Norwich for their employment.

Community: A Complex Phenomenon

That is the nature of many rural communities. We use the term 'community' of them, but there is little common life beyond residing alongside each other in the same location. One of the mistakes made in building new estates after the Second World War and into the 1960s was that it was assumed 'community' grew naturally as a result of people simply living alongside each other. We have learned at some cost that this is not so. Yet in many government statements or policies about rural communities there is an assumption that 'community' exists quite naturally in such locations. Perhaps this is part of the rural myth. While there is a good deal of 'investing in communities' in urban areas, community life is sometimes presumed to exist naturally in rural locations. What is also frequently noticeable is that the role of the parish church is often ignored, even in publications aimed at those engaged in parish governance.

In the *Good Councillors Guide* (Countryside Agency, 2002) as a resource for town and parish councillors, there are just two references to parochial church councils (and none at all to parish churches) in its 74 pages. The impression is given of a very neat and clear-cut division between the civil and ecclesiastical parish. The material responsibilities are distinctive. No one assumes the parochial church council is responsible for bus shelters, street lighting and allotments. But the description of a quality parish council found in the guide brings with it aspirations which seem almost theological:

- A quality parish council represents all parts of its community and creates a sense of belonging.
- It provides community leadership and a vision for the future.
- It listens to local people and articulates their needs.
- It works closely with community groups.
- It keeps them informed of what it does and why.
- It performs in a professional manner; this means that its finances are properly managed; it conforms to high standards of behaviour; and it is served by a qualified clerk.
- It works in partnership with other organizations, especially principal authorities and other parish councils.
- It is committed to ongoing training and development.
- Most important, it is active and elected by its community.

Here it becomes clear that the parish council is not simply concerned with the provision of services and facilities within the village or town. Governance is more than government. It is about providing community leadership and generating a sense of vision and purpose for all who live within the parish. It is charged with creating a sense of belonging, a task which, if articulated at all, was previously seen to belong to the parish church and the local school, often the two working together.

It is assumed in this description of the quality parish council that the community already exists. But what common life is actually found in some of our rural parishes? The mere fact that a wide range of people reside in the same location does not make them a community. A community only comes into being where there is common life, a network of relationships, common interests, and a degree of personal interaction.

The Parochial Church Council (Powers) Measure 1956 declares: 'it shall be the duty of the minister and the parochial church council to consult together on matters of general concern and importance to the parish'. The functions of the parochial church council include co-operation with the minister in promoting in the parish the whole mission of the Church, pastoral, evangelistic, social and ecumenical, and the consideration and discussion of matters concerning the Church of England, or any other matters of religious or public interest.

The difference between the parish council and the parochial church council in relation to the wider parish is that the former assumes the existence of the community within the parish as a whole, whereas the latter emerges from a community already gathering on a regular basis and which (in theory) embraces different ages, backgrounds and interests. It arises out of a common faith, though often one expressed in a host of different ways. What is significant about the Quality Parish Council Scheme is that it ignores entirely the significance of religious belief, the presence of the churches or a sense of the holy in building a sense of community and belonging to one another. It assumes that these things are achievable without any reference to religion at all. The aims of the parish council are expressed in terms common to an understanding of spirituality (belonging, vision) but believes these goals will be obtained through efficient, professional and democratic local governance. As Christopher Moody said in his book, *Eccentric Ministry*:

> The case has yet to be proved that a way of organising society which banishes a sense of a holy to the outskirts of its ways is any better at bringing down the barriers between people than one which respects it. (Moody, 1992: 74)

The Church on the Margins

Many parochial church councils have accepted this marginalization and get on with the inner world of church life. Maintaining the church building, raising the parish share, coping with change in patterns of worship and ministry, such tasks take enough energy without looking more widely. Some parochial church councils would undoubtedly warrant the disliked description 'sleeping' if the Countryside Agency were to review them. Rather than councils for the parish they have become management committees for a congregation, and the wider aspirations for which they were created are not often realized. Like civil parish councils, they frequently believe themselves powerless and that 'the diocese', 'the General Synod', 'the Church Commissioners' or indeed, 'the bishop' does not understand them.

Despite this, the parochial church council has some inherent qualities that are not always appreciated even by its own members. Unlike the civil parish council, which raises much of its income from the precept upon council tax payers, the parochial church council takes responsibility for raising its own funds voluntarily. The budget of a rural parochial church council may often exceed its civil counterpart. Parochial church council membership may thus generate a more active commitment, not least because of this direct responsibility for producing the resources for mission, ministry and the maintenance of church buildings. The danger is that this active commitment becomes very introverted and limited to the church itself rather than stimulating a sense of wider responsibility for the parish and all its people. Hence, the parochial church council itself, while being active, may collude with the marginal status granted it by those who simply see the ecclesiastical parish and its church as catering for a religious minority.

Yet this very marginalization (and it is experienced elsewhere in the Church of England despite its establishment status) may have its value. The way in which our churches live their corporate life on the margins of modern society, even in rural areas, may give them a different perspective on the character of the wider community. Returning to the aspirations set for quality parish councils, there seems to be a great confidence (whether imaginary or real) expressed within them. The confidence derives from the ambitions of institutions which believe themselves to be at the centre of society and upon which its desires are focused. Perhaps, though, the more historic communities at the margins may have a better understanding of the much less visible networks of memory, history, feeling and belief that persist and shape people's hopes and fears. These are deeply significant for community life.

Vision, Belonging and Hope

What is it that gives spirit to a place? What generates vision? Inspired individuals and visionary leaders rarely work through councils and committees. But they do connect with the history, character and feelings of those whom they lead and inspire, however that may be done. Unless they lead by fear and oppression, there is often a deep connection with the unspoken aspirations of the people. Churchill's wartime leadership, for example, derived not least from speeches in which he articulated the feelings and hopes of the British people and gave them a language to express them. He caught their vision and expressed it in a way that was inspirational because it matched their most profound desires and fears. They could not have put it themselves in the way that he did, but they knew when they heard him that what he said rang true. Visionary leadership requires interpretation.

Not every parish will find a Churchill. Charismatic and individualistic leaders do exist in some villages, but they are not always easy people with whom to live and work. If a vision for community life is to find expression, though, there does need to be some understanding of this almost metaphysical reality. There has got to be an ability to interpret the life of the community in order to articulate a vision, let alone enhance the experience of 'belonging', in itself an integral part of the dynamic of community. There also needs to be an appreciation of the complex web which constitutes the community network, even in a small rural parish. The identity of such a community frequently relates to its history and often finds its focus in the parish church, which may have a significance in the landscape and corporate memory much greater than the numbers worshipping in it on any given Sunday may suggest. Rural parish churches are frequently full for weddings and, even more significantly, for funerals.

In one of her novels, Susan Hill describes the feelings of a young woman whose husband has just been killed. This young widow is at his funeral in a village church.

She became aware not of the presence of the village people sitting or kneeling behind her, but of others, the church was full of all those who'd ever prayed in it; the air was crammed and vibrating with their goodness and the freedom and power of their resurrection, and she felt herself to be part of some great living and growing tapestry, every thread of which joined with and crossed and belonged to every other, though each one was also entirely and distinctly itself. (Hill, 1977: 113)

This sense of community stretches well beyond our present life and circumstances. Each individual is of huge importance, the more so because of being part of a movement in history. Continuity and community have more in common than we often recognize.

Communities have a history and a future. In worship the Church is constantly remembering the past, presenting itself as a living sacrifice in the present, and directing attention to the coming kingdom of God, already anticipated even if in a shadowy way in the liturgy. Belonging and vision have to do with more than transient connectedness to those among whom we may happen to live.

Building Community and the Democratic Process

One of the encouraging features of the Quality Parish Council Scheme is that it recognizes that there is more to building community and creating a thriving social environment than simply keeping the footpaths clear and the cemetery tidy. What, though, of the place of democratic elections at parish level? Why is this dimension given such an enhanced status in this context?

Partly it is because some parish councils seem to have become impenetrable, a sort of local politburo, where no matter how significant the revolution was years ago, nothing is now allowed to change. Dominant local personalities may use the parish council to prevent any alteration in the balance of power in local life. Free and fair elections, it is argued, may change all that, especially if local people from all backgrounds are encouraged to stand.

Like the parish council, the parochial church council is an elected body. But in rural parishes, elections are the exception rather than the rule. There are no statistics collected centrally (or even on a diocesan basis) to illustrate this point, but I have not met anyone with wide experience of the rural Church who believes otherwise.

Many rural churches have not had an election to the parochial church council for decades. In some cases I expect there never has been a competitive election since the very introduction of the parochial church council. Some clergy (more often in urban parishes and market towns) generate an election as a means of increasing the liveliness of the parochial church council. Surely elections bring with them competitiveness and are a sign of an active council, one in which people are keen to participate? Other clergy are equally keen to avoid an election at all costs, using co-options and other tactics to prevent a candidate feeling excluded. This is commonly regarded as weak leadership, and it may be so in some cases. However, in the countryside it may also reflect an accurate understanding of the nature of rural community life. Representative democracy works tolerably well where a constituency is large and relationships are inevitably distant. The majority of people living in a parliamentary constituency will not have met their member of parliament personally, nor would they necessarily expect to do so. Yet at parish level elections may create community divisions as well as giving an opportunity to the local electorate to exclude mavericks and the ill-intentioned.

One of the strange conjunctions of British political life at the beginning of the twenty-first century is that growing opportunities for the electorate to vote have been met by an increasing reluctance of the same electorate to do so. Whether for the European Parliament, a directly elected mayor, the Westminster Parliament or a local parish council, turnouts are disappointing and mostly in decline. This does not necessarily mean democracy is cherished less by the population at large. For democracy is not simply about elections. It is about people taking responsibility for themselves in public life by contributing to corporate decision-making for the well-being of all.

While turnouts in local elections may be low, this other level of democracy is appreciably more alive and well at parish level. Its vigour may be reflected in the governing body of the local school, the Women's Institute, the local horticultural society, the local history society, or in a hundred and one other organizations. In some rural parishes the sort of groups I have mentioned may be enfeebled or non-existent. In others they may be dynamic. All this may seem at first to have little to do with parish governance, but it is frequently in these contexts that the taking of responsibility for fellow citizens finds a focus. This is where the organic character of community life has its ingredients. The most imaginative parish councils (and parochial church councils too) work with the grain of such community life. Perhaps the most inclusive and creative forms of parish democracy may emerge where the liveliest and most publicly responsible of such local groups are given a voice and a hearing in matters beyond their immediate interest. One of the potential dangers of an increasing bias toward professionalization and democratic election in parish councils is that they will become more isolated from the organic character of local public life if creative partnerships are not established.

This exploration of the aspirations and potential pitfalls of current developments in parish governance is not determined by a nostalgic longing for some past golden age. None of this is a plea for the return of the good old days when the rich man was in his castle, and the poor man at his gate, and you knew where you were in rural community life. It is a warning that the recipe of increased professionalization and competitive democracy alone may lack some of the essential ingredients for generating active, inclusive and empowered rural communities. They leave out too many of the salient features and characteristics of vibrant community life, ones in which the Church of England (and other churches too) does not simply have an interest but a long track record. One of the challenges we face ourselves is that the rural Church often does not believe that the treasures that it possesses are much more than those to be found in the heritage of its buildings. The treasures are in the history, fabric, networks, feelings and sympathy of the church community, the community to be defined not simply as those found at regular worship Sunday by Sunday, but including all those who are sometimes caught in the web of Christian life. That is still a very substantial proportion of the population in many of our rural parishes.

REFERENCES

Beresford, J. (ed.) (1978), *James Woodforde: The Diary of a Country Parson 1758–1802*, Norwich, The Canterbury Press.
Countryside Agency (2002), *Good Councillors Guide*, Cheltenham, Countryside Agency.
Department of the Environment, Transport and the Regions (2000), *Our Countryside: The Future, a Fair Deal for Rural England*, London, Stationery Office.
Hill, S. (1977), *In the Springtime of the Year*, Harmondsworth, Penguin.
Linnell, C. (1961), *Some East Anglian Clergy*, London, Faith Press.
Moody, C. (1992), *Eccentric Ministry*, London, Darton, Longman and Todd.
Russell, A. (1980), *The Clerical Profession*, London, SPCK.

5. Private Property and Public Good

DAVID S. WALKER

Summary

This chapter examines the pressing question to whom rural Britain belongs. For theologians this question raises important issues about our relationships to pieces of land, 'belonging' in general, and the rights and responsibilities that go with it. The Old Testament takes these issues very seriously and they are overdue for re-examination in the present context. The New Testament builds on this tradition, but with a stronger emphasis on 'communities of belonging', among which the Church itself is a principal example. The first section of this chapter, 'Belonging', seeks to harness the scriptural and theological tools at our disposal.

The second section, 'Ownership and access', gives an account of the legal position, in particular those aspects that have developed under the pressure of the various stakeholders. We look, *inter alia*, at rights of way, trespass and access agreements as they have come under the twin influences of an ever-greater ability of non-residents to travel to rural areas and the increasing expectations of privacy that characterize our culture.

In our third and last main section, 'Rights and responsibilities', we look at the historical background to rural Britain as a natural resource before in turn addressing the private and public, individual and institutional stakeholders in the countryside together with the current drivers for change and growth. We seek to assess their place within a theological and explicitly Christian framework and give some pointers to churches seeking to understand and participate in debates and planning decisions.

Belonging

The Christian life can be expressed in three modes: believing, behaving and belonging. While at any time we will be operating in all three dimensions, it is the contention of this chapter that, when we address questions about the balance between public and private rights in the countryside, we are predominantly concerned with what it means to belong.

Belonging or ownership

When we employ the language of belonging we either speak of those things that belong *to* a person, indeed they are often given the title 'belongings', or we speak of the things *to* which a person belongs. This creates at the outset a one-way model that does not do justice to the mutuality between the two parties of a belonging relationship. Most modern Christian scholars would hold to the view that the biblical narratives do not support the contention that we can say of any object, 'This is mine. I can do just what I like with it.' For this reason we shall use 'belonging' as our theological tool in this chapter, whereas 'owner-ship' will refer to a narrower legal relationship and the exercise of claims over property. Wherever possible we will use the term 'belong-ing with' rather than 'belonging to', as this better captures the sense of mutuality that we are seeking to express.

Belonging with God

From a Christian perspective, the prime belonging from which all others derive is a belonging with God. The Old Testament expresses this through a series of covenants. The covenant relationship with Israel is determinative of that nation's identity. It places obligations on God, on the people and on individuals. The Jubilee laws, set out in Leviticus 25, make God's centrality clear. 'The land belongs to me,' says God, before laying down how each family is to regain its ances-tral land every 50 years. In the later Old Testament period, and into the New Testament period, we see the eschatological dimension of this belonging become ever more prominent. In Acts 4 we read of how those joining the early Jerusalem Church give back to God all their belongings in anticipation of the coming of God's kingdom, while throughout the Gospel of John run the nuances between the belonging we shall have with God in the future and that which the Church has with God here and now.

Belonging with people and places

Jesus summarizes the law as 'love God and love your neighbour as yourself', indicating that our second chief belonging is with people. Central to this is the notion of a 'household', a group of people who express their belonging together through inhabiting a shared space. The precise boundaries of what constitutes a household vary from culture to culture, with the modern western understanding being notably narrower than that of most other places or cultures. In order to enact this belonging in the context of present-day Britain the following conditions are important: that the space (or home) is defensible; that those who live there can exercise control over both who is a member of the household and who can have access to it; that its inhabitants have unfettered access and some degree of security of tenure; that the dwelling place contains facilities for washing, sleeping, consuming food and mutual interaction; and that it provides sufficient access to wider facilities such as shops, work, education and voluntary associations. It is important to note that already we can see the necessity for both the private and the public.

Belonging with the land

When in Jeremiah 32 the prophet buys a parcel of land that is to lie under enemy occupation, he is making a profound statement. His aim is to declare prophetically that the people of Israel will regain their inheritance. That he chooses land as the appropriate symbol is indicative of the significance of places to our sense of belonging. Nor can anyone with even a cursory knowledge of the present-day Middle East overlook the importance attached to gaining or retaining territory. Ties between human beings or communities and the pieces of land with which they experience belonging can bring out from us the most remarkable acts of violence or self-sacrifice. It is this belonging that inspires the farmer to continue to work marginal land in the teeth of accountants' advice. Where belonging is complex, as when public rights of way cross private land, the capacity for conflict is far beyond what otherwise the potential gain or loss of amenity might suggest.

Ownership and Access

Public access

The pattern of land ownership with which Britain began the twentieth century owes much to the Enclosure Acts of the eighteenth century and the rapid urbanization of the nineteenth century. By 1900 most working-class men and women were several generations away from having had any piece of land with which they could claim a special belonging. Their lifestyles and those of the small minority who owned large parts of non-agricultural rural land had grown further and further apart through the preceding 200 years.

It can be no coincidence that the generation that went off in unprecedented numbers to fight for their homeland in the war of 1914–18 returned determined to assert possession of it. The experience of war had served to heighten in them a sense of belonging that would no longer accept the degree of privatization and enclosure of rural uplands they found on their return. The right to stand on England's summits and look down upon the towns and villages in which they lived and worked, as well as on the beauty of the country-side, was not something that could be restricted to those who could claim title to the territory. A brief summary of inter-war developments is given in Ann Holt (1995). For those who took part in the events that led up to and followed the mass trespass on Kinder Scout in 1932 this was no campaign for the right to exercise; there was plenty of that in the mines, mills and factories, as well as on the sports fields. It was a declaration of belonging, and as such challenged the rights of land-owners as to the extent and nature of their own belonging.

In the following years, the opportunities to gain access to rural Britain have multiplied through such factors as the lessening of work-ing hours, the advent of widespread private transport, and much greater disposable wealth. At the same time, long-distance travel and mass media such as television have increased the area with which any of us may feel a sense of belonging. In the hackneyed phrase we are global villagers, and we expect to be able to walk across our village green. According to the Ramblers' Association (2001) the 1996 General Household Survey showed that 44.5 per cent of adults claimed to have gone for a walk of over two miles in the previous four weeks. Walking was estimated in the 1998 Day Visits Survey to have been the principal activity on approximately 930 million trips in England and Wales in that year. As an activity rambling stretches across almost the entire social spectrum. Legal rights of access are meaningless unless they come with genuine accessibility and provide access to something desirable. Visitors seeking unrestricted and way-marked footpaths and bridleways are in many cases also looking for conveniently situated car parking, places for refreshment and lavatories. They want resting places, like shops, buildings or sights, that engage their attention along their walk. Church visitors' books bear witness to the number and variety of those who either seek out or happen upon what is often the most prominent and historic building in the community, and of the impact their visit has upon them.

The 2001 epidemic of Foot and Mouth Disease made visible for the first time the extent to which public access to the countryside is now a more significant factor in the rural economy than farming. Government figures for 2002 estimate agriculture contributes £7.1 billion, and countryside day trips £9 billion to the United Kingdom economy. There can be no vision for a sustainable rural Britain that does not place at the top of its list how to develop further the range of services and activities provided for visitors. The challenge will be how to achieve this in ways that do not, through the creation of massive car parks, tourist facilities and opportunistic retail outlets, destroy the very countryside that attracts visitors in the first place.

Private space

Privacy in the home is an integral part of belonging there. The right to control who gains access to our premises contributes to our sense of identity and creates space in which we can foster relationships with those whom we invite in or with those who share our living space. The desire or need for private space is not, however, a static phenomenon. One of the most striking features of the last century has been the increasing distance we keep between most other people and ourselves. Average British citizens of a century ago would have shared their dwelling with several times today's typical household size. Most would have been educated in classes of 40 or above and then have worked cheek by jowl with the next labourer. Leisure in the early twentieth century exhibited similar limitations on private space; the cinema, music hall and public house were busy jostling places and football grounds regularly squeezed in twice the capacity the same space will hold today. Moreover, the houses themselves were smaller, with the likelihood of at most a small yard rather than an enclosed garden.

As we become more private in each aspect of our lives, it is hardly surprising that we increasingly see others as intruders into that privacy. Ownership, which historically was always hedged with rights and responsibilities, and in Christian terms is more commonly considered as stewardship, is seen more and more as an absolute. Moreover, as the population becomes more mobile, and as a larger proportion of rural dwellers are those who have chosen to move out of urban and suburban areas precisely in order to find peace and quiet, it is natural that those who infringe that vision by exercising rights of access become the objects of concern. Hence in recent years the focus of debate has moved away from that of access to agricultural land. There are still complaints about litter, leaving gates open, damage to crops and harassment of livestock, along with the occasional blocking of footpaths, but these are no longer to the fore. By and large most farmers accept that rights-of-way are here to stay and that any nuisance caused is minor. Indeed many rural landowners are sufficiently dependent on the wider rural economy to recognize that visitors bring substantial economic benefits. It is only when panic sets in, as in 2001 with fears that Foot and Mouth Disease would be carried from farm to farm on the boots of ramblers, that public access along rights-of-way is perceived as a significant threat.

Car parking, noise from customers leaving country pubs in the late evening, and congestion near well-known tourist traps all play their part in creating visitor-generated nuisance for rural dwellers. Most significantly in terms of the privacy of individuals, the Ramblers' Association indicates a significant rise in requests that footpaths be diverted because those walking along them can see into private homes. The underlying complaint is that personal space is being violated and belonging is being threatened. There is clearly an implication that what is acceptable in urban, or even village centre, locations in terms of being overlooked by passers-by on roads and pavements ceases to be so once the setting becomes sufficiently rural. In principle the removal or relocation of a right-of-way so that it no longer overlooks a property may add to the market value of the home.

Rights-of-way and trespass

In Scotland there is no law of trespass outside the domestic cartilage. However, in England and Wales it remains, under successive Acts of Parliament, a civil offence to stray from a right-of-way or to use one other than for passage, re-passage and purposes reasonably incidental thereto. Having said this, the use of the law of trespass is quite rare, not least because plaintiffs have difficulty in establishing that they have suffered damage.

The most frequent complaints or requests for assistance received by the Ramblers' Association with regard to rights of way relate to the duties of landowners, and of local councils as highways authorities, to see that all footpaths, bridleways and roads are passable. Landowners are by and large not averse to the existence of paths across their ground, and few go as far as the deliberate blocking of paths, but many resent having to expend energy, effort and money to maintain them. One common complaint to access organizations relates to the temporary blockage of rights of way by crop planting.

The Ramblers' Association also reports significant variation as to the vigour with which highways authorities enforce the law. There are a few rural county councils whose performance in this respect suggests that they give a very low priority to spending public funds on maintaining access for the benefit of others. The legal process required to enforce an authority to fulfil its legal requirement is sufficient to deter access organizations from pursuing it except in the most flagrant of cases.

While a case can be made along the lines that one person (the landowner) should not have to pay for a benefit that accrues entirely to others (rural walkers), it remains a principle of English law that property ownership brings with it legal responsibilities and that the cost of fulfilling these is reflected in the market value of the land. Similarly, the requirement on local authorities to maintain footpaths and bridleways would be hard to separate from their parallel responsibility for the road network. It is a problem that at present, while responsibility for maintaining rights-of-way rests with local councils in rural areas, the benefits are substantially received by the inhabitants of neighbouring urban authorities. As regional government structures develop across England, it may be worth considering whether those responsibilities that relate more to leisure than working life would more properly pass to the higher tier.

Under a provision that was new to the Highways Act 1980 path diversions can be sought where they are in the interests of the owner. Many of these are uncontroversial and may well both increase the enjoyment of the route for walkers while making path and crop management easier for farmers. There is some evidence of diversions being sought to increase domestic privacy and enhance property values, but these are a minority and will normally be opposed by organizations such as the Ramblers' Association which see a presumption in favour of the historic pathway as being itself a piece of heritage, unless adequate cause is shown.

Access agreements, conservation and the right to roam

The National Parks and Access to the Countryside Act of 1949 introduced a framework that allowed local authorities to provide access to specific areas through purchase, agreement or order. Even in the place where these were most used, the Peak District, the impact was relatively slight, with 19 agreements covering 76 square miles (see Holt, 1998).

With the rise of concerns over the impact of visitors on 'the preservation and enhancement of natural beauty' following the Sandford Report (1974), these largely fell off the agenda in favour of the prioritization of conservation. Over the next 15 years a highly politicized debate with claim and counter-claim as to the actual impact of visitors to open country on conservation was waged, though a dominant view emerged, as expressed in the Sidaway Report (1990), that the way forward lay in sensitive management rather than access restrictions. Access to the most obviously 'open' country, mountain, heathland, moor and downland, as well as to registered common land was finally granted, subject to reasonable restrictions for up to 28 days per year, in the Countryside and Rights of Way Act 2000. By this stage most researchers were no longer seeing conservation and access as inevitably opposed.

In the initial phase, as authorities seek to map which land is used for farming and which is eligible for access, the Country Landowners and

Business Association (2001) has received many reports from land-owners that some designations are inaccurate. Although some are being speedily rectified, there are worries that not all such disputes will be resolved amicably. There may well also be a low level of ongoing disputes in the future, as marginally economic land is taken in and out of agricultural use. There will need to be thoughtful work put into handling the small number of sites attracting large numbers of visitors that are thrown up by the Act. Some landowners are likely to respond to increased access by setting up farm shops or related businesses. Concerns remain to be addressed about liability for injuries caused by long-forgotten mine workings and other 'non-geographical' features. In practice though it is likely that the countryside will quickly settle down to the new access arrangements. There is no evidence that land values are being affected by the change.

In many ways the passage and implementation of these Acts of Parliament illustrate the balance to be found between different interests: the visitor who may wish to achieve access, the landowner who may have shooting or other commercial interests to protect, and the public interest as a whole, which seeks to minimize degradation by both owner and visitors and to maintain such things as biodiversity, geographical features, patterns of land use and physical attractiveness.

Winners and losers

Taking stock of the access and ownership debate at the start of the twenty-first century, we find a picture less of winners and losers among the interest groups but of geographical areas in which most will fall into the same category. Where the economy is robust, tourism and resident/owner interests will have much in common. Perhaps inevitably the greatest tensions between landowners and walkers occur in those parts of the country where both farming is marginal and the land less accessible. (It is where we find our own belonging to be threatened or challenged that we are most likely to resent and resist the assertion of belonging by others.) Hence where farmers feel more vulnerable they may be more likely to present negative attitudes toward those exercising rights of access over their land. In the same vein it is disproportionately those rural inhabitants seeking escape rather than engagement with rural society and economy that most resent what is perceived as intrusion into their privacy.

Rights and Responsibilities

A historic resource

The great British misconception, as true for the Church as for other aspects of national life, is that things had always been just as they were 20 years ago, and it is only the present generation that is inflicting fundamental change on them. The countryside has undergone tremendous changes over the last millennium, as it continues to play a major economic role in the life of the nation. In medieval times the great forests that covered much of northern England were destroyed in order to create land for sheep to graze. The woollen trade was so preeminent in creating the wealth of Britain that it was expressed ritually in the seating of the Lord Chancellor on the woolsack. Parts of rural North Yorkshire reached levels of population in the thirteenth and fourteenth centuries that they have never regained in subsequent years.

While sheep continue to graze in many fields and on many hillsides, other significant calls on the countryside have been made in later centuries. Industrialization produced demands for stone, coal and iron, and new towns grew up almost overnight to service the extractive industries. Population growth and mass transport combined to cover many agricultural areas with housing. Whole villages disappeared under reservoirs to provide water for the burgeoning towns.

New demands continue to emerge and grow. Public concern about renewable energy resources opens up the possibility of exploiting the countryside through wind farms and for the production of biofuels. The expanding of commercial leisure activities has seen shooting and fishing rights become highly valuable in certain areas. The question as to how economically dependent the countryside is on hunting remains hard to calculate.

At the same time conservation interests have never been stronger. Landowners, through the Country Land and Business Association, complain that their legitimate rights to exploit their land, and to contribute to rural employment in the process, are given too light a weight in the balance when set against the discovery of any creature whose habitat might be threatened by change.

The history of the countryside demonstrates how a simple distinction between private and public interests is impossible to make. Often the balance to be found lies between the interests of one part of the public and another; or between the interests of the present moment and the future. So, for example, an initiative that would bring manual jobs into a rural area will be welcomed by poorer families struggling to stay in the country, but opposed by those who have recently purchased a rural retreat.

A strong recent trend is for those objects traditionally seen as of value in their own right to be treated first and foremost as capital assets. Nowhere has this trend been more evident than in the case of land and property, as reflected in the way in which the media consider house price inflation as something to be welcomed, whereas inflation overall is treated far less favourably. The impact of viewing land and property assets as economic, rather than inherent, goods distorts the ways in which we use them.

Increasingly planning processes (in urban as well as rural areas) are influenced by stakeholders' views on whether a proposed development will add to or reduce the capital value of their asset, rather than wider considerations.

While it is a minority Christian stance that the acquisition of wealth is in itself to be avoided as either sinful or the cause of sin, the tradition is almost universal in warning against allowing it to dominate moral decision-making. There is clearly a call for the Church to be counter-cultural here, and there are impressive, if not widespread, examples of individuals and church-related communities that have engaged in the planning process in ways that demonstrate priorities other than the narrowly financial.

An important question for this volume is whether there are guidelines that are of particular use to Christians who either seek to engage in these debates or who have a need to respond to a particular situation arising in their own community. We will look briefly in turn at what rights and responsibilities may broadly accrue to the rural community, to individual property owners, and to the wider nation. Within this topic we select for examination the issue of house building, where the diversity of interests and the underlying aspirations of different stakeholders in the rural community is often exposed at its keenest. Underpinning our discussion will be the theology of belonging with which this chapter began.

Community belonging

If we wish to have rural communities within which people belong, then those communities need to be economically sustainable. That which destroys community also destroys belonging. The rural economy must work.

Expensive transport costs, lower levels of competition, and lack of economies of scale are obvious examples of one perennial rural disadvantage. This is not only an issue for farming; 16 per cent of rural jobs are in the manufacturing sector, where the combination of national sector decline with competition from urban areas closer to motorway and rail networks creates a particularly acute threat. However, if rural sustainability is not to be subject to political whim, it cannot be something artificially held in place by a massive degree of external revenue subsidy. The economy must naturally regenerate, creating new jobs as old ones disappear.

Rural economic sustainability requires a planning framework that views positively the main drivers for rural job growth, including diversified use of agricultural premises, light industry, home-working supported by information technology, and tourism, together with the support services each requires. The Country Land and Business Association argues that the changes of land use required to achieve sustainable levels of economic growth are not large, but to respond to opportunities as they arise will almost certainly require rather more than we are accustomed to in the way of joined-up thinking between those with responsibility for economic issues on the one hand and conservation or habitat preservation on the other hand.

Economic sustainability must also go along with its social counterpart. Belonging requires the rural community to have reasonable local access to schools, leisure and meeting facilities, places to celebrate rites, and basic shops. It is also necessary to sustain a level of voluntary associational activities in the countryside. It is particularly important to test whether the community provides a sustainable lifestyle across the age range. Young people, for example, can often be poorly served both in terms of what is available for them in their local community and in respect of access by public transport to facilities further afield.

From their presence in the rural community, local churches are well placed to notice where the social fabric is thin. The Church has comparatively short and accessible communication lines between the local parish and specialists at diocesan level, or directly to the staff of the ecumenical Arthur Rank Centre in Warwickshire. These in turn engage at senior level with Department for the Environment, Food and Rural Affairs and other government departments.

Land for house-building

The demographic profile of the community will have a large part to play in determining what social facilities are or are not sustainable. It is in this area that one of the hardest fought battles over land presently takes place. Land in and near to communities, urban or rural, is a resource for house building. In particular, given the immense discrepancy between agricultural land values and the cost of land with residential planning permission, rural land is a natural resource for building affordable housing. The landowner is still able to realize a significant profit, while the property costs are kept well below full market value. Although figures for council housing are not available at sub-authority level, anecdotal evidence suggests that only a tiny fraction of the rural council housing stock remains publicly owned. This would imply that there is significant opportunity to meet local need and sustain local infrastructure by releasing land for housing association development.

A numerically smaller but important related issue is the provision of retirement housing for rural estate workers. As people live longer and in frail health, the typical estate cottage becomes less suitable. Present planning rules do not make it easy to construct appropriate retirement properties on the estate itself, forcing individuals and families away from their natural community at a vulnerable point in their lives.

Rural clergy regularly report stories of intended developments which they would support in principle, but where the vehemence and polarization of local opinion makes it almost impossible to commend publicly. Clergy attest that opposition to development comes disproportionately from those who have moved to the countryside in recent times, a fact which cannot fully be explained away by the newer arrivals being either more articulate or better used to using legal and planning processes than their longer-established neighbours.

Rural sustainability will not be achieved without diversity. Jesus himself makes it clear in the parable of the good samaritan that neighbourliness is to be found in how we interact with those unlike us, not in the huddling together of those with strong common interests. Mixed communities are essential, and will not arise without diverse patterns of housing tenure. Planning law provides a framework in which such diversity can be delivered, but the implementation is poor. All too often specious objections to affordable housing at a case-by-case level override the wider needs of the community.

Owners and entrepreneurs

Owners of property and land in the countryside cannot be placed in a single category. While any categorization runs the risk of caricature, a few examples may be helpful. One category consists of those integrated both into the rural economy and rural society. Often they have been significant landowners in their communities for many years or generations. Their network of relationships within the community will tend towards recognition of the rights and needs of others. Given the natural human tendency for rights long possessed to be worn more lightly than those recently acquired, they are relatively less troubled by the presence of footpaths on their land. Such noise and nuisance as is consequent upon economic activity is seen as a price worth paying, not least since they are largely beneficiaries of such activity. In any economic regeneration of rural areas they are likely to play a lead role. Within this group we would place the historic, individual and corporate landowners. Many of these have inherited and continued a strong desire to maintain rural services such as shops, schools and affordable housing. Moreover, they do so often to their own financial disadvantage.

A second category consists of rural entrepreneurs, the high technology home-workers mentioned briefly earlier. It is increasingly possible to run many small businesses from home. Some businesses are naturally best sited in a rural environment, some spring up where the entrepreneur is already settled, and some are deliberately relocated as a business develops. Some of these will grow and begin to offer administrative and other lower paid employment in the local community. They may also provide support for local businesses in the catering and related trades. They can help maintain sustainability of rural communications infrastructure, including post offices and mail delivery.

A third category consists of those for whom the countryside is not a place of engagement, but a place of escape. Some continue to commute to the towns and cities for work. Most look outside the rural environment for social relationships, shopping and participation in organized activity. Some will live part-time in the country, perhaps mainly at weekends and holidays. They are less likely to welcome the noise and intrusion that goes with economic and leisure activity, as these may have been principal factors in their leaving the urban environment. For some there are also dimensions of 'trophy living', where a rural home in private grounds is acquired as a sign of success and affluence. These persons will tend to be both articulate and used to expressing their wishes and aspirations forcefully and effectively. Beyond paying council taxes, and in a few cases employing domestic staff, they make a disproportionately small contribution to local sustainability and to rural belonging.

Rural living continues to attract many former urban dwellers. And it does so with lifestyles that contribute very little towards either economic or social sustainability. At a time when the language of 'social capital' is being developed (see Alan Smith in Chapter 11 of the present volume) we can properly ask what contribution, other than the cost of house purchase, should be expected as the price of living in the countryside.

The refusal of a significant proportion of residents to belong, as opposed simply to own and to inhabit, diminishes the belonging of others. While it would be impossible to enforce community participation on rural inhabitants, there are good examples of the use of planning law in urban areas, for example to limit the erection of hedges and fences, that might with sensitivity and imagination be used as models for rural Britain, so as to restrict unnecessary isolation and over-privacy.

The Church

No study of rural land and property owners could fail to address the part played by the Church, not least because the Church Commissioners for England remain one of the most significant historic landlords.

The Church Commissioners' prime responsibility is to manage both capital and revenue in order to maximize their financial contribution to the ministry of the Church of England. Much of the Church

Commissioners' revenue is directly applied to supporting parish ministry in poorer dioceses or to discharging historic liabilities such as pensions for clergy service. It is possible in law for the Church Commissioners to forego certain types of activity or investment that might bring the Church into disrepute, or substantially impair its mission, including for example, investment in armaments and the alcohol industry. However, it is not possible in law for the Church Commissioners to operate in ways that support other good aims at the expense of their prime responsibility. The same is true for other asset-owning church bodies such as dioceses and individual parishes, whose combined assets well exceed those of the national institutions.

In terms of managing their substantial rural assets, chiefly land, the Church Commissioners and other asset-holders broadly follow the pattern of responding to positive ideas that emerge locally inasmuch as they are consistent with good asset management. These would include permissive access or paths where proposals are initiated by tenants, for example through countryside stewardship schemes, and assisting tenants in rural diversification schemes, including instances where the Church Commissioners have themselves become investors in the scheme. Recent examples include converting buildings into offices and an organic milk processing plant. Current tenancy law puts succession rights at risk where diversification income exceeds that from farming. The Church Commissioners are aware of and in sympathy with moves to change the legal position on this risk.

The Church Commissioners also respond permissively to demands regarding rural sports and activities. This includes occasional approaches for cycling and metal detection, together with a quite marked diversification into horse livery and related activities.

There are several examples of the Church Commissioners using exception procedures to gain planning consent for low-cost rural housing. Proposed changes in planning law, increasing the require-ment on developers to include low-cost, social or key worker accommodation make it likely that in future landlords, including the Church Commissioners, will expect to sell at full market value, leaving the social element to the developer and planners. Again, although there are examples of the Church Commissioners' land being sold to provide local facilities, this is mostly achieved through Section 106 agreements between developer and planners.

It would be quite a culture change were the Church's rural assets to be managed in a more proactive fashion. Tenants in particular might resist a new style that sought to impose conditions or priorities upon them that do not accord with their own perceptions of their interests. There would also be legal concerns should changes in policy be deemed to reduce either revenue incomes or capital values. These objections should not override a strong moral case. Much could be learned from the example of the National Trust which, like diocesan bodies and the Church Commissioners, is substantially running and managing land that formerly belonged more locally. It would be timely for the Church of England to commission a working party to investigate how it might use its position as a major rural landowner in order to promote best practice both for itself and for other church bodies so as to maximize the social capital as well as economic value of its assets.

Many of the assets held by church institutions at diocesan and national level derive from rural land and property holdings. There is still resentment in many rural parishes at what is seen as a diversion of these assets into maintaining the urban Church, with the consequence that many rural parishes are now seen as 'non-viable'. Whether it is seen as direct subsidy to maintain rural social capital as reparation for past diversions of assets, or as a combination of both, the rural Church has a legitimate call on resources now held at a wider level.

The public stake

We have mentioned earlier some of what the wider public expects of rural Britain. Accessible leisure, with all of the support facilities to enable that, must come at the top of any list. We also expect the countryside to conserve some of what we have lost from urban areas by way of wildlife and flora. We demand cheap and visually attractive foods, and in so doing create an agricultural economy which has its own effects on land. And there is the re-emerging need to look to the countryside to contribute to our energy needs as offshore supplies of fossil fuels become less cheap and plentiful. It is important also to ask at this stage what new expectations are being made, and what areas are likely to expand in the future.

At a time when the numbers held in the prison system are expanding and when government provision for dealing with asylum claims is perceived to be inadequate, the countryside is looked to as a location where society can place those whom it wishes to keep, literally, at arm's length. Inappropriate suggestions of locations for such prove particularly complex for the Church to respond to. The distinction between opposing an inappropriate site and rejecting the people concerned can easily be lost in the heat of an intense media campaign. This is evidenced by the experience of the diocese of Worcester in opposing a large asylum facility at a remote location.

Remoteness is also a desirable feature sought for military training and for testing defence systems and technologies. In an unstable world, with United Kingdom troops regularly engaged in action across the globe, and with the scaling down of training facilities in Western Europe, it remains to be seen if military needs can continue to be confined to their traditional grounds with no wider impact than at present.

Water supply is an increasingly political topic as several factors combine to increase demand. Modern agriculture is ever more water intensive. Climate change and global warming may deplete rainfall at points in the farming cycle when it is most needed. Modern industrial processes consume more than their precursors. And we expect our homes, our belongings and our bodies to be cleaned more frequently than previous generations. Government websites already carry information as to the parts of the United Kingdom in which the situation is becoming most urgent. While intensive reinvestment in existing provision, especially through seeking to reduce water losses in transit, could produce some savings, it is highly unlikely that we can forestall for long the need to make strategic decisions about how to increase supply. For the United Kingdom capturing more rainwater is likely to remain a cheaper option than desalination or better recycling. If this is achieved through the creation of a new generation of large reservoirs the contentious issue will be the consequent flooding of tracts of land. If we seek to increase extraction from rivers, this will impact upon existing extractors and leisure users. If we take greater supplies from groundwater, this may have detrimental effects upon the water table.

It is likely that trends in rural sports will come and go. There is evidence from the Country Land and Business Association and others of a growth in river use by canoeists. If this accelerates, there may be issues to settle where canoeing is seen as detrimental to the exploitation of fishing rights or where rivers pass close to domestic property.

Quid pro quo

One emerging strand covers the public benefits that may be sought in return for public subsidy. There are a number of examples of such agreements in other sectors. Bodies such as English Heritage may require commitments to public access in return for grants made towards the renovation of churches. European funding for community facilities often stipulate a minimum number of years for which the private owner must provide a public benefit. There are examples of public access to private buildings or to works of art being granted in lieu of inheritance taxes. Planning law has for some years sought to tap the windfall gains made by landowners in order to derive a local public benefit.

Within the agricultural sector, the current policy of the European Union Commission Agricultural Policy represents a decisive move away from subsidy to land management grants, available in return for compliance with certain standards of management. A further example of development in this direction can be seen in the present debate about whether set-aside land should come within the terms of the access rights given in the Countryside and Rights of Way Act 2000. If such land were included it might be seen to set a precedent for access arrangements and improvements in other cases where landowners are in receipt of public monies.

The theological stance of this chapter is that the relationship created by the gift and receipt of subsidy is a relationship of belonging, and that it is reasonable to explore what obligations can legitimately arise out of that belonging. From a practical perspective this fits with the evidence from existing and developing schemes that there needs to be a strong link between the asset for which the subsidy or grant is given and the public good that is sought in return.

There remains considerable scope to develop the practice of linking revenue to requirements that sustain and enhance the rural community, or that deliver objectives that the wider national or international community consider desirable. Alongside land management these could include enhanced living conditions for livestock, or more controversially, the replacement of blood sports by humane alternatives.

Conclusion

Rural Britain remains, as it always has been, deeply connected with the economic and wider life of the whole nation. The very special nature of land, and our relationship to it, means that the questions with which we must interrogate rural policies and practices often arise at a deeper level of our self-understanding and can be clouded by the emotional attachments we may hold quite subconsciously. There is a need for Christians to engage theologically with such issues, and the concept of 'belonging' has proved a simple but useable tool, which may be developed and adapted for specific issues.

Unsurprisingly some of the interests expressed will not be easily reconciled, and here particularly clergy, preachers and teachers will need to weigh carefully the point at which they cease to help their congregations understand and participate in the debates and when they become advocates of a particular cause themselves. Nonetheless, the fact that subjects are contentious cannot be justification for the Church to ignore them.

REFERENCES

Country Landowners and Business Association (2001), *Rural Regeneration: A Policy Framework for Business Diversification*, London, CLA.

Holt, A. (1995), *The Origins and Early Days of the Ramblers' Association*, London, Ramblers' Association.

Holt, A. (1998), *Managing Conflict Over Access to Open Country: A Case Study of the Peak National Park*, London, Ramblers' Association.

Ramblers' Association (2001), *Rights of Way: A Guide to Law and Practice*, London, Ramblers' Association.

Sandford Report (1974), *Report of the National Park Policies Review Committee 1974*, London, Department of the Environment.

Sidaway Report (1990), *Birds and Walkers: A Review of Existing Research on Access to the Countryside and Disturbance to Birds*, London, Ramblers' Association.

6. Globalization and Local Autonomy

RICHARD CLARKE

Summary

The chapter begins with the suggestion that 'globalization' should be seen as a vehicle for the injustices of free trade today, rather than their moral cause.

In Britain and Ireland we are undoubtedly benefiting from the global economic forces of the present time but, ironically, as we damage the economic progress of other countries, our own farming sector (in particular in Ireland) is itself being destroyed. Globalization means also that countries, even so-called developed countries, are at the mercy of multinational corporations who may, at will, move their business interests to and from particular countries and localities. The notion of the 'nation state' is thereby being eroded, as governments have ever less control over the internal economic structuring of the state. The world has become 'delocalized'.

Whereas a return to a pre-global utopia is far-fetched, the Church has an obligation to challenge the directions in which an untrammelled free market has taken us. The Church must assert that increased production (and consumption) of goods is not axiomatically a desirable good, that justice and rationality are not necessarily co-terminous, and that the biblical demand for communion and community, as proclaimed in the theological construct of *koinonia*, has still a prophetic resonance for the world of today. Even if globalization remains, the encouragement of local community remains also an imperative.

Introduction

We need to be very clear at the outset of our discussion as to what we may attribute directly to the phenomenon we casually call *globalization*. After all, for as long as members of the human race saw fit to take faltering steps beyond the borders of the local self-sufficient village community, we have had globalization, to a lesser or greater extent. The first steam ship, the first telephone call, the first electronic credit transfer, were all, in their time, crucial steps in the process of reducing the world to more manageable proportions. What we have encountered in our generation, however, is a quantum leap in human ability to *move things*, the movement of capital, of produce, of ideas and of instructions. Today, money can be transferred across the world at the press of a button, goods of any type can be moved from continent to continent within hours, and global communication is electronic and instant. Whether or not these are the ultimate techno-logical steps in the business of globalizing is not for us to decide. To us, at this moment, it seems this way. But a little further into the future, who knows whether what we now portentously call 'globalization' may not all seem endearingly primitive and antiquated? Technology well may have many more leaps to make.

The horrors that have stemmed from the opportunities presented to capitalism by globalization as we now know it are sufficiently well documented, although brief reference must still be made to some of these for the purposes of this chapter. We need to ask at this point, however, the central question as to how much of the misery is intrinsic to globalization *as such*, and how much due to the opportu-nities presented to an unfettered capitalism and a global free market which is virtually without regulation of any kind. The classical theory of economics, propounded by Adam Smith over two centuries ago, is (with some oversimplification) the hypothesis that if we allow open competition in all production of goods, we will increase efficiency, and therefore productivity, and therefore total wealth, and that everyone will thereby benefit. A further step in the argument is that the larger a market, the 'better' it will inevitably be. A larger market allows for greater specialization and therefore for greater efficiency in pro-duction. The removal of bureaucratic interference in the means of pro-duction will, it is argued, automatically ensure greater effectiveness.

In a world where there are such vast opportunities for economic expansion (a world never dreamt of by Adam Smith), the World Trade Organization was brought into being in 1995, to ensure what was to be regarded as a 'level playing field' in terms of trade. There is, however, a rather unfortunate flaw in this argument. Remaining with the analogy of a playing field, the strict rules of a field game are of little relevance if one side has the services entirely of 18-stone trained professional athletes and the other side the use only of those recently released from a spell in concentration camps where they lived on starvation rations. And free trade by a code of strict rules does not axiomatically mean fair trade. Indeed cruelty and injustice may even be *expanded* through market forces which are untrammelled and unchecked. This globalized form of market, when it is unrestrained, is, of its very nature, inhuman and inhumane. It does not manufacture or produce goods in order to meet genuinely human needs, but in order to meet the needs *of the market*, almost as an entity in itself. There are examples enough around us to make it unnecessary to give more than a few brief glimpses of the human misery that results from uninhibited market forces.

Advantage to Us, Disadvantage to Others?

In Britain and Ireland we expect to pay as little as possible for our food, and we have been very successful in this. The proportion of the family budget spent on food for the home in the United Kingdom is little more than a third of the equivalent spent 50 years ago (Atkinson, 2002). A handful of supermarkets in both our islands control the vast bulk of the supply of grocery foodstuffs, and make it well worthwhile for us to use up prodigious quantities of fuel and time on Saturday mornings as we drive past our local shopkeeper in search of ever better value. Many of our foods that we do not think of as 'foreign' have in fact been flown thousand of miles to us, because the costs of transportation have plummeted in recent years. Earnings in African or Asian countries are infinitesimal compared with European wages, and the food from these countries can be placed on supermarket shelves in Europe at lower prices than if those goods had been produced locally.

An already celebrated supplement in *The Guardian* newspaper demonstrated the economics and technology of how this happens (Lawrence, 2003). A ready-packed tray of vegetables in a supermarket, for example, may have been flown in from Kenya, following

an email order sent out, on the basis of the computerized record of
sales from the electronic tills in the shop, on the previous day. There is
no written contract with the Kenyan suppliers and the amounts of produce required may vary dramatically. The vegetables will have been
packed by women on 12-hour shifts in a factory close to Nairobi airport, working for the equivalent of £1.60 per hour (not that this is
regarded as a particularly low wage in Kenya). The vegetables will
have been grown on large intensive farms, and with a high degree of
dependence on pesticides. Some of these workers, again without contracts, may be paid as little as £40 per month. As land cannot produce
indefinitely under such intensive conditions, an environmental disaster
looms in the near future and, when these acres of land then cease to
be cost-effective, the farm work (ill-paid as it is) will disappear completely. As an ultimate irony, Kenya was actually self-sufficient in food
until the 1970s; today it is a far poorer country and is a net food-
importer.

On these Islands

As we look at the reverse side of the coin, there is more incongruity to
be encountered. Although there are a number of farmers on these
islands who have made a great deal of money farming (see Anthony
Russell in Chapter 8 of the present volume for further detail), nevertheless a large number of those whom we classify today as poor in
Britain and Ireland, in our indices of wealth and poverty, are farmers.
Historically, the farmer was the essential and respected cog in the
apparatus of food provision. Today he or she must bargain for fuel,
cattle feed, fertilizer and machinery, in order even to begin the task of
farming. When the farming is done, he or she must then haggle with
hauliers, supermarkets and restaurants in order to get a reasonable
deal on the food that has been produced. The farmer is thus often
squeezed between two sets of powerful business forces, many of them
multinational. The average age of the farmer of Britain or Ireland is
now middle-aged. Very few young people are prepared to stay on
farms and to endure the risks and privations that are now part and
parcel of running the business. If a crop fails, the farmer does not get
extra consideration from those to whom he or she sells. The risks are
entirely his or hers. The serious profits are other people's. In Ireland a
recent national farm survey (Teagasc, 2001) has established that the

average family farm income (excluding off-farm income) is less than €16,000 (well under £12,000). Three-quarters of farmers have an income of less than €20,000. These farmers have little real control over their own destinies. Indeed, less than half of the farmers in the country can rely on farming alone to survive. This is but another aspect of a free market which is given the awesome motor of globalization.

Although World Trade Organization rules have brought a level of justice to certain features of global trading, there are also troubling aspects. There are occasions when one country (or groups of countries) will set higher farming 'standards' than others and may suffer economically as a result. So, for example, European Union law, under World Trade Organization rules, may apply only to countries within the European Union and whereas animal welfare standards can be (and are being) improved within the European Union, there can be no legal ban on imports from non-European Union countries where these rules do not obtain. So, for example, the use of battery cages for hens is now being banned by the European Union (although the final ban will not come into effect until 2013) but, under World Trade Organization rules, the import of battery eggs from non-European Union countries cannot be banned. As battery eggs are less costly to produce than free-range eggs, the European Union ban will, as things stand, mean the near destruction of poultry farming, egg-production in particular, within Europe.

On Top of the Globalization Heap

What of those who have enjoyed the fruits of the global free market? May they also be victims, albeit not in the short term? Until very recent times, Ireland appeared as almost the major economic success story in terms of the developed world (White, 2001). The term 'celtic tiger' became the ubiquitous cliché. Two areas in particular powered this economic upsurge. In the mid to late 1990s, the chemical and pharmaceutical sectors expanded to such an extent that the share of total exports attributed to these products grew from 18.9 per cent in 1995 to 31.9 per cent in 1999 (Irish Central Statistics Office, 2000). But these are American-based companies. The other major sector that made for this economic miracle is the computer software industry. In 2000, Ireland passed the USA as the largest exporter of software. But none of these companies is Irish-owned. They have been attracted to Ireland by low corporate taxation. Ireland has 'done well' out of it, but it is a very insecure strength. If another country were to provide a cheaper workforce and even better tax incentives, would these multi-national corporations have any reason to stay in Ireland? Goods, whether computer software or medicines, can be transported from anywhere to anywhere on this planet with relative ease. Are we in Ireland in any better position than Kenyan farmers to ensure our financial future?

Sentiment will not be sufficient to keep investment high in Ireland. In recent times, although clearly the population of the Republic of Ireland as a whole was deeply unhappy about Irish involvement of any kind in the invasion of Iraq in 2003, the facilities of Shannon Airport remained available to the forces of United States of America, and the Irish government was extremely careful not to be outspoken on the matter of the war. It was not merely the deeply cynical who pondered over the long-term future of major multinational corporations in Ireland (with the obvious effects on employment and financial health), had Ireland shown a genuine political independent-mindedness on the matter.

The locating of much of the new industry in a very small area, all near and around the capital city of Dublin, has had dramatic effects on the demography of the country. The population of the two counties bordering on Dublin, Meath and Kildare (which incidentally comprise a fair proportion of the diocese in which I work), both grew by more than 20 per cent between the years of 1996 and 2002 (Irish Central Statistics Office, 2002). But this is precisely because these two counties are adjacent to Dublin. The area, long associated with farming, now contains vast number of commuters, and the business of farming has become more and more precarious. Many of those who live in the counties of Meath and Kildare spend hours of each day travelling to and from work in or near Dublin. They are 'bed and breakfast' residents only, in what are genuinely *dormitory towns* in the formerly rural counties that surround Dublin.

The Irish response to the globalized free market has been, in general, to 'go with the flow', and to enjoy, where possible, the material advantages. We need to appreciate, therefore, that not all those on the 'providing end' of the free market resent the fact. Some may accept globalization smugly for its benefits, without thinking either into the more distant future or considering those who are the victims of its inherent lack of humanity. But Ireland, perhaps rural Ireland in particular, has been changed for ever by the global free market. The entire culture of a so-called 'developed country' has been changed irrevocably. It has made Ireland far less insular and far more cosmopolitan, both developments which may well have improved the country, but yet any sense of local identity and of autonomous control on what is happening to the local community has been steadily eroded. The notion of a single home or a single locality in which to spend one's entire life, has disappeared from the consciousness or the aspirations of all but the older generation.

There is far less interest in political life in Ireland. As in the United Kingdom, it seems that few young people have any interest in political parties or in elections, whether local or national. People and communities have simply become *delocalized*. And, although the *average* standard of living in both Britain and Ireland may have grown on most indices, the *gap* between rich and poor has grown to a considerably greater degree. In 1996, Britain had the highest proportion in Europe of children living in poverty, with 300,000 worse off than they had been 20 years earlier (Sacks, 2003: 29). Certainly, for any of our churches to remain complacent in the face of the obvious deprivation confronting us today in our own society, and as the result of the delocalizing influences of our economic structures, is to turn our backs on the entire Judaeo-Christian tradition that the needy and the stranger are our God-given responsibility:

> You shall not deprive a resident alien or an orphan of justice; you shall not take a widow's garment in pledge. Remember that you were a slave in Egypt and the Lord your God redeemed you from there; therefore I command you to do this. When you reap your harvest in your field and forget a sheaf in the field, you shall not go back to get it; it shall be left for the alien, the orphan, and the widow, so that the Lord your God may bless you in all your undertakings. (Deuteronomy 24.17–19)

What Is a Country Today?

One of the most disturbing features of the new free market is the sense that the concept of *nation state* has ceased to have much meaning as a controlling mechanism over the economic structures of a country. Many of those who are at the top of the economic pyramid are financial conglomerates far stronger financially than many sovereign states (including some countries that are far from tiny or impoverished). General Motors is, for example, economically more powerful than Norway, and Mitsubishi than Saudi Arabia. In fact, the 200 largest business corporations have greater combined revenues than the 182 countries which contain 80 per cent of the world's population. Over half of the world's largest economic structures are multinational corporations rather than nation states (Sacks, 2003: 34).

In such a world, the notion of countries making all the decisions for the well-being of their own citizens (or, indeed, the peoples of other countries) becomes hypothetical. With no frontiers on the movement of money, a large multinational corporation may move its resources continually in search of the best deal going. In short, those with wealth will, if left to their own devices, invest where the highest rate of return is to be found. If this return drops for whatever reason, and a better financial return is to be found elsewhere, investment will be transferred. There is thus a pressure on developing countries in particular (but increasingly on developed countries also) to lower minimum standards not only for wages, but also for the care of the environment, and for public services, as a necessary price for providing an attractive environment for investment from outside. Globalization has made this situation logistically simpler to effect than it could ever have been in the past. Ethical considerations, as always, will be secondary, if indeed they appear at all.

In recent years the Fair Trade Federation has directly connected poorly paid producers in developing countries with the consumer markets of the developed world. It makes these consumers aware of how paying very little more for fairly traded products can ensure not only reasonable wages but also safe conditions for the workforce within the developing world. The Federation would be the first to admit that this is still a small-scale venture although happily it is a growing operation. Turning from the practical response to theological appraisal, it is undoubtedly one of the tragedies of our generation that some of the truly great social teaching of Pope John Paul II, perhaps in particular the encyclical *Centesimus Annos* (1991), has been submerged amid other less prophetic declarations from the Church.

Alienation and Delocalization

Attempting any assessment of this without some reference to Marxist theory is all but impossible. It is ironical that, with the total collapse of a discredited and corrupted Eastern bloc which had departed far from the principles of true communism, Marxism seems, if not more attractive, then certainly more *compelling* in its analysis of economic forces at work in the world. And it is certainly true that, with the departure of communist states, however decadent they may have become, the lack of an alternative political ideology has meant that the force of world capitalism has had no counter-balance or counter-influence to restrain it. The onward march of the unrestrained free market makes it very clear that a motive power behind developments in human history may indeed be, as Marx argued, primarily economic. The idea of the just society (so much part of the Marxist as well as the Christian tradition) has all but disappeared from public discourse. Indeed, with the collapse of communism, a dimension of moral reasoning within society has ceased to be a matter for debate. Similarly, the Marxist concept of a distancing, the 'alienation', between the worker and the means of production may no longer be a matter for serious discussion, but it is nevertheless a reality we see all around us. Words written in 1848 by Marx and Engels have, *mutatis mutandis*, a startling resonance for a world familiar to us today.

> Meantime, the markets kept ever growing, the demand ever rising. Even manufacturers no longer sufficed. Thereupon, steam and machinery revolutionised industrial production. The place of manufacture was taken by the giant, Modern Industry; the place of the industrial middle class by industrial millionaires, the leaders of the whole industrial armies, the modern bourgeois.

> Large-scale industry has established the world market, for which the discovery of America paved the way. This market has given an immense development to commerce, to navigation, to communication by land. This development has, in turn, reacted on the extension of industry; and in proportion as industry, commerce, navigation, railways extended, in the same proportion the bourgeoisie developed, increased its capital, and pushed into the background every class handed down from the Middle Ages. (Marx and Engels, 1992: 7)

What is as critical as the lack of a sense of *virtue* as a component of authentic community, is the actual collapse of any sense of *being community* in much of the western world. But *delocalization* is not confined to Britain or Ireland. In particular the globalization of the media means that the local may well be mediated through the focus of the alien. Via satellite, people may well learn of the bombing of another part of their own country from the 24-hour news coverage of a media organization within the very country which is doing the bombing.

As I have suggested, globalization (properly understood) is not of itself the moral cause of this complex reality, but rather the vehicle through which the free market can hold such utter sway. As Europeans, can we look to the broader context of Europe to provide a stronger platform for challenging the onward drive of capitalism? The outlook at present is far from promising. The continent of Europe, for all that the European Union is now a fact of life for so much of Western Europe, is still fractured and fractious. When there is a lack of common purpose, suspicion and cynicism follow close behind and, in the European Union of today (and I write as a truly committed and enthusiastic European), there seems little interest in any *common good* but rather a determination from within each country that it will not be damaged by the malice of others or by a threatening alliance of other countries. For all the honest and honourable calls for Europe to find a *soul*, there is little indication that these pleas are being properly heeded.

Has the Church Anything to Say?

The Church has in many ways lost out at both ends of the globalization process. Globalization has tended to have a fracturing effect on the cohesiveness of the western Church. There is now far greater exposure to the reality of other cultures and other faiths. In Ireland, where, as the result of considerable immigration within the past few years, the number of Irish residents who are Muslim increased fourfold in a decade (Irish Central Statistics Office, 2002), Islam is not a genteel study for those interested in comparative religions. It is a visible and present reality not only on the televisions screens, but in the local school and at the local mosque. At the localized level of church life, in Ireland as in England, there have been two mutually exclusive responses.

The first is counter-cultural, in a new fundamentalism which stresses non-negotiable truth as the foundation of true religion. The second is a syncretism which carries with it an inevitable tendency to relativism. Both are destructive, for neither is persuasive, and they share in common a refusal to meet head-on the challenges of globalization. They are also deeply antipathetic to one another and can use sophisticated techniques, now so freely available as the result of globalized communication framework, to mobilize their own factions and, by so doing, to make the ecclesial community, both local and central, more splintered than it has been for generations. In the rural communities this has had its effect, and not only in terms of bringing the Church into deserved derision or a place of utter marginalization. It has affected the entire local community which can no longer relate to the Church as a credible focus of decency and integrity. The local church community would, I believe, have served such a valuable and valued purpose even in highly secularized communities, whether rural or urban, until very recent times. Today, it is only in the context of a tragedy which has been globalized, whether the Soham murders of 2002 or the premature death of Princess Diana a few years earlier, that the Church within western culture can fulfil anything approaching this function.

Coupled with the fracturing and degrading of religious communities in the context of western Christianity is a new and somewhat alarming 'top down' attempt to centralize the faith. It has been visible in Roman Catholicism from the nineteenth century when globalization meant that railways and the telegraph could carry messages to and from Rome as far as the outer reaches of the Church with a new speed. More centralized control became a genuine possibility. Amid the advances of the globalization process today, we see signs that the Anglican Communion is, for the first time, attempting strenuously to turn itself into a global multinational conglomerate. Local autonomous decisions, particularly on matters of ethics, are not only suspect but are now being blamed for endangering the communion of Anglicanism. In addition, the playthings of globalization, particularly instant media exposure, are regarded as *sine qua non* for the running of any community which wishes to be taken seriously, and the Church has been unusually quick in seeking to take advantage. (It is well enough known that the number of media experts at the Lambeth Conference of 1998 far outnumbered the theological consultants.) But resort to the technology of global communication is very much a two-edged sword. The communication techniques, which may show the Church to apparent advantage as a slick, effective and articulate machine, may as easily hold the same Church up to deserved contempt on the following day.

The new dislocation between centrism and localism so apparent in western society, and therefore in the western Church, does not however seem to have affected other parts of the globe as readily. Part of this displacement in western society is due to the socio-historical connection between Church and state which, as the nation state itself has become degraded, has had an inevitable impact on the relationship of Church to society. In Ireland, where Islam appears more monolithic than might be the perception in areas of the United Kingdom where many Muslims are British-born, it certainly appears that our western brand of Christianity has no emotional parallel to the Islamic *Ummah*, that sense of mutual belonging and total spiritual solidarity which transcends national boundaries because it was never dependent on national frontiers. A Muslim in Dublin is *personally* diminished and damaged by the murder of a Muslim child in Bethlehem, almost as though this were his or her own child. Western Christians would not feel anything of the same degree of personalized involvement in the murder of a Christian (whether by other Christians or not) in a distant country. There may be a generalized sense of outrage but no sense of truly *interior* solidarity. It may indeed be argued that globalization, particularly in its advances in communication, both media and electronic, has united some religious groupings but has fractured others, of which Islam must be placed with the former and Christianity with the latter.

If we accept that the current stage of globalization, for all that economic profit may have been the incentive to its huge technological advances in recent years, is of itself value neutral, we must still subject the economic theory behind the free market to ethical analysis, if we are to rescue *communality*. There are various features of neo-liberal economic theory that must be confronted, as they are far from value neutral.

Principles to Consider

In the first place, the unrestrained application of market principles in an environment of such rapid movement, both of goods and services, is simply incompatible with the maintenance of real community. The cliché of the so-called *global community* needs to be challenged firmly. Community in its biblical understanding assumes a degree of justice and of mutual supportiveness. It is not possible to produce such a community on a global scale where market forces are not restrained.

Second, increased production and consumption of goods is not axiomatically a desirable end. Neo-liberal capitalism has successfully sold to the world images and icons of a good life which is predicated entirely on riches and goods without limitation or end. The idea that reasonable security and unpretentious means may actually be sufficient for a satisfying life seems emaciated and unconvincing to most people. Need this be so? The idea of global sustainability is however of far greater ultimate importance. For example, if present rates of increase continue, the number of road vehicles in the world will increase almost fivefold, to well over 2 billion, within 30 years. A secure and just future for the world is not merely a desirable aspiration but an essential if the free market is not to wreak destruction on the planet. There are indeed two global conversations taking place, one a vision of sustainability and sustainable development, and the other a vision of a world society where production, consumption and commerce are unfettered by local or long-term considerations. The latter conversation is drowning out the former. We therefore need to look for more appropriate indices of 'success' within nations than Gross National Product (GNP) or Gross Domestic Product (GDP) – the usual indicators. There are already a number of alternative indices for sustainability, notably the United Nations' Human Development Index (HDI), which factors in the *health* of a nation in far more holistic terms, including nutrition, literacy and health. Similarly the Index of Sustainable Economic Welfare (ISEW) includes the effects of economic activity on the environment and considers such non-profitable matters as childcare (Community of Religious of Ireland, 2002). So for the United Kingdom, Gross National Product has doubled in the past 50 years but the Index of Sustainable Economic Welfare has shown almost no improvement. The true 'wealth of nations' can be seen as something entirely different from an aggregate of Gross National Products.

Third, what is coldly rational is not necessarily just. This is unfashionable and therefore largely unsaid. The creation of community and the doctrine of sustainability are not, for our culture, axiomatically good ends *per se*. The fact is that western culture has moved from thinking primarily in religious terms (in pre-modern times) to thinking in scientific constructs, and today has moved to making economics the principal yardstick for human improvement. The response of religion, in the case of scientific modernism, was first to seek to bully science into submission, then to ignore science and ultimately to capitulate to science, just at the moment when science was learning its own limitations. None of these responses by religious communities was healthy or useful. What the ethicist can contribute, however, is to challenge modern neo-liberal economic theory on the grounds that it is inherently destructive of real community. Christianity asserts the centrality of community as a basis for human dignity. *Community* may not be restricted to the local, but community cannot exist on any wider scale if it has been destroyed in the locality.

Fourth, we must as Christians reflect biblically (and publicly) on the meaning of communion, *koinonia*. Community or communion without sharing and generosity is a contradiction in terms. When Paul (or a Pauline disciple) wrote to the Corinthians of the generosity of Christians' contributions to the needs of others, the word employed for these gifts is linked with *koinonia*: 'Through the testing of this ministry you glorify God by your obedience to the confession of the gospel of Christ and by the generosity of your sharing *(tes koinonias)* with them and with all others' (2 Corinthians 9.13). But, as we also know, *koinonia* is that which unites us with the body and blood of Christ: 'The cup of blessing that we bless, is it not a sharing *(koinonia)* in the blood of Christ? The bread that we break, is it not a sharing *(koinonia)* in the body of Christ?' (1 Corinthians 10.16). Community with God and with 'local' is inextricably related to a communion of generosity to the outside world.

The notion of returning to a culture of localization may sound Luddite in its implications and yet there is a viewpoint which expounds such a vision fluently and persuasively (Hines, 2000). Is there a genuine alternative to globalization that is not a return to protectionism? In this context it should be remembered of course that classic protectionism sought to protect a local home market but never expected other markets to be similarly closed. Yet only some form of protocol that would permit the siting of a multinational corporation only in a country where it will undertake a reasonable proportion of its sales can ever break the stranglehold of the global noose. This would require considerable courage and political will on the part of governments in the developed world (and could only be envisaged while they still retain any semblance of control over the internal economics of their nation state). It would also assume that groups of countries would co-operate together. If there were any conscious and phased return to the idea of localized production forced upon multi-national corporations, then the levels of taxation would come back under proper democratic control, and labour and environmental standards could more readily be enforced. Where there can be no local production, as for example in the area of some foodstuffs, there might be governmental enforcement of the standards of fair trade as distinct from free trade. The Fair Trade Federation has shown us one route.

This espousal of greater localization might indeed seem to be a vain attempt to turn the clock back to a utopian, green and golden age. But the alternatives are terrifying. If China were to become fully part of the globalization spiral (and this is already the likely scenario), the economics of the entire world would be totally destabilized. Cheap food would flood into China, the global textile industry would be based entirely in that country, but the internal economy of the country would be imperilled with the collapse, in the face of international competition, of millions of jobs in their less efficient industries and production methods. Furthermore, the economies of many Third-World countries would, through international competition with a country containing the population of China, be utterly annihilated.

If the local church community has indeed something to say that is even tenuously prophetic, it must surely be to repudiate again and again the notion that there is no alternative to the most powerful forces of this world. The prophetic Christian voice which once helped to overthrow slavery, even against its own vested interests, should surely speak again against the new slavery which provides its own finances and boosts its own income and the lifestyle of its western adherents.

REFERENCES

Atkinson, S. (2002), *The Money-Go-Round: Globalization and the Destruction of Farming*, Leicester, The University and Colleges Christian Fellowship.

Community of Religious of Ireland (2002), 'Sustainability' [online], available from: http://www.cori.ie/justice/soc_issues/sustain.htm [accessed 10 Jun 2004].

Hines, C. (2000), *Localization: A Global Manifesto*, London, Earthscan

Irish Central Statistics Office (2000), *Economic Reports*, Dublin, Stationery Office.

Irish Central Statistics Office (2002), *Census 2002: Preliminary Report*, Dublin, Stationery Office.

John Paul II (1991), *Centesimus Annos*, London, Catholic Truth Society.

Lawrence, F. (ed.) (2003), 'Food: Why We Eat This Way', *Guardian*, 17 May, supplement.

Marx, K. and Engels, F. (1992), *The Communist Manifesto* (first published 1848), Oxford, Oxford University Press.

Sacks, J. (2003), *The Dignity of Difference* (second edition), London, Continuum.

Teagasc (2001), *Irish Agriculture and Food Development Authority, Annual Report*, Dublin, Teagasc.

White, T. (2001), 'Globalization and the Preservation of Local Identity', [online], International Studies Association, available from: http://www.isanet.org/archive/white.html [accessed 10 Jun 2004].

7. Biodiversity

JOHN OLIVER

Summary

This chapter addresses the meaning of biodiversity and looks briefly at the prehistoric statistics, at enormous variations which have taken place, at times of extinction and speciation. It considers the effects of human intervention, with specific examples from prehistoric time to the present day. It then attempts to answer the questions of why biodiversity is so important, and why Christians in particular should care about it. Biodiversity is essential for survival (soil fertility and sewage disposal), but there are spiritual and ethical, as well as economic and practical imperatives. There is a brief discussion of the treatment of biodiversity at the Lambeth Conference 1998, and of the potential for interfaith co-operation. There is then the examination of the pressures which lead to species extinction: poverty, greed, intensive farming, monoculture, urban expansion, pollution and climate change. There is a brief survey of action programmes to counteract the loss of biodiversity, in Europe, the United Kingdom and worldwide, following the Rio and Johannesburg Conferences, and through the reform of the Common Agriculture Policy. Finally, there is a survey of the uncertain future of the planet, the twin threats of habitat destruction and climate change, the need for education and for a conversion experience for the whole human race.

The Meaning of Biodiversity

The word biodiversity is one which would have been unknown to our grandparents. It has come into use only very recently, the first recorded usage being in 1986, but it has very rapidly become a central concern for all those who are in any way sensitive to the pressures on the environment, the enormous rate of species destruction which has been taking place for the past 100 years, and the severe threats which exist to life on this planet.

Biodiversity simply means biological diversity, the variety of life forms in the environment. It embraces all living things, including viruses and bacteria. The United Nations Convention on Biodiversity was signed at the Earth Summit in Rio de Janeiro in 1992. Klaus Toepfer, Executive Director of the United Nations Environment Programme, has explained the significance of biodiversity in the following way:

> The natural environment provides the basic conditions without which humanity could not survive. Life on the blue planet is contained within the biosphere, a thin and irregular envelope around the Earth's surface, just a few kilometres deep around the radius of the globe. Here, ecosystems purify the air and the water that are the basis of life. They stabilise and moderate the Earth's climate. Soil fertility is renewed, nutrients are cycled and plants are pollinated. Although scientists are now able to appreciate the complexity of this web of interacting natural processes, we are still a very long way from understanding how they all fit together. What we do know is that if any part of the web breaks down, the future of life on the planet will be at risk. Biological diversity, the variability of life on Earth, is the key to the ability of the biosphere to continue providing us with these ecological goods and services and thus is our species' life assurance policy. (Convention on Biological Diversity, 2002)

Scientists have only limited understanding of the enormous variation in the number of species which have existed since the beginning of geological time, but it is known that there have been at least five episodes of mass extinction, some of them relatively short (lasting from one million to ten million years). The most significant period of mass extinction, at the end of the Permian era (250 million years ago), eliminated a very large proportion of species, estimates varying from 77 per cent to 96 per cent. But apart even from these mass extinctions, the background rates of extinction and speciation (the creation of new species) are not constant. Within the past 250 million years relatively high rates of extinction have occurred nine times, at intervals of approximately 26 to 28 million years.

It could be said that global biological diversity is now close to its all-time high. Floral diversity reached its highest level ever several tens of thousands of years ago, and the diversity of marine fauna has risen to a peak in the last few million years. It is important to notice the enormous time-scale involved in these calculations, and the contrast between them and the remarkably short time-scale in which very severe extinction of species has taken place during very recent times – that is to say in the past 100 years. But that is not to say that humanity has not contributed to species extinction for very much longer than the modern period. Between 25,000 and 15,000 years ago the hunting of large mammals caused or contributed to significant extinctions in North and South America and Australia. These three continents lost something like three-quarters of the species of 'mega fauna', that is to say mammals weighing more than 44 kilograms. For at least 50,000 years intentional burning has occurred in vast areas of Africa, and at least 5,000 years ago in Europe deforestation and the conversion of wild lands to pasture began. There is evidence in North America that for as long as 4,000 years the indigenous peoples' influence on structures and forest communities caused at least local species extinction. In Central America very large areas of forest had already been removed before the Spanish conquistadores arrived (Groombridge, 1992).

Very rapid extinction has often taken place when dominant alien species have been introduced, such as the Polynesian rat, the domestic pig and the domestic dog, and as a result of systematic hunting. Human colonization in New Zealand began about AD 1000, and at least 13 species of large flightless birds and 16 other indigenous bird species disappeared before any European arrived in New Zealand. The fifteenth and sixteenth centuries saw an enormous expansion of European colonization, and the introduction of European livestock, crops, weeds and diseases increased the loss of flora, particularly in isolated island communities, very much more rapidly than had previously been the case. But it is also true that the new patterns of travel by human beings involved the introduction of new species in very large numbers to many areas which had not hitherto known them. One of the most striking cases of the influence of European travellers was on the previously uninhabited Mascarene Islands (Mauritius, Reunion and Rodrigues). In the mid 1600s the Dutch settled in these islands, and in the following 300 years 20 species of birds, including the emblematic dodo, and eight species of reptiles were lost. An extreme example of the possibility of extinction of a native species took place on the very small Stephen Island off the coast of New Zealand, where the lighthouse keeper's cat was single-handedly responsible for the extinction of the flightless Stephen Island wren (World Resources Institute Website, 2004).

While hunting has been responsible for the destruction of some notably well-publicized species, there is no doubt that habitat destruction is in the long run far more damaging. Tropical forests contain between 50 and 90 per cent of the world's plant and animal species, despite the fact that they cover only 7 per cent of the earth's land surface. Deforestation is the most serious cause of loss of biodiversity in the present day, and in 1993 it was estimated that forests were being felled at the rate of about 4,500 acres every hour. An area of tropical forest equivalent to four times the size of Denmark was lost each year during the 1980s (Ryan, 1992: 7). Temperate forest, such as stretched originally from California to Alaska, and once covered very large proportions of Europe, has almost disappeared. The loss has been 90 per cent in Europe since prehistoric times. In Britain 45 per cent of ancient broad-leaved woodlands were lost between 1945 and 1985.

Why Does It Matter?

At the most basic level the human race should care about biodiversity because it is the basis of all life. The maintenance of soil fertility, the disposal of sewage and the continuation of conditions on the planet in which the human race can survive are all dependent on an immense range of species. All perform a role, as part of complex ecosystems and in production and consumption cycles, in maintaining, stabilizing and regenerating the so-called 'biosphere'. The human race is highly dependent on the stabilizing forces at work in the natural world to remedy and repair ecological disasters and pollution incidents. The way in which the oceans recover following an oil spill is one example of this, so there are the most compelling pragmatic reasons, from the point of view of the human race, for believing that we have a responsibility for arresting the present very rapid rate of species extinction. But there are also extremely important spiritual and ethical reasons, and these need to be spelt out in some detail.

The theological basis for caring about biodiversity is most commonly described as stewardship, although that word is loosely employed in many contexts without clear definition. There is also a sense in which the Christian and Jewish faiths have been accused, not without some justification, of taking a rather cavalier attitude toward the created order, of regarding the human race as the primary focus of God's concern, love and saving acts. This attitude derives from texts in the book of Genesis, which are commonly translated into English in terms of the human race 'having dominion over' the created order. But the underlying sense of the Hebrew is 'to have responsible care for' rather than to lord it over, or treat with arrogance or contempt (in particular, Genesis 1.28). The rediscovery by Christians of the theological imperative for caring about the created order, and in particular about biodiversity, is one of the most important changes to have occurred in Christian thinking in the second half of the twentieth century.

In the Anglican Communion, successive ten-yearly Lambeth Conferences have dealt with environmental issues. The 1998 Conference passed a number of resolutions that spelt out the biblical vision of creation, according to which, 'Creation is a web of interdependent relationships bound together in the Covenant, which God the Holy Trinity has established with the whole earth and every living being' (Lambeth Conference, 1999: 86).

The Lambeth Statement and Resolutions were based on the following three fundamental theological principles (Lambeth Conference, 1999: 379):

- The divine spirit is sacramentally present in Creation, which itself ought to be treated with reverence, respect and gratitude.
- Human beings are both co-partners with the rest of Creation and living bridges between heaven and earth, with responsibility to make personal and corporate sacrifices for the common good of all Creation.
- The redemptive purposes of God in Jesus Christ extend to the whole of Creation.

The idea that the whole of creation should be seen as of sacramental value implies profound respect for all of it; if the divine spirit is present in any part of it, then Christians may not treat it with scorn, contempt or indifference, nor may they (without very good reason and without having weighed the consequences in terms of the lesser evil) destroy any species or allow it to be needlessly lost. In setting out an eco-theology for Lambeth XIII (the 1998 Conference), the report recognizes that:

> the gravity of the present challenge to the global ecosystem arises from the technologically enhanced impact of human intervention on our planet. Scripture was inspired in a different world, but biblical insights into the nature of the God-human-world relation provide a firm foundation for a contemporary ecological theology. (Lambeth Conference, 1999: 89)

Even if people know about the cyclical species extinction which has over geological time been a notable part of the history of biodiversity, it is not the prerogative of the human race to pre-empt what, for example, the next ice age might bring about. We are called to care for creation as we have inherited it, and to care for it humbly, responsibly and lovingly.

This leads on to the second theological principle, that human beings are co-partners with the Creator; the report uses the phrase 'co-creators':

> Whereas other creatures adjust to the given world, the human being desires to create its own world, transforming raw materials into new realities . . . Human beings are called to be priests and pastors of creation, living bridges between heaven and earth. They are to pronounce God's blessing on creation, and they are also the means of expressing creation's praise and longing to God. (Lambeth Conference, 1999: 90)

The report goes on as follows: 'Nowhere is the priestly ministry of humanity brought more clearly into focus than in the eucharistic feast, which is indeed "the Eucharist for all things" ' (Lambeth Conference, 1999: 91). The Eucharist embodies the conviction, not only that elements of earthly reality, bread and wine, can become means of grace for human beings, but that also, as they are offered up to God by human beings, the elements themselves receive new meaning and status. The offertory prayer declares:

Blessed are you Lord God of all creation,
through your goodness we have this bread to offer,
which earth has given and human hands have made.
It will become for us the bread of life.

This is a very high doctrine of humanity, but it implies an equally high doctrine of the created order. It derives from the symbolism of Genesis, chapter 2, where God forms *adam*, the first earth creature, out of the very dust (*ha'adam*). This idea goes back to the teaching of Maximus the Confessor (580–662) that the human being is the microcosm of creation, the hypostasis of the whole creation community.

Third, it follows that if the whole created order is to be seen sacramentally, the redemptive purposes of God in Jesus Christ extend to the whole of creation. What this means is not spelled out in detail, but there is emphasis on the idea of the Sabbath Feast of 'enoughness'. There is a plea for the recovery of the sense of rhythm which the Sabbath brought, and its emphasis on the importance of rest. The Genesis narrative emphasizes that creation reaches its crown and consummation not in the creation of humankind on the sixth day, but in the peace of the Sabbath on the seventh day. And the Sabbath concept, when related to the fallow season for the earth, introduces a constraint on human intervention in nature, and thus sets limits to the human exploitation of the natural order. The report calls for the reinvigoration of the Sabbath: 'not as a nostalgic symbol of a religious past, but as a feast of redemption and anticipation of the ecological harmony and sustainable equilibrium of Christ's Kingdom' (Lambeth Conference, 1999: 92).

In addition to theological reasons for caring about biodiversity, there is also what many scientists would describe as an ethical imperative. There is a non-material evaluation of biodiversity, which has a very powerful influence over a great many scientific minds. Scientists and conservationists are not merely concerned with the defence of biodiversity because of potential material gains or benefits for the human race: drugs, new fibres, new foods, new genetic capabilities, all of which may well derive from unexpected sources in the natural world, sources which have survived by chance, neither recognized nor understood during human history, but suddenly becoming apparent as a result of some scientific investigation, or even of some accidental discovery. But scientists also recognize the value of

intellectual enquiry, spiritual fulfilment and recreational satisfaction
that can be derived from the immense richness of the earth's biodiversity. It is impossible to put a financial value on the potential
benefits which can stem from a proper and careful conservation of biodiversity, and still less is it possible to put any kind of value on the
intellectual, ethical and aesthetic importance of maintaining biodiversity as far as is humanly possible.

Much Christian debate on the subject has centred around the
anthropocentric reasons for protecting biodiversity, that is to say, the
benefits to the human race that can accrue from the immense variety
of life forms which exist. This may look at first sight to be a narrow,
selfish or inadequate justification for caring about biodiversity, but
further consideration reveals how immensely important this argument
is, and how far it may be pressed. There is an excellent discussion of
this in Michael Banner's *Christian Ethics and Contemporary Moral
Problems*. Banner points out that:

> anthropocentrism, properly understood, is not necessarily a licence
> for ruthless exploitation of the natural world, but may offer a
> reason for treating it with a degree of care and caution, and this for
> the simple reason that where human well-being is reasonably held
> to be by no means independent of the well-being of the environ-
> ment, human self-interest will itself dictate a concern for the
> interests of others than humans alone. (Banner, 1999: 167)

Where regard is paid to the need for maintaining a healthy planet, and
for ensuring the well-being of future generations, it becomes vitally
important to protect biodiversity rather than to exploit it in ways
which relentlessly diminish it. But there are limits to the point to which
anthropocentric arguments can be pressed, and as Banner himself
says: 'what is lost in the anthropocentric perspective is the quite simple thought that certain ways of treating the environment are not only
ill-advised or imprudent humanly speaking, but quite simply wrong'
(Banner, 1999: 172).

It may properly be argued on theological grounds that the well-
being of non-human life on earth has an intrinsic value of its own,
quite independent of any instrumental usefulness it may have for the
human race.

It is not simply the Christian faith which is concerned with environmental matters and with the issue of biodiversity. This is an area where interfaith co-operation can be remarkably fruitful, and the Association of Religions and Conservation is a body which has both tried to encourage philosophical and theological debate, and also to sponsor and celebrate flagship achievements by different world faiths in terms of environmental protection or improvement. In the political domain there was a significant meeting at Trieste in March 2001, when the Italian government imaginatively invited world faith community leaders to meet with the environment ministers of the G7, a significant recognition of the fact that those who are charged with political responsibility for protecting the environment have much in common with those who value it for religious reasons. This is an area where much progress could be made even in the United Kingdom, and it is a very fruitful topic for interfaith dialogue and practical co-operation.

The Main Threats to Biodiversity

It is important to understand the very wide range of pressures which are bearing down today on biodiversity in the world, because unless there is a proper understanding of the factors which are damaging and diminishing biodiversity, there can be no effective action to reverse the trend.

There is no doubt at all that deforestation is the most serious threat to a very wide range of species, simply because so many species exist only in rainforest or temperate forest. It would be fair to say that both poverty and greed are motives for the destruction of rainforest. On the one hand, there is the slash and burn technique practised by landless peasants, or people in desperate need of more land to cultivate, driven by poverty or by extreme inequalities of wealth and land distribution in South America, notably in Brazil. Greed is also a powerful factor, particularly in the destruction of rainforest in order to exploit the hard woods, or to create cultivable land for transnational corporations which want to practise ranching of beef cattle. The very well-publicized threat to some of the great mammals of Africa and Asia, notably rhinoceros, elephant, lion and tiger, is to do with the enormous value on the world market of products derived from these animals even when, as is often the case, trade in them is illegal. Many developing countries are beginning to realize the potential value and importance of eco-tourism, but the more uncertain long-term rewards to be derived from this particular form of conservation, involving very large tracts of protected land, are difficult to weigh against the immediate short-term gain of poaching for ivory or skins, or some very desirable derivative of an endangered species (House of Commons, 1993/94).

It has long been the case that deforestation simply for the reclamation of wood fuel has been a cause of habitat destruction and soil erosion in many developing countries. This problem continues, despite the gradual introduction of other sources of energy in developing countries. The harnessing of solar power for lighting and cooking is one way in which technology promises to provide at least part of an answer to the huge problem of deforestation for fuel. Delegates to the Anglican Communion Congress on the Stewardship of Creation, which took place in South Africa in August 2002, heard about an imaginative and successful scheme from a retired Ugandan bishop, who is the Co-ordinator of Solar Light for Churches in Africa, an organization which has developed an extremely efficient and cost-effective way of harnessing solar power for lighting. Similar successes have been achieved with very simple technology to produce solar-powered cookers, but there is a significant problem in their use, in that the time when solar power is available for cooking is at midday, but the traditional African time for cooking is in the evening. A huge social change would be needed to take advantage of this particular technology, while more sophisticated use of solar power or photovoltaics, which would enable power to be stored and used according to demand, would be infinitely more expensive and unachievable in economic terms.

In the developed world, one of the most serious threats to biodiversity has been intensive farming and monoculture. This has developed progressively over a long period from the middle of the nineteenth century, and is seen at its most extreme form in the American Mid-west. Here there may be some justification for monoculture, making the best use of available land and disregarding the effect of such farming on biodiversity, because enormous tracts of America are conserved in national parks, areas large enough to enable a huge range of biodiversity to survive and flourish. The problem in Europe is rather different, for here conservation has to go hand-in-hand with farming. The dramatic decline in biodiversity in farming areas in Britain in the last 30 years has been directly attributable to the encouragement of intensive farming under the Common Agricultural Policy, the misguided encouragement to farmers to grub up hedges to create larger and more efficient fields, and the very widespread use of large amounts of herbicide and pesticide to optimize crop yields. It is ironic that policies emanating from the European Union have simultaneously attempted to espouse the cause of biodiversity in ways which will be discussed in the next section, while at the same time encouraging its destruction through the particular nature of subsidies offered to farmers, and the translation of such policies into techniques which have been deeply damaging to biodiversity of farmland species. There has been an increasing awareness in recent years of the need to modify this malign influence of the Common Agricultural Policy, and to develop ways in which farmers can be encouraged, either by exhortation and advice, or by carefully targeted financial inducement, to have more regard for biodiversity on their land (House of Lords 1998/1999). The implementation in 2005 of the next step of the reform of the Common Agricultural Policy, involving the decoupling of subsidy from agricultural production and its redirection toward agri-environment schemes, will bring some relief in terms of biodiversity.

A further threat to biodiversity has of course come from enormous urban expansion, which has been going on all over the world. The relentless rise in the size of cities, and the amount of land taken for house building and industrial development, have had a severe impact on areas formerly rich in biodiversity. The United Kingdom has one of the most enlightened and highly developed planning policies of any industrialized country, and the pursuit of nature conservation, not least through green belts round towns and cities, has to be seen as a considerable success. The comparison between the reasonably compact and contained urban areas of Britain with the urban sprawl which has been allowed to develop in France, Spain, Portugal and Italy, is instructive. The contrast is even more marked in the United States of America, where huge areas of old industry have simply been abandoned, in such places as the Rust Belt city of Buffalo, and replaced by vast expansion on green field sites round the periphery of the city.

A further destructive factor in its impact on biodiversity has been pollution of various kinds. This is one of the most immediate results of the industrial revolution, and the almost complete extinction of life in the rivers in industrial areas was one of the most striking results of the careless disposal of effluent from industrial processes. This problem is at last being addressed, and considerable success has been achieved in cleaning river water and reintroducing a wide variety of species into rivers which were previously lifeless. But these are very small successes when measured against the continuing problem of increasing pollution in the world at large, not least in the oceans, which have for a long time been used as dumping grounds for enormous quantities of toxic materials, and have suffered increasingly in the petrochemical age from spillages of oil and chemicals. Despite the extraordinary power of the natural world to absorb pollution and regenerate, the decline of biodiversity in many marine environments is deeply serious.

One of the richest areas of biodiversity has been shallow coastline water and salt marsh and wetland associated with it. Partly as a result of urban expansion, partly as a result of an enormous increase in the amount of trade, and the development of huge container ports in previously undeveloped estuaries, there has been a serious loss of marine biodiversity round the coasts of the United Kingdom. The great expansion which has taken place in the ports of Immingham, Felixstowe, Harwich and Southampton has had a very damaging effect on the marine ecosystem, most notably in the availability of areas for migrant birds, particularly waders.

In relation to deep-sea biodiversity the Common Fisheries Policy of the European Union has also been deeply damaging. The well-publicized decline in the population of herring, cod and other previously commonly available species of fish is only the best known example of the damage which has been done to the richness of marine life by ruthless overfishing, and by the introduction of new techniques of factory fishing, sucking up enormous quantities of fish, much of which is then rejected or wasted.

One threat to biodiversity which has only recently been taken seriously, is that posed by climate change. Although some far-sighted people have for a long time been warning against the danger of climate change created by human activity, it is only in the last ten years, or even less, that the issue has assumed a high public profile. The publication of the Royal Commission on Environmental Pollution Report (2002), *Energy and Climate Change*, drew public attention to the reality and the threat of climate change. How climate change will precisely affect biodiversity is not clear, as species have a remarkable ability to adapt, and many will have time to migrate to areas where the changing climate is more congenial to them. There are limits to this process, and the increasing incidence of extremes of weather, either of rainfall and flooding in the winter in temperate zones, or very great heat and drought in the summer in equatorial areas, cannot be calculated. The likelihood is that considerable areas of land will become completely uncultivable because of drought and heat, whereas other areas at present uncultivable because of cold may well become sufficiently temperate to allow cultivation along with colonization by temperate species driven from their former habitats. Climate change is also likely to lead to a steady rise in sea levels, partly through the melting of Arctic and Antarctic ice, but mainly through the warming of sea water, which leads to its expansion. This will lead to the further elimination of many low-lying coastal areas, at present rich in biodiversity, which will be covered by the rising sea or devastated by surges of sea water due to extremes of weather. This process is already being seen in Bangladesh and in some Pacific islands.

The Worldwide Fund for Nature (2002) has summarized some of the effects of human activity and climate change on a range of significant species in their *Living Planet Report*. They have measured the decline in biodiversity over the past 30 years: forest species down by about 15 per cent over that period; marine species down by about 35 per cent; and freshwater species down by about 54 per cent. These are extraordinary and dramatic declines which are largely attributable to human intervention. The Worldwide Fund for Nature projections for the future have taken into account likely human population increase and carbon dioxide emissions. We must expect an increase in global population to just under nine billion by 2050, and while carbon dioxide projections are uncertain because of such action as the Kyoto Protocol and the other possibilities which exist of curbing and limiting greenhouse gas emissions, the likelihood is that the process of climate change will continue and indeed accelerate, with a devastating effect on biodiversity.

This is a brief summary of the very serious threats to biodiversity which have been at work in recent years, and threaten to grow more damaging unless dramatic action is taken. The next section examines some of the efforts which have been made and are being made to deal with these threats.

The Fight for Biodiversity: Statutory Action

In the face of the relentless threats to biodiversity in the twentieth century, there have been some decisive measures to try to stem the destructive tide of human influence. One of the first significant international agreements was the RAMSAR Convention (1980) for the conservation of wetlands. Drainage of wetlands for agricultural use and building development, and the ecological devastation in areas such as the Black Sea, the Aral Sea and Lake Chad, prompted determination to try to protect what remained of important wetland habitats. This initiative was the precursor of the major United Nations programme, begun in 1989, which culminated in the Convention on Biological Diversity, which was finally signed following the Rio Conference in 1992 by 163 nations, and ratified by most of them in December 1993. This was real cause for celebration in the conservation world, and marked the most significant achievement by the human race in terms of recognizing and trying to reverse the destructive impact of human life on biodiversity. It was also the first time that there had been proper recognition of the significance of climate change, and the Kyoto Protocol, which was signed by most of the developed nations, with the notable and scandalous exception of the United States of America, offers hope that during the second decade of the twenty-first century there will be some modest reduction in carbon dioxide emissions by some of the most polluting countries.

It is deeply disappointing that the successor conference to Rio 1992, the World Summit on Sustainable Development (WSSD) at Johannesburg in 2002, achieved so little. Considering the ten years during which issues of conservation and biodiversity had been widely publicized following the Rio Conference, and considering the increasing awareness on the part of scientists of the seriousness of the degradation of the environment, it was particularly disheartening that very few specific targets were set at the Johannesburg Conference. There was a certain amount of worthy aspiration, but most of the scientists and conservationists who went to that summit with high hopes came away disillusioned.

There was a valuable and significant development from the point of view of the Church's contribution to this area of concern in the fact that the Global Anglican Congress on the Stewardship of Creation took place near Johannesburg in the week preceding the World

Summit on Sustainable Development. This brought together 70 people from many different parts of the world, representatives of the Anglican Communion in both developing and developed countries. Among the major speakers were representatives from the United Nations, distinguished academics from South Africa, the Caribbean, Australia, Madagascar and the United Kingdom. Resolutions were passed on biodiversity and climate change issues, including a commitment to the study of contraction and convergence, a post-Kyoto strategy for achieving a reduction in greenhouse gas emissions and an equitable and worldwide energy policy, involving emissions trading on an unprecedented scale and in a form which would be of real benefit to the poorest and most disadvantaged countries.

In the European Union, the development of a biodiversity strategy has been taking shape for the past 25 years, notably with the Birds Directive (1979) and the Habitats Directive (1992). There is provision for the establishment of Special Areas of Conservation, but the response of most member states has been deeply disappointing. The deadline for the communication of candidate Special Areas of Conservation to the Commission was May 1995, but by May 1999 not one single member state had submitted a complete national list and maps. For most member states such areas are not afforded any protection under Article 6 of the Directive until they are formally adopted by the Commission. This means that many highly important sites remain unprotected because of the failure of member states to keep to the agreed schedule. There has to be serious doubt as to whether national governments are indeed truly committed to European Union policies and to the principle of sustainable development in a coherent territorial approach. In principle, European initiatives should be particularly valuable, because they cover a large area of landscape, one which is extremely diverse, and also include a vast amount of important, and at least in parts entirely unspoilt, coastline. (See minutes of evidence taken before the European Communities Committee (Sub-Committee C) of the House of Lords, May 1999.)

The previous section looked at the damaging effect of the Common Agricultural Policy on the character of farming in Europe over the past 30 years. At last, there is to be substantial reform of the Common Agricultural Policy, with a single farm payment being made from 2005, superseding the existing immensely complex system of subsidies and agri-environment schemes. Product subsidies have been the bane of European farming since the formation of the European Union. They have encouraged farmers to produce more than can be sold on the world market at a reasonable price, they have encouraged dumping of surplus European Union produce on developing countries with a devastating impact, in some cases, on local agriculture; and they have more than outweighed any good that has been done by the relatively small scale, limited and quite complex agri-environment schemes. Under the unreformed Common Agricultural Policy, production-related subsidies have a budget 50 times greater than either the agri-environment programme or the less favoured areas compensation scheme.

The Countryside Stewardship Scheme in Britain is a significant contributor to the improvement in biodiversity which has been taking place in some areas of farming, but it requires financial input by the farmer, and is complicated both to arrange and to police. Environmentally Sensitive Areas are a simpler form of agri-environment scheme, because they include all the farmers in a particular designated area. But the areas themselves are relatively small in number and in extent, and no new ESAs have been designated for some time. From 2005 the single farm payment will replace the whole panoply of subsidies and agri-environment inducements, with a single 'broad and shallow' entry level stewardship requirement, which many farmers will meet without too much difficulty; there will then be higher tier forms of support for farmers who are prepared to buy into an increasingly complex menu of environmentally desirable practices. This will involve an increasingly stringent cross-compliance regime, according to which payments are made only if farmers deliver environmental benefits.

The new Common Agricultural Policy system will be a great deal simpler to organize and enforce, and there has over the years been an increasing readiness on the part of most farmers to be seen as guardians of the countryside, people who manage the landscape in a sustainable way. This has something to do with the process of shedding the traditional pride in farming as a craft business, and with the growing awareness on the part of farmers of their wider place in the economy and social life of the country.

Finally, there are important points to be made about the contribution to biodiversity by hunting and game conservation. Both require the maintenance of diverse habitats, and run counter to the pressures of intensive farming. The present deeply polarized debate about hunting in the United Kingdom cannot conceal the fact that country which is hunted over is more likely to be rich in biodiversity than country which is given over entirely to cultivation and the rearing of livestock. Game conservation is even more important in the protection it offers to woodland, and to cover for game birds. This is not the place to enter into a debate for or against the morality or desirability of hunting, but it is beyond dispute that hunting and game conservation contribute significantly to biodiversity, and if they were to be banned or reduced in scale, there would undoubtedly be a negative impact on the biodiversity of the United Kingdom landscape.

An Uncertain Future

We know very little indeed about biodiversity, but of the complexity and interrelatedness of all life, there can be no doubt. Edward O. Wilson in his book *The Diversity of Life*, says this of the unexplored biosphere, referring in particular to the vast number of species of insects and flowering plants, and to their complex interrelationships:

> The immense diversity of the insects and flowering plants combined is no accident. The two empires are united by intricate symbioses. The insects consume every anatomical part of the plants, while dwelling on them in every nook and cranny. A large fraction of the plant species depend on insects for pollination and reproduction. Ultimately they owe them their very lives, because insects turn the soil around their roots and decompose dead tissue into the nutrients required for continual growth. So important are insects and other land dwelling arthropods that if all were to disappear humanity probably could not last more than a few months. Most of the amphibians, reptiles, birds and mammals would crash to extinction about the same time. Next would go the bulk of the flowering plants and with them the physical structure of most forests and other terrestrial habitats of the world. The land surface would literally rot. (Wilson, 2001: 123–4)

Fortunately, it is not likely that this will happen, but we need to be reminded by such analyses that significant loss of biodiversity through species extinction is a very serious matter indeed for all life. We have to ask the question whether there is any hope that the human race can succeed in reversing the present catastrophic decline in biodiversity, which is occurring almost entirely through deforestation and habitat destruction, and is likely to accelerate as climate change impinges on the planet.

It therefore becomes clear that habitat destruction and climate change are the two decisive factors with which the human race has to grapple. Anything which helps to reverse the diminution of biodiversity, or to delay or even reverse climate change, must be welcomed. As has already been pointed out, success will only come if there is a dramatic and worldwide determination to address these issues. But it is also true that every little helps.

As far as habitat destruction is concerned, high-minded resolutions achieve nothing unless there is a determination to act. It is particularly important to concentrate attention on what are known as 'megadiversity habitats', the conservation hotspots of the world. These are to be found particularly in Brazil, Columbia, China, Mexico, Australia, Indonesia, Peru, Malaysia, Ecuador, India, Zaire and Madagascar. These are countries where there are habitats or ecosystems that harbour a particularly large number of species, and where the threats to their destruction are considerable.

Brazil is perhaps the most important of all. It is credited with having more species than any other country on earth, over a fifth of the world's flowering plant species, for example. The Brazilian Amazonian Rainforest covers 60 per cent of Brazil, and so far just over 10 per cent has been lost. Deforestation in Brazil has slowed down since its 1987 peak. But the Atlantic Forest, which once ran all along the Atlantic coast of Brazil, covering 12 per cent of the country, has suffered much more severely. Because it covers an enormous distance from north to south, it includes a remarkable variety of soils, climates and altitudes, and thus contains a mosaic of sub-regions or habitat types, coastal plain forest, sand dunes, mangroves and grasslands, which together make the Atlantic Forest uniquely rich in plant and animal life. Because it is much more accessible than the tropical rainforest, it has been much more heavily exploited, and only 8 per cent of the original forest cover remains, in isolated fragments. Perhaps only 1 per cent is primary uncut forest. Conservation efforts being made by the Brazilian government do not appear to be having much success, but this Atlantic Forest is one of the most important megadiversity hotspots. Many of the plants and animals in the area are indigenous and unique, and many are on the verge of extinction. Seventeen of the 20 primate species found there are indigenous, and all 17 are endangered. It is clear that the economic and social problems of Brazil, which are leading to such devastating destruction of its biodiversity, are of importance to the whole world. It cannot be right to leave to the Brazilian government responsibility for safeguarding resources which are of potential benefit to the entire human race. This is why the United Nations Convention on Biodiversity is so important, and why there is an urgent need to raise the profile of this whole issue, and to achieve much more effective action to counter the understandable but destructive impact of development of many different kinds (House of Commons, 1993/94).

Climate change is a problem so vast that it is barely comprehensible, but once again efforts by individuals are well worth making. Energy conservation is the most effective way of reducing carbon dioxide and greenhouse gas emissions, together with a great reduction in the use of transport, particularly as long as transport depends on the burning of fossil fuels, either directly in the form of oil or petrol, or indirectly through electricity whose generation is often by fossil fuel means. Air travel is one of the great polluters, and has only recently come to be recognized as a very serious issue. There is a direct conflict in the United Kingdom between the government's desire to increase airport capacity, so that the United Kingdom does not lose out in terms of its share of air traffic, and its Biodiversity Action Plan and Energy White Paper, both of which recognize the need to reduce dramatically greenhouse gas emissions. That there is such conflict at the heart of government is a fundamental problem, which can only be solved by the right kind of political will, which needs to be enforced through fiscal policies, and motivated by what it as heart an altruistic, or even spiritual, concern for a proper care of creation.

Education is of vital importance. It is fascinating to notice the enthusiasm of young children for studying the environment, and their deep concern about what is happening to it. There is a salutary lesson in the idealism of the young, which is so seldom sustained through later years of adolescence and into adulthood. But if we are to safeguard the future of pharmaceuticals derived from plant life, or if we are to follow agricultural policies which are far more environment-friendly than those of recent decades, if we are to handle properly the contentious subject of intellectual property rights, and if we are to develop and adequately manage eco-tourism, there has to be a fundamental conversion, not only of those who are in positions of responsibility in government, but of those to whom they are answerable.

If political decisions about the environment are to be limited to electoral cycles, and therefore to be essentially short term, there is very little chance indeed of developing effective means of safeguarding biodiversity. Dr Norman Moore, whose own personal achievement in increasing biodiversity in a small area of Cambridgeshire is well described in his book, *Oaks, Dragonflies and People* (Moore, 2002), writes with passion of how we are probably the last generation which has a chance of taking adequate and decisive action. He recognizes the particular difficulty of reconciling the long-term future requirements of the planet with the short-term day-to-day pressures on government. He recognizes how recent is the development of the term 'biodiversity', although the concept behind it is not new; conservation has always been about the value of the variety of life and the need to conserve it, but the development of one single word has encapsulated this complex truth in a form which makes it much more accessible to a much greater number of people. What is needed now is a term which defines the particular political activity which can bring about the safeguarding of the future, by achieving a willingness on the part of the whole human race to give this objective the priority it demands. He suggests the term 'Future Care' politics. If this term could be brought widely into circulation, people would begin to enquire about its meaning, and to understand its significance and its impact on them. Future Care politics would transcend party divisions and would be embraced by all politicians as an indispensable philosophy in tackling the degradation of the environment. As Dr Moore says: 'The future of the environment is a matter of life and death, and so political parties should be able to put aside differences and achieve an effective long-term campaign on behalf of future generations' (2002: 103).

The fact is that the demands of the present have always to be weighed against the demands of the future. Is it possible to put enough emphasis on the latter to limit and transform the former? While it is true that self-interest would carry us a long way towards the goal, those who care about the future must want to see something in the nature of a comprehensive conversion experience of a kind that needs to be sustained by religious fervour.

REFERENCES

Banner, M. (1999), *Christian Ethics and Contemporary Moral Problems*, Cambridge, Cambridge University Press.

Convention on Biological Diversity (2002), *Sustaining Life on Earth*, Montreal, Quebec, World Trade Centre.

Groombridge, B. (ed.) (1992), *Global Biodiversity: Status of the Earth's Living Resources*, Dordrecht, Netherlands, Kluwer Academic Press.

House of Commons (1993/94), *Biodiversity*, London, House of Commons Library Research Paper.

House of Lords (1998/99), *Biodiversity in the European Union: 18th Report*, London, Select Committee on the European Communities.

Lambeth Conference (1999), *The Official Report of the Lambeth Conference 1998*, Harrisburg, Pennsylvania, Morehouse Publishing.

Moore, N. W. (2002), *Oaks, Dragonflies and People*, Colchester, Harley Books.

Rolston, H. (1995), 'Duties to Endangered Species', in R. Elliot (ed.) (1995), *Environmental Ethics*, Oxford, Oxford University Press, pp. 60–75.

Royal Commission on Environmental Pollution (2002), *Energy: The Changing Climate*, London, The Stationery Office (CM 4749).

Ryan, J. C. (1992), *Life Support: Conserving Biological Diversity*, Washington, DC, Worldwatch Institute.

Wilson, E.O. (2001), *The Diversity of Life*, Harmondsworth, Penguin Books.

World Resources Institute Website (2004), 'A History of Extinction' [online], available from: http://pubs.wri.org/pubs_content_text.cfm?ContentID=519 [accessed 2 July 2004].

Worldwide Fund for Nature (2002), *Living Planet Report 2002*, Cambridge, UNEP-WCMC.

8. Farming in a Time of Transition

ANTHONY J. RUSSELL

Summary

This chapter emphasizes the difficulty of writing about farming at a time of sharp decline following a long period of prosperity. The chapter begins by tracing the history of British farming, which became an exported industry in the nineteenth century with the extension of the American railway to Chicago. At the beginning of the First World War, Britain was only 17 per cent self-sufficient. The next period of prosperity in British agriculture began with the Agricultural Act of 1947. Britain entered the Common Market cautiously in 1973, but farming benefited from this move. By the 1980s, however, changing perceptions of farmers, and questions about aims and objectives of the Common Agricultural Policy were becoming a source of unease for farmers, and in the early 1990s the period of prosperity was coming to an end. Cheaper sources of food were now to be found abroad, and disease outbreaks were compounding the downward trend. All of this exposed the necessity for structural changes which should have occurred much earlier.

The final section of the chapter examines the 'triple bottom line' in agricultural policy, economic, environmental and social concerns, and its implication for the future. Common Agricultural Policy reforms continue to determine the economic picture, and non-food crops, especially energy crops, are becoming increasingly important. Differing views on what the countryside is for are heard in environmental policy-making. Understandings of the nature of the countryside and the rural community are determinative in future social policy.

Thus, at a time when it has become isolated, and a small player in a European and global agricultural context, British farming must grapple with social and ethical problems which have become central topics in agriculture.

Introduction

There can hardly be a more difficult time to write about farming. Many of the moral, scientific, ethical, political and social issues which face society at present can be seen in sharp focus in the farming world. The problems and issues of contemporary agriculture have been in the forefront of public debate in recent years, while at the same time farming itself has moved from a long period of prosperity into a sudden and sharp decline.

If at present there is some modest indication of a recovery in certain commodity prices, it is a recovery from historically low levels, and the consequences of the sudden dramatic fall can be seen all around. The Department for the Environment, Food and Rural Affairs' figures indicate that if 100 is used as the profitability index during the period 1994–97; by 2001–02 farm profitability had declined on average to 29 (on predominantly livestock farms 30; predominantly arable farms 10). At the end of the last decade, United Kingdom farm incomes were more than 40 per cent lower at the end than at the beginning.

The evidence of an industry in decline and crisis is all around. Agriculture's share of the GDP has reduced to less than 1 per cent. Only 0.3 per cent of Britain's population are now employed in full-time agriculture; while this is a very small percentage of the national population, it also represents only 1.2 per cent of the rural population. Recent figures from the Office for National Statistics for 2002 record that 52,000 farmers and farm workers left the land during that year. Thus farming is losing its workforce at approximately a rate of 1,000 per week. The average age of farmers is 59; half the farmers in East Anglia are part-time, and a similar number have no identified successor. Many agricultural colleges have diversified into such areas as horticulture, equitation, recreational and environmental studies, and in some cases, have no farming students. It has been said that the present crisis is as much about *farmers* as it is about *farming*, and certainly many farmers feel that they operate in a world in which they have lost control, and that they have been abandoned by politicians to their fate.

At harvest 2003, some cereal prices have shown a modest increase, yet despite this they are still at nearly half the level of the late 1990s. Such is the international market in agricultural commodities that, while farmers watch the local weather with close attention, they are also interested in the weather in the main grain-growing areas of Europe and North America. During 2003, unusually hot weather and prolonged droughts were likely to give lighter harvests across Europe. From France and Spain, to Russia and the Ukraine, high temperatures and lack of water were likely to have an adverse effect. However, the principal area of uncertainty resided in the implications of the reforms to the Common Agricultural Policy, widely known as the mid-term review, which promises to shift the focus of agricultural support from production subsidies to whole farm subsidies, coupled with support for the environment and the rural community.

Moral Values

Farming, like any other human activity, does not take place in a moral vacuum, and the decisions that an individual farmer takes, and the activities of international grain and food organizations, arise from complex motivations. All religious traditions share a concern for the God-given environment, and seek to harmonize the natural and human world to the detriment of neither, and to restrain unbridled greed and exploitation. In the biblical tradition, God placed man in a garden to tend, keep and protect it, and much of the biblical tradition is about the restraint of exploitation, and fairness and justice in distributing the products of agriculture. Large parts of the book of Deuteronomy are in fact a farming manual, and provide advice at a time of change from nomadic livestock farming to settled arable communities.

The Christian tradition has often been caricatured as legitimizing an unbridled exploitation of the natural environment, but that is to misunderstand the Genesis account, and to ignore the biblical tradition of stewardship allied to responsibility. In traditional society, men and women were much closer to the natural environment, and their ability to intervene had clear limits. The natural world was seen as hostile, something to be kept at bay and always threatening to take over. The modern history of farming has been an account of the way in which developing technology and scientific discovery have allowed men and women to exercise much greater control over the natural processes of growth. Modern plant-breeding, the development of powerful herbicides and pesticides, and increasingly sophisticated agricultural machinery allow a high-yielding, clean crop of cereals to be grown year after year in the same field. The only significant variable is the weather, and while that cannot be controlled, its effects can be significantly reduced. With greater control comes responsibility for the effects of human actions on the natural world, and that lies at the centre of much of the environmental debate.

Farmers are fond of quoting from Genesis 41, the account of Joseph's time in Egypt as Pharaoh's steward, and the dream of the seven fat, followed by the seven lean, cattle. The cyclical nature of farming is regarded as one of its few constant features, and provides a way of accounting for the varied fortunes of agriculture. The modern history of agriculture since the agricultural revolution of the eighteenth and early nineteenth centuries can be seen as a long contest between rural producers and urban consumers of food; between *protection* (to support home production) and *free trade* (to facilitate low cost imports). The current debates about the future of the Common Agricultural Policy are but a contemporary expression of this historic contest.

Historical Perspective

At the end of the Napoleonic Wars, the new Corn Law of 1815 protected farmers against a fall in cereal prices by prohibiting the sale of foreign corn until the price reached certain thresholds. The pressure from urban consumers in the reformed Parliament led to the repeal of the Corn Laws in 1846. However, such was the expansion in the urban population that agricultural prices remained relatively high. By 1853, the golden age of Victorian 'high farming' set in. It was characterized by high rents, high returns, and high levels of investment in drainage, fertilizer, farm machinery and buildings, together with the breeding of improved stock. The enclosures of the previous century had allowed the development of ring-fenced farms outside the village (the previous medieval pattern had been for farm buildings to be located in the village, and the land to be dispersed outside), and it is from this period that the modern pattern of English farming developed.

After 20 years, there was a sudden and dramatic change. In 1873, the railway reached Chicago, allowing relatively cheap American, and later Canadian, wheat to be exported to Europe. In England, the price of wheat fell by half between 1871 and 1898. This was quickly followed by imports of meat and dairy produce from New Zealand, Australia, Canada and Argentina, and a consequent sharp decline both in domestic price and production. This process was encouraged by the government (now largely representing the urban interest), for the importing of food from overseas generated finance which allowed the purchase of machinery and factory-made goods from urban England. In a sense, the British farming industry was exported, and agricultural commentators see in present events a similar pattern.

By the onset of the First World War, domestic food production had declined to such a degree that Britain was only 17 per cent self-sufficient. The 1920s and 1930s were a period of significant agricultural depression, in which farm land in Hampshire and Wiltshire could be bought for £3 an acre unfenced, or £5 fenced. At the low point in any agricultural cycle there are considerable changes in farm structure and ownership, and the 1920s and 1930s saw the emergence of many of the large farming families who have played such a significant role in recent agricultural history. No account of contemporary farming is complete without an assessment of the legacy of the years of agricultural depression and its lasting effect on the attitudes and memory of the farming community. By the 1930s, sour, soggy and degenerating land, full of speargrass, bracken and brambles, together with dilapidated and out-of-date buildings, was common in many areas. On the lighter, less fertile soils, such as in north Norfolk, farmhouse windows gazed emptily over derelict fields which were rapidly disappearing under a covering of gorse, thistle, dock and ragwort. In some areas, ditches and drains slowly filled, hedges began to thicken into copses, copses became woods. Landowners were forced to forgo the rent in order to ensure that tenants remained on the farm. The principal crop of a significant area of Huntingdonshire was rabbits, sent by train to London.

As a consequence of the Atlantic blockade, the increase in home food production became a matter of national survival during the Second World War. When the war was over, farmers were determined that they would not slide back into another period of depression, and the Agricultural Act of 1947 was the foundation stone for the next period of British agriculture. The Act established a system of securing guaranteed prices (subject to the annual February price review) and a system of grants and subsidies for capital projects. Food rationing (in certain commodities) was not lifted until 1953, and much of the planning for the future of European agriculture was based on the memory of food scarcity and starvation during the period immediately after the Second World War. Around 15,000 people died of starvation in Holland immediately after the end of the war, and there were food riots in Paris. The severity of post-war rationing was in part to facilitate the feeding of the German population.

Every encouragement was given to the expansion of food production at a time when Malthusian concerns about population outstripping food production were again being heard. This was a time of much concern about world population growth, resulting in campaigns with such slogans as 'feed the world'. The principal response of western governments was to increase investment in agricultural research; thus, between 1947 and 1951, agricultural production grew by 20 per cent, and by 1978 the average yield of wheat had doubled.

Initially, the farming community was cautious about entering into the Common Market in 1973. In reality, farming has been the main beneficiary through the Common Agricultural Policy, which was based on the Mansholt Plan, developed in response to the need for European food security and support for rural regions (Commission for European Communities, 1968). Subsequent events have tended to obscure the fact that the Mansholt Plan was primarily a social and political policy aimed at restoring and reinvigorating the depopulated rural areas in the post-war period. In the elections immediately after the Second World War, 35 per cent of the population of rural France voted communist. The extent to which the English countryside was suffering was well illustrated by the research of C. S. Orwin, Director of the Agricultural Economics Research Institute in Oxford, and published during and after the Second World War (Orwin, 1949). Economists agreed that by increasing the profitability of farming, new wealth would be dispersed throughout the rural community.

While agriculture took some time to adjust to post-war conditions, by the time of Britain's entry into the Common Market it was clear that the farming cycle was moving again into prosperity. There followed a 25-year period which may in retrospect be seen as another golden age of British farming, encouraged and sustained by the formerly derided Common Agricultural Policy. However, by the 1980s three concerns were being increasingly heard. Advances in livestock and plant-breeding were coupled with new crop protection technology and greatly enhanced machinery capacity. The implications of this, allied to improved management techniques, created an over-supply in many of the temperate crops. This was the era of 'grain mountains', 'beef mountains' and 'wine lakes', in which considerable quantities of food were bought into intervention, and then disposed of (often being dumped in communist Eastern Europe or in developing countries). For a time, a significant proportion of the Common Agricultural Policy budget was needed to address the problem of these surpluses, with the triple cost of subsidized production, storage and disposal. For a time, it appeared that Adam Smith's dictum, that the object of economic activity is not production but consumption, had been forgotten.

Many voices were raised against what appeared to be the injustice of European agricultural surpluses and famine in sub-Saharan Africa. It is said today, that while in the poorer areas of Africa average daily subsistence amounts to 80p, every European cow is subsidized to the daily value of £1.64. Other critical voices note that the two original planks on which the Common Agricultural Policy was founded, European food security and the financial support of rural areas, no longer bear the weight of argument which they carried 30 years before. Increasingly, the Common Agricultural Policy is portrayed as a very expensive cartel, which provided throughout Europe high incomes for the farming community and relatively cheap food for the urban consumer.

As human power to intervene in the processes of nature grew, the environmental impact of agriculture caused increased concern. Farming was no longer a small-scale, domestically based operation, but had become an industrial process based on arable specialization and intensive livestock farming. For generations, and particularly during the Second World War, the farmer had been portrayed as the heroic provider of the nation's food. Now farmers were increasingly seen as the destroyers of the countryside, the killers of flora and fauna, who restrained public access and enjoyment of rural areas, and who were paid very considerable sums to produce food about whose safety consumers had increasing doubts.

The late 1980s and early 1990s saw policy mechanisms designed to restrain levels of agricultural production and their associated costs. On 3 March 1984, milk quotas were introduced across Europe in an attempt to restrain overproduction. In 1988, set-aside (a device which had long been a feature of American agricultural policy) was introduced in Europe, whereby a percentage of arable land was taken out of production, which it was hoped would confer environmental and ecological benefits.

Contemporary Crises

By the early 1990s, it was clear that the long golden period of post-war prosperity was coming to an end, and when the collapse came, it was sudden and far-reaching. By the middle of the decade, farm incomes had dropped by 80 per cent; wheat that had been sold for £120 per tonne was selling at half that price. One bank recorded that approximately a quarter of farm businesses were technically insolvent, and half no longer provided sufficient income to sustain the farm family. There are many reasons for the sudden change and the downturn in commodity prices, but among the contributory factors, British agriculture was disadvantaged by the euro-sterling exchange rate. Increasingly, food was purchased from the cheapest worldwide source, and domestic cereal prices were significantly affected by the development of new areas of production, such as the Ukraine and the Black Sea coast. Ukraine alone accounted for 7 per cent of the wheat traded on the world market in 2002. Pig meat from Holland and Denmark, and dairy produce from France and Germany were all produced and marketed in the United Kingdom at lower cost. Cheap international air freight (there is no tax on aviation fuel) brought the produce from areas of the world where growing conditions and labour costs gave a significant financial advantage. British farmers frequently comment that there is no 'level playing field' in food production, as the domestic demand for higher standards of welfare, feed and slaughter conditions disadvantages home production. However, at the same time, urban consumers feel at liberty to purchase cheaper imports, particularly in the catering industry which accounts for 50 per cent of the total food market, and where traceability is less evident.

The downward spiral of British agriculture was compounded by a series of disease outbreaks and the accompanying publicity, which has seriously damaged public confidence in farmers and farming. Despite the earlier outbreaks of salmonella in eggs and the classical swine fever outbreak in East Anglia, nothing prepared the farming community for the two major catastrophes. On 20 March 1996, it was announced in Parliament that scientific opinion now held that there was a reasonable presumption of a link between Bovine Spongiform Encephalitis (a cattle disease) and new-variant Creutzfeldt-Jakob's Disease. The outbreak of BSE had a devastating effect on the domestic livestock industry, and United Kingdom farming lost its annual export of 350,000 animals. Despite the much-publicized photograph of the Minister of Agriculture feeding his daughter a beefburger at an agricultural show, the domestic beef market collapsed.

This was followed by the outbreak of Foot and Mouth Disease, which had an even greater effect on livestock farming, particularly in the west and north. The outbreak was notified on 20 February 2001, and within three days the Ministry of Agriculture, Fisheries and Food had banned animal movements, and a policy of slaughter for all affected animals was pursued. By mid-March, the disease appeared to be out of control, and the slaughter policy was extended to livestock on neighbouring farms. Six million animals were slaughtered.

Many people found the burning and mass burial of cattle, sheep and pigs to be a profoundly disturbing event. There can be no doubt that this further accelerated feelings of unease about the direction in which the farming industry was moving. Confidence in British food and farming markedly declined, and this affected the political environment in which farming operated.

The long period of prosperity had protected British farming against some of the structural changes that should otherwise have taken place. There were many small farms (particularly in the livestock sector) which in all likelihood had been on the edges of non-viability for many years. While it is not evident to the casual observer, the countryside has changed significantly in the past five years, as elderly farmers have sold up. Recent statistics have indicated that 56 per cent of the present purchasers of farms come from urban areas. In many cases, what looks like a traditional landscape is in fact a pattern of farmhouses lived in by new residents, while the land is farmed by large-scale farming businesses. At the beginning of the twentieth century, only 12 per cent of the land area in Great Britain was owner-occupied; by the latter part of the century, following the break-up of the landed estates, this had increased to 70 per cent. Thus, the majority of farmers were also landowners (and not tenants). Farming became an increasingly distinctive industry, as the farmer both owned and operated the farm. However, one of the recent consequences of Foot and Mouth Disease and low commodity prices has been a considerable increase in 'rented' farm land occupied under a range of terms, including farm business tenancies, share farming, and contract farming arrangements.

Among the responses of government to the agricultural downturn has been the reconfiguring of Ministry of Agriculture, Fisheries and Food (MAFF) as the Department for the Environment, Food and Rural Affairs (DEFRA). 'Farming' and 'agriculture' no longer have a place in the new title, unlike nearly every other European Union country, and the farming community no longer has a designated Minister of Cabinet rank. The agricultural crisis prompted the government to establish a major inquiry into the state of British agriculture, chaired by Sir Donald Curry (2002). The report has highlighted a number of the fundamental problems: that agriculture has become detached from the rest of the economy and the environment; that international competition will increase; that technological developments in agriculture will continue to produce productivity improvements outpacing demand for food; that high growth in consumer demand for convenience foods ensures that farmers remain producers of low cost raw materials, to which others add significant value; and that the fragmented structure of the farm sector contrasts sharply with that of other links in the food chain, namely processors, manufacturers and supermarkets. The implications of this can be seen in the low profitability of farming, compared with other sectors in the food chain.

The Curry Report and other recent reports on agriculture have seen farming as operating at the intersection of three areas of policy and public concern: economic, environmental and social dimensions, often referred to as 'the triple bottom line'. The present state and future of British farming may be considered under these three headings.

Economic

Since 1973, British farming no longer operates within a national framework, and has been subject to the rules and direction of the Common Agricultural Policy. Both within and outside the farming community, opinions about the Common Agricultural Policy differ widely. Despite its complex rules and bureaucracy, farmers acknowledge that it has played a significant role in maintaining the profitability of British farming (certainly throughout the 1970s and 1980s), and point to the relative cheapness of food in this country. In 1950, it took the average Briton 90 days to earn enough income to pay for a year's food supply. Today, it takes 44 (and of these days, only five represent the earnings of the farmer). Much is made of the cost of the Common Agricultural Policy, which amounts to 70 per cent of European Union funding, though it is equivalent to just 1.3 per cent of total public spending in the European Union. Although recent statistics have shown that the Common Agricultural Policy costs an individual household approximately £90 per annum, this is less than farm support in the United States of America, which costs an American household £122. While some regard the Common Agricultural Policy as in need of far-reaching restructuring, others see it as fundamentally unreformable, and regard it, in the words of a recently retiring government minister, as 'a grotesque protection racket'. The uncertainty of the present situation is compounded by the volatility of currency markets, by the inevitable impact of European Union enlargement, and principally by the effects of the current reform of the Common Agricultural Policy, proposals for which were agreed on 26 June 2003.

The essence of this agreement is to restructure agricultural support so that it is no longer based primarily on production subsidies, and at the same time, to make money available for environmental and social programmes. This was the substance of the MacSharry proposals (European Union, 1992). The process, known as 'decoupling', will initially affect three-quarters of the payments in the arable sector and half the total value of payments in the sheep and beef sector, to be in operation from 2005 (the dairy sector follows in 2007). The decoupled single farm payment will be based on the average payments claimed over the three-year reference period, 2000–02. The single farm payment will be reduced by 3 per cent to create a national reserve for hardship, exceptional circumstances, and farms 'in a special situation'. A further 10 per cent of payments will be 'modulated' (effectively top-sliced) and made available for environmental and rural development programmes.

It is clear that this is a complex process, but the intention is to make agriculture more market-sensitive, leaving farmers free to determine their cropping systems and also to reduce the current bureaucracy. It is too early to suggest the precise impact of these changes, but one East Anglian farmer with 1,200 acres of arable crops received £100,000 in subsidies in 2002 for his cereals; he estimates that in the future the sum will be cut by 30–40 per cent. He will hope to make up the shortfall by participating in further environmental improvement schemes, by new farm diversification projects, and by a wider crop mix, including energy crops.

Perhaps it is remarkable that the term Common Agricultural Policy has been retained, when it is clear that countries, within the broad concepts of decoupling and modulation, may implement its proposals with wide variations. For instance, implementation is due in this country in 2005, and in France in 2007. The enlarging of the European Union, as ten more countries join in 2004, will have a considerable impact. It is hard to see how the assurance can be honoured that farm spending will not rise as a percentage of European Union spending. Some see in the new proposals attempts to weaken European control of agriculture, and partially to renationalize farming.

The declining viability of British farms has led to two principal responses. First, there is a change in farm structure, as older farmers retire and their sons and daughters are not being encouraged to continue. Second, particularly in arable areas, there is an inexorable drive towards farming larger units, over which fixed costs can be spread. What is emerging can be termed two-tier farming. On the one hand, there are large 'broad-acre' farming businesses with considerable acreages, using the economies of scale and the latest scientific advances to produce high-quality crops at world prices. On the other hand, there are smaller farms, often livestock holdings, producing specialist products for a niche market, in many cases using organic methods.

For some time, the production of non-food crops, including crops for energy, chemical and pharmacological uses, has been seen as the prospect that will transform British agriculture. Farmers remember that in the mid-nineteenth century, 30 per cent of the land was used to grow crops to feed horses, and suggest that with the possibility of known oil stocks running out around 2050, farming may return to a similar situation. Many novel and new crops appear to have limited markets, and enthusiasm is short-lived. However, in three areas considerable advances have been made. Oilseed rape (canola) was a novel crop in the early 1970s, and has become a major source of oil for domestic and many other uses. New crops, such as crambe (Abyssinian mustard), which has a high oil content of exceptional purity, are being experimented with. Second, hemp is being grown extensively as a fibre source, and is found in a wide variety of uses in the building trade (where it replaces asbestos), and in car manufacture (where it replaces fibre glass). Third, the much-heralded advent of bio-fuels, given encouragement in the recent Energy White Paper, is regarded as now technically feasible, and requires an adjustment in tax to make it commercially viable (Department for Trade and Industry, 2003). It is suggested that if 25 per cent of the land in the United Kingdom were planted with industrial sugar beet and wheat, the country could be self-sufficient in biofuels. A number of continental countries are already further advanced with bioethanol and biodiesel (there is no tax on biofuels in France and Spain). Currently United Kingdom wheat is being exported to Spain to be turned into bioethanol. In certain areas where there is a suitable power station, farmers are growing willow and miscanthus. However, many developments in new crops are hampered by the fact that they are inevitably small in scale and consequently vulnerable to market changes. Recently, the modest quantity of evening primrose, formerly grown in this country, has disappeared, as China has established a major area of production which effectively supplies the world market.

The authors of the Curry Report believe that reducing costs and increasing efficiency, getting closer to the end purchaser, joining in farm co-operatives, adding value to the product, diversifying into new agricultural and non-agricultural areas, will all provide pathways out of the present crisis, and that this will provide a way out of the present agricultural depression.

Environment

Traditional societies saw the environment as essentially hostile, always ready to reclaim modest human efforts to clear and cultivate the land. In the late eighteenth and early nineteenth centuries, advances in agricultural practice considerably extended human ability to control and harness the natural world, to the point where concerns were beginning to be expressed about the extent and effect of human intervention. Agriculture, the practice of encouraging two blades of grass to grow where one grew formerly, is essentially about inter-vention in the natural environment. However, by the mid-nineteenth century, it was clear that not every intervention was benign, and that men and women now had access to power and chemical resources capable of making a much more profound impression on the natural environment. It is no coincidence that the word 'ecology' first appeared in the English language in 1873. The following period saw the foundation and growth of a large number of voluntary organizations concerned with environmental protection, animal rights and other related issues. From the point of view of agriculture, the formation of the Soil Association in 1946 by Lady Balfour has been the most influential, and has given rise to an approach to farming now known as 'organic'.

Behind much of the debate about the nature of the environment lies the question, 'What is the countryside for?' For farmers, the answer is simple: it is the shop floor of Britain's largest industry. But it is clear that many see the countryside in a different and competing light, valuing it principally as a habitat of flora and fauna, as a place of space and landscape, a place of recreation and refreshment. The Foot and Mouth Disease crisis demonstrated how much the countryside is valued as a recreation and tourist resource, on which much of the rural economy now depends.

Increasingly, farmers have been portrayed as destroyers of the rural environment in order to receive large sums of subsidy from the Common Agricultural Policy, as in books like *The Killing of the Countryside* by Graham Harvey (1997). Harvey records the significant loss of biodiversity, particularly on arable farm land, now devoid of weeds and many insects. This has led to a decline in seed- and insect-eating birds, such as skylarks, finches, buntings, lapwings, tree sparrows and grey partridges. Despite much that has been done recently by such organizations as Farming and Wildlife Advisory Groups (FWAG) and other organizations, it is difficult not to conclude that there is an inevitable conflict between commercial farmers and those who see the countryside principally as a habitat for flora and fauna, increasingly reflected in the constraints that are placed on farmers as a response to public awareness of these issues.

The debate between a scientific and technological approach to the countryside, and an environmental one is posed sharply by the emergence of genetically modified technology. In June 2003, the government initiated a national debate on genetically modified crops and food at six regional launches. While genetically modified crops are extensively grown in North America, there has been a strong consumer resistance in this country. There is little doubt that the way in which genetically modified technology was introduced, without notice or explanation, has contributed significantly to this. What is currently being debated is whether permission should be given for genetically modified crops to be grown commercially, and it is clear that there is still considerable opposition.

There have been four areas of concern regarding the commercial growing of genetically modified crops: food safety, the impact on the environment, questions related to genetic ownership, and the related question of the power of biotech companies. While there are few doubts that food grown from genetically modified crops is safe (there has been no litigation in the United States of America), there is concern about superweeds and genetic transfer, and these matters are still being considered. Protagonists point to the environmental gains (less spraying), higher productivity, and other advantages of genetically modified technology, particularly in growing crops for industrial and pharmacological use. Organizations such as Friends of the Earth and the Soil Association point to the uncertainties and risks which they perceive to exist. What is certain, is that there is little consumer enthusiasm in this country, and much eloquent resistance from environmental groups. Some areas, such as Ryedale, have designated themselves as 'genetically modified-free zones'. One of the principal non-agricultural issues concerns insurance, and the anxiety that if unseen problems emerged, insurers could be facing problems on the scale of asbestosis.

A reaction to the heavy dependence of agriculture on agrochemicals in the post-war period has been the development of organic farming. 'Organic' is not a term which has a scientific definition, and in practical farming terms, 'organic' is now defined by the United Kingdom Register of Organic Food Standards (UKROFS). In the eyes of the general public, it is seen as a method of farming in closer harmony and co-operation with the processes of nature. While some spraying is permitted in certain circumstances, those chemicals that are used are regarded as being of a more benign nature. It is estimated that approximately 2 per cent of the land is farmed organically, and this represents 1 per cent of United Kingdom food production.

Organic farming has established itself as a significant niche and specialist market. However, it is an area that has become particularly vulnerable to cheap overseas imports, which now account for 75 per cent of all organic food sold in this country. Its most successful proponents have been those who have developed local markets, selling either through the recently established farmers' markets, or direct selling to the public through 'veg box' schemes. However, in the main, organic farmers have found that the higher prices they require to compensate for adhering to United Kingdom Register of Organic Food Standards have been eroded. Producers of organic milk have suffered most, and the premium they require for profitability has been consistently eroded. Under the government's £49 million Organic Farming Scheme, started in 1999, farmers have been paid up to £450 per hectare to convert to organic production. In March 2003, there were 4,104 registered holdings. Farmers must remain in organic production for a five-year period, but recent statistics have indicated that many of those who initially transferred (particularly those in the dairy sector) are now preparing to return to conventional methods. In many commodities, the 'organic premium' has been eroded, while production costs remain significantly higher. The high level of imports, consumer resistance to higher prices, and concern about the frequency with which the rules which determine what is 'organic' are modified, are regarded as contributing to this situation. Recent Department for the Environment, Food and Rural Affairs statistics have shown that, while in 1999 there were 1,142 agreements which provided funds for farmers to change to organic methods, by 2002 the number had declined to 278.

The high summer temperatures and low rainfall experienced across Europe in 2003 may be exceptional, but few now doubt that evidence exists to support the global warming hypothesis. In the course of time, this will mean that climatic and agricultural zones will move northward, and that areas that previously could not grow temperate crops will now be able to compete in the European market. Perhaps most serious is the allied problem of water supply. The very high temperatures in Europe in 2003 (in parts of Central Europe the hottest for 200 years) led to droughts across most of the region, for instance, the River Po in Italy reached its lowest level for 100 years. There is no doubt that the availability of water is likely to be one of the main constraining factors in the future development of agriculture. Many farms now have their own water supplies and reservoirs, and the cost of water is a significant factor in such crops as potatoes and field vegetables.

With their large resources and sizeable memberships, organizations representing the interests of heritage, countryside and environment, and animal 'rights' are now able to influence political decision-making in a major way. It is widely recognized that they are likely to have an increasing effect on farming in the future. The chairman of the Countryside Agency, speaking at the Royal Agricultural College at Cirencester, said, 'I suspect in ten years' time, people, politicians and policy-makers will no longer equate the countryside with farming and food.' If this is an extreme statement, it nonetheless represents the direction of future rural policy. For the majority of the population, the answer to the question, 'What is the countryside for?' is increasingly offered in environmental terms, and these are priorities to which farming in the future will have to accommodate itself. These may well become the priorities around which agriculture will have to fit.

Social

Originally, the Common Agricultural Policy was conceived principally as a social policy, aimed at relieving the evident poverty and depopulation in many European rural areas, and the process known in France as 'desertification'. It was envisaged that the maintenance of high commodity prices would be a way of supporting the rural community, for money made available to farmers would percolate into the local community. One of the principal changes which has affected agriculture in the past 20 years in this country, is that politicians no longer see agricultural policy as delivering social goals. The effect of this has been to change attitudes toward agriculture as a part of national life, and at the same time, to abandon any form of coherent rural policy. Effectively, the countryside is seen as an urban back garden, rather than as an area with its own discrete needs, problems and concerns. This is in distinction to rural policy in France and Germany, on which the original thinking of the Mansholt Plan was based.

The nature of the rural community in the twenty-first century has changed significantly. It no longer comprises those who depend upon the farming community, and within the typical village, commuters, the retired and second-home owners dominate the community. It is likely that these people have no direct connection with the farming industry, and indeed regard aspects of modern farming practice as detrimental to the peace and rural beauty which they came to seek. Many of those who live in the contemporary countryside commute to urban jobs, or have retired to a rural area, and their way of life and their view of the countryside bears little relationship to that of the farming community. Often in an idyllic and arcadian way, they view the countryside as a place of residence, retirement and landscape beauty. By contrast, the farming community sees the countryside principally as the shop floor of Britain's largest industry.

Some observers now maintain that it is not possible to talk about rural society in England, because so much of English village life has become suburbanized. However, while this may be so of the 'urban shadow' and 'accessible' countryside immediately around the major urban centres, it is less the case in the more remote and marginal rural areas. For instance, in parts of Wales, the farming community still represents 30 per cent of the total population. However, in England, a notable feature of the present situation is the way in which farmers have become isolated, even within the modern rural community with which they no longer share a common understanding or way of life. Farming has become a distinct socio-economic community, with its own mores, codes and understandings. Many farmers are isolated by virtue of where they live, and by the hours which they work. For generations, farmers have had little contact with the consumers of the food they produce, selling directly to merchants and markets. The loss of food-processing in the nineteenth century, which became a separate industry, separated off farmers, who became essentially producers of the primary raw material in the majority of cases.

At the time of the Mansholt Plan, agricultural policy was seen as a major way by which rural policy could be developed and conditions in rural areas ameliorated. While in some countries this is still an appropriate response, in much of Western Europe, the numbers now employed in agriculture, and the significance of farming in the local economy, no longer make this possible. In Cambridgeshire, there are more people employed by Cambridge University than in the whole of Cambridgeshire farming. For a developed urban country, it is inevitable that farming no longer has the central role of being the vehicle of social policy in rural areas. However, despite two recent Rural White Papers (Ministry of Agriculture, Fisheries and Food, 1995; Department of the Environment, Transport and the Regions, 2000), the modern countryside effectively lacks a social policy, which means that many rural residents have to struggle with the mutually reinforcing problems of deprivation and lack of access which characterize the less accessible countryside, and which were identified in

Faith in the Countryside, the report of the Archbishops' Commission on Rural Areas (1990).

Farming today lies at the intersection of a whole range of political, social, economic, environmental and ethical problems, and this is a particularly difficult time at which to chart its future. While in the 1960s and 1970s the principal problems that faced agriculture were of a scientific and technical nature, and concerned with increasing the productivity and the profitability of modern farming, today the problems are of a very different nature.

Globalization brings considerable threats to all primary producers, but its impact on farming has been particularly far-reaching. The power of supermarkets, who control 80 per cent of retail food sales in this country, is such that they can both drive down producer prices in this country, and purchase from the cheapest international supplier. It can be argued that the United Kingdom government no longer controls British agriculture, which operates within a global and European framework. Alongside the economic issues, there are clear ethical issues in the interrelationship between the developed and the developing world.

Changes in public attitudes towards the countryside and its use principally as a recreation and leisure resource, and the rural village as a place of retirement, have had their impact on farming. At the same time, the recent crises in agriculture have posed their own problems, not least in the area of animal husbandry. Today, the problems that agriculture faces are increasingly those of a social and ethical nature, and this is the area with which the farming community will need to engage in the coming years.

REFERENCES

Archbishops' Commission on Rural Areas (1990), *Faith in the Countryside*, Worthing, Churchman Publishing.

Commission for European Communities (1968), *Reform of Agriculture in the European States*, Brussels, European Union.

Curry, D. (2002), *Farming and Food: A Sustainable Future*, London, Stationery Office.

Department for Trade and Industry (2003), *Our Energy Future: Creating a Low Carbon Economy*, London, Stationery Office.

Department of the Environment, Transport and the Regions (2000), *Our Countryside: The Future, a Fair Deal for Rural England*, London, Stationery Office.

European Union (1992), *Common Agricultural Policy Reforms*, Brussels, European Union.

Harvey, G. (1997), *The Killing of the Countryside*, London, Jonathan Cape.

Ministry of Agriculture, Fisheries and Food (1995), *Rural England: A Nation committed to a Living Countryside*, London, Stationery Office.

Orwin, C. S. (1949), *History of English Farming*, London, Nelson.

9. Eating Well

JAMES JONES

Summary

The British landscape has developed over thousands of years through our relationship with the land. Agriculture has played a major part in this process. As farmers worked the land to provide the food that fuelled our passage into the twenty-first century, they were also responsible for creating much of our beautifully diverse landscape. Perhaps somewhat unfairly, we take it for granted that today's farmers will maintain this tradition.

In the current climate of globalization new pressures are being exerted on farmers all over the world. In an industry steeped in tradition there is tremendous pressure to change. As the world shrinks the competition grows. Here, recent crises have taken their toll, and globally the arrival of new technologies has brought new pressures to bear. An industry which was once labour intensive is now being streamlined to maximize productivity and to minimize expenditure. Small farmers are being swallowed up by more competitive landowners. People who have farmed for generations are being forced off the land into lives of uncertainty. We expect our food to be convenient and cheap. But at what cost?

This chapter examines some of the tensions involved in modern agriculture and advocates a way forward. Decision-makers are challenged to examine their motives. Consumers are challenged to take more responsibility by engaging their purchasing power to steer the food markets and to enable farmers to continue in their role as stewards of the landscape.

Introduction

When it comes to eating, society changed immeasurably during the last century. Additional pressures on people and the movement of more women into the workplace meant that convenience became the holy grail in many households. Less time spent in the kitchen meant more time available for other priorities and pastimes. Fresh produce gradually gave way to frozen foods and the preparation of meals with individual ingredients was eclipsed by 'oven ready' options. The advent of the microwave was hailed as a long-awaited breakthrough and more and more meals were prepared outside the home. Whereas in 1980 the average meal took an hour to cook, by 1999 most of our meals were ready to eat within 20 minutes (Food Standards Agency, 2004a). Through the intensification of food production methods the proportion of consumer spending tied to the purchasing of food reduced considerably. But, at what cost?

People are born natural consumers. Both science and theology agree on this. The picture of Adam and Eve in the garden clearly exposes them as natural consumers, yet at a time when both famine and obesity abound, issues of the human diet have never been more pressing. Science unearths the complexities of our nutritional requirements and technology grapples with the task of delivering them equitably. Meanwhile, the Bible warns us to be discerning consumers who are called to make choices within certain ethical boundaries.

The earth was cursed through Adam's disobedient and selfish consumption of the fruit of the tree of knowledge. According to Jewish tradition the tree of knowledge of good and evil stands there in the Garden of Eden as an inhibition, to put and to keep the human family in its place. In the book of Genesis God responds to Adam's eating of the forbidden fruit from the tree of knowledge by cursing the earth beneath his feet saying 'cursed is the ground because of you; in toil you shall eat of it all the days of your life' (Genesis 3.17). By setting a physical boundary between Adam and the 'tree of life' (Genesis 3.24) God then protected that most prized of fruits by placing it out of Adam's reach.

In the New Testament, the Lord's Prayer urges us to seek God's will on earth and his provision of our daily food. The Gospels also tell of how Jesus himself 'came eating and drinking'. He ate and drank to such an extent that his opponents were outraged by his lifestyle and accused him of being a 'glutton and a drunkard' (Matthew 11.19). Indeed, they compared him to his ascetic cousin John the Baptist, who apparently ate no bread and drank no wine, in order to belittle him. Not only was Jesus not an ascetic, he took rituals of consumption, eating and drinking and elevated them to liturgical heights. Through the taking and breaking of bread and the drinking of wine at the passover meal Jesus gave his disciples a physical means through which to remember him. By consuming 'the body and blood of Christ' they received the sacrament of redemption, the key that opens the way to forgiveness, freeing the earth from its curse incurred through the disobedience of Adam.

It is clear then that consumption can be a means of both sin and redemption. It is also clear that as natural born consumers we have boundaries within which we must operate. The question is, what are these boundaries?

Vegetarianism: Rooted in Eden?

Evidence suggests that our evolution as human beings and our omnivorous diet were intrinsically linked. Indeed it has been claimed that, although a fully vegetarian diet is perfectly possible (Ford, 2000), our unusually large brain size and function could only have been achieved in evolutionary terms through eating meat (Aiello and Wheeler, 1995). Our ancestors were opportunistic in their eating habits as there were great dividends in utilizing all available sources of food. Any supply of meat, however irregular or scarce, would have helped supplement the nutritional value of a largely vegetable diet. As a species, this enabled us to expend less energy on digesting low-quality diets and more on evolving a larger brain (Aiello and Wheeler, 1995).

Our omnivorous diet is also documented throughout the Bible. In the Garden of Eden Adam was given the fruits of the trees to eat (Genesis 3.16) and after the fall he was forced to eke out an existence outside Eden relying on wild plants for sustenance (Genesis 3.18). However, Adam's offspring soon saw the potential in eating meat. The first murder in biblical history was sparked by Abel's offerings of the first lamb being favoured by the Lord over the offerings laid before him by Cain the farmer (Genesis 4.3–5). Indeed, God seems to endorse meat eating when speaking to Noah and his sons by stating, 'Every moving thing that lives shall be food for you; and just as I gave you the green plants, I give you everything' (Genesis 9.3).

So there would seem to be both a scientific and a biblical basis for continuing to eat meat. Yet, there are many cultures that depend solely on a vegetarian diet and increasingly, in western countries, people are turning away from eating meat. The arguments for adopting a vegetarian diet include the following three points.

The consumption of meat compounds world famine because animals are fed food which could be given directly to people (Garcés, 2002). With one-fifth of the world's arable land being used to grow cereals which are then fed to farm animals it is clear that in modern commercial agricultural systems intensively reared animals are fed grain and beans which might arguably be more beneficially fed directly to the world's human population. However, in traditional mixed farming systems where livestock is used to convert waste vegetable matter into edible animal protein, while providing a quickly available source of organic manure, animal husbandry has obvious benefits. It is also beneficial in environments where sustainable agriculture is difficult to achieve but where limited sources of plant material can be converted into animal protein and therefore made useful through grazing.

Meat-eaters have higher rates of heart and kidney disease, cancer, obesity and osteoporosis than vegetarians (Schwartz, 1998). It is difficult to separate the effect of dietary intake from environmental factors and lifestyle issues. Increases in the above conditions have undoubtedly accompanied an increase in the availability of meat and dairy products in western cultures. Other potentially harmful foodstuffs have, however, also become more abundant. Many of the ingredients used in 'modern' foods pose a threat to our health and lifestyles have become generally far more sedentary. Although government agencies have advised against the intake of excessive amounts of fatty acid which are associated with red meats and dairy products (Food Standards Agency, 2004b), it is clear that this is just one issue in the battle against the obesity that is reportedly threatening the western world.

Some individuals and organizations claim that eating meat is inhumane and even immoral. Yet throughout the Bible there are references to the killing and eating of animals. In the Gospels we are told that Jesus himself ate meat and fish (Luke 24.42). It is important to remember that the stories of Noah and Jonah both draw our attention to the high regard in which God holds the whole of the animal kingdom. God regards every species of animal as being good, and worth saving, and charges Noah and his family with the responsibility of ensuring their continued existence (Genesis 7.1–5). The covenant, of which the rainbow is a sign (Genesis 9.12), is not just with the human family but is also with every living creature and the whole earth.

In the story of Jonah, God expresses concern, not only for the people of Nineveh, but also for the many cattle (Jonah 4.11). Jesus, holding the whole of creation in high esteem, all things having been 'created by and for' him (Colossians 1.16), reminds us that 'not even one sparrow is forgotten by God' (Luke 12.6). Although celebrated as 'the Lamb of God' Jesus uses the bread, and not the lamb and bitter herbs served at the passover meal, to represent his body. This makes the act of communion a vegetarian act of remembrance.

In fact the animal kingdom is woven deeply into the fabric of the Gospels. There are 27 references to animals in Matthew's Gospel alone. These include locusts, birds, dogs, pigs, wolves, sheep, foxes, snakes, doves, sparrows, vipers, fish, camels, donkeys, colts, hens, chickens, vultures, goats and a rather infamous cockerel. And in the Old Testament the new creation is rather beautifully described as a place where 'The wolf and the lamb shall feed together, the lion shall eat straw like the ox; but the serpent, its food shall be dust! They shall not hurt or destroy on all my holy mountain' (Isaiah 65.25).

Through his many insights Andrew Linzey explores the place of animals in God's world. The chapter on 'Vegetarianism as a Biblical Ideal' in his book *Animal Theology* begins by stating, 'Of all the ethical challenges arising from animal theology, vegetarianism can arguably claim to have the strongest biblical support' (Linzey, 1994: 125–37). He expands his argument that 'the radical message of the Noah story . . . is that God would rather not have us be at all if we must be violent' and goes on to explain God's words to Noah and his sons (Genesis 9.1–4) as being a concession made to a fallen humanity. In conclusion he argues that through the adoption of a vegetarian diet we may move 'forward . . . not backward into Genesis' (Linzey, 1994: 137).

This assertion certainly becomes compelling when you consider some modern methods of meat production. In Britain 95 per cent of all chickens are destined to live only seven weeks of their seven-year life span (Anglican Society for the Welfare of Animals, 2002). Broilers, the chickens so many Christians go home to say grace over after church on Sunday, have been bred to be one of the world's most rapidly growing organisms. Reared in batches of up to 50,000 birds at a time, they are kept on concrete floors in windowless sheds. Artificial lighting is carefully controlled to avoid over activity in the birds. Movement is restricted through cramped conditions, with each bird having the equivalent of an A4 sheet of paper within which to live and move and have its being. A carefully controlled diet, supplemented with a cocktail of antibiotics, is designed to maximize the productivity of each batch of birds. Once their maximum potential is reached, the broilers are then crammed into crates and transported to the slaughter house, leaving empty sheds to be scraped clean and sterilized ready for the next batch of chicks to be trucked in.

This litany does little to conjure up the imagery of Isaiah! Neither is it representative of all modern meat production systems. However, it is difficult to defend. Surely systems such as this are driven by money rather than ethics.

In his study of *Livestock Ethics* Gordon Gatward (2000) does defend intensive methods of livestock production arguing that 'intensive systems cannot always be equated with cruelty and extensive practices do not always epitomise kindness' (Gatward, 2000: 15). Cataloguing mutually beneficial outcomes such as improved human health and improved animal welfare he points out that the majority of farmers have the greatest respect for their animals. However, he does go on to express concern over the exceptions to the rule, where animals are kept under unacceptable conditions, and acknowledges that some activities, for example, beak clipping (Gatward, 2000) are inhumane and perhaps serve to undermine the reputation of the industry as a whole.

Instinctively many feel the arguments put forward by Linzey are strong. Perhaps the route back to Eden is marked by a meatless diet. Certainly, cruelty to animals is now frowned upon and legislated against. Yet, as an article in the *Economist* once pointed out, 'increasing numbers of people in rich countries have doubts about modern farming methods. But few, so far, are willing to give up the cheap food these methods have brought' (*The Economist*, 1996: 93–5).

It seems clear then that the first step for those of us who have not taken the route of vegetarianism, but who are concerned about cruelty to animals, is to recognize the practices which fall below those ethical standards of stockmanship outlined by Gatward. For many of us, to reinstate our recognition of the interdependence of the human family and the animal kingdom will require us to reassess radically our place in creation, to re-evaluate our relationship with nature. It will require nothing less than a paradigm shift in the way a large proportion of the world's population think and act. Those evocative scenes described in Isaiah must, for now at least, be far beyond our reach.

Organic Farming: Striding Forward Into the Past

In striving for efficiency and maximum productivity modern agriculturalists have tended to turn their attentions toward technology and chemicals. Through her famous book *Silent Spring*, Rachel Carson (1962) alerted the world to the dangers of an overdependence on synthetic pesticides. By charting the demise of songbird populations she provided a graphic illustration of the kind of consequences the world could expect to see if agriculture continued to disregard nature's boundaries. Species come and go in the history of evolution but the excessive use of chemicals over recent decades has endangered species at an alarming rate destroying delicate balances within the natural world. In *Something New Under the Sun*, John McNeill (2000) details a startling account of the development of the agrochemical industry beginning in 1842 with the production of the first superphosphate.

Prior to Englishman John Lawes' experiments with sulphuric acid and phosphate rock the world's agricultural activity had been restricted to what is now known as 'organic' farming. It was reliant on naturally occurring resources that were managed through principles developed over generations. Crop rotation, and the incorporation of organic matter, enabled farmers to keep their soils healthy and productive. By ensuring that even the most unpleasant waste products were recycled, people were able to sustain themselves. Through hard work crops were prevented from being overwhelmed by weeds, and pests were kept at bay by encouraging the presence of their natural predators. Nature provided the means by which people lived but it also set the boundaries within which their lives were sustainable.

Relatively recent advances in the agricultural industry appear to have reduced our reliance on nature. Our ability to increase greatly crop yields, through the application of fertilizers, has resulted in 'crucial chemical alteration of the world's soils with colossal economic, social, political and environmental consequences' (McNeill, 2000). The development of a vast spectrum of pesticides is also complicit in this. Indeed, McNeill predicts that without recent advances we would need at least 30 per cent more good cropland to feed the current world population. In other words, two billion out of the six billion people alive on earth today simply might not be alive were it not for the agrochemical industry. Yet even in the face of these technological advances starvation and suffering are commonplace.

Surprisingly, despite having to pay up to 70 per cent more for organic products, the organic sector is the fastest growing sector of the British grocery market (BBC News, 2000). So what is this growth based on?

According to Prince Charles, patron of the Soil Association, 'Organic farming delivers the highest quality, best-tasting food, produced without artificial chemicals or genetic modification, and with respect for animal welfare and the environment, while helping to maintain the landscape and rural communities' (Soil Association, 2004). The Soil Association website states that organic farming is an agricultural system that encompasses management practices which sustain soil health and fertility; the use of natural methods of pest, disease and weed control; high standards of animal welfare; low levels of environmental pollution; enhancement of the landscape, wildlife and wildlife habitat and the prohibition of all genetically engineered food and products. This website then outlines three reasons why organic farming is so important, focusing on human health, environmental health and animal welfare.

Human health

Many of the vast array of agrochemicals used to produce food in intensive farming systems are poisonous to people. Though legislation is in place to limit human exposure to these chemicals, studies have shown that higher residues do occur in a proportion of the food we eat. The long-term effects of these chemicals, especially when taken in combinations, are not yet properly understood.

It is also claimed that organic food contains more vitamins and minerals and that the use of chemicals on crops has resulted in a decrease in antioxidants which are beneficial to human health. Furthermore, nitrates and pesticides from intensive systems finding their way into watercourses means that, unless properly cleaned, the water coming from our taps could also be affected.

Environmental health

According to Azeez (2000), organic farms have been found to contain five times as many wild plants and 57 more plant species on average than conventional farms. Pesticides are designed to work on organic material so, although it is claimed that some are environmentally safe, it is clear that the overall effect is destructive to nature. Although a small minority of creatures can be regarded as being 'pests', by encouraging wildlife on to their farms organic farmers benefit from the presence of natural predators which help to control 'pest' species. Pollination also benefits from this increased diversity. In total 76 per cent of the United Kingdom's land is used for agricultural purposes. As around only 3 per cent of British agricultural land is farmed organically the cumulative effect of intensive farming on British wildlife has to be detrimental.

An overreliance on intensive farming has also resulted in the degradation of soils all around the world. A stark example of this is currently taking place in parts of India. During the so-called 'green revolution' Indian rice growers were seduced into turning away from traditional 'organic' farming practices and instead began to use 'new' crop varieties and cocktails of agrochemicals to maximize yields. Sadly, short-term benefits were soon overshadowed by long-term environmental damage with habitat destruction, the pollution and depletion of watercourses and the erosion of soil, leaving barren land and starving people in their wake. The realization that short-term gain does not always guarantee a brighter future has led to farmers in India turning away from intensive farming to adopt again the more sustainable mixed farming approach to land management they once relied upon.

Animal welfare

The Soil Association's system of accreditation insists on stringent animal welfare standards. On farms which have been accredited with the Soil Association mark of approval, animals have access to fields and are allowed to express their natural behaviour patterns. They always have comfortable bedding, usually straw, and plenty of space when they are housed. Also organic standards minimize the negative effects of transporting animals (Soil Association website).

Another consideration is that animals reared organically are not subjected to regular doses of antibiotics. Antibiotics are used routinely on some farms, and in many cases are fed daily to animals in intensive systems to keep them healthy, thereby ensuring maximum growth rates. Unfortunately, the result of this has been to raise resistance in bacteria living within these animals making treatment more difficult. As many of the antibiotics used in the treatment of human illness are similar to those used to treat animals this means that the effectiveness of human medicines to treat bacteria can also be reduced.

GM: The Great Debate

> Animals, plants and microbes are the consummate engineers. They have found what works and what lasts. After 3.8 billion years of evolution, failures are fossils, and what surrounds us is the secret of survival. (Benyus, 2002)

Humanity has learned to work with this natural capital to unlock its potential. Since the dawn of agriculture farmers have been manipulating the gene bank through selective breeding to produce new breeds of plants and animals designed to meet human needs. By influencing evolution, plants have been transformed and animals made almost unrecognizable. It could be argued that nature has become less natural and that people have stepped into God's shoes! However, during the last few decades our ability to tinker with nature has breached boundaries that never before have been crossed.

Genetic engineering has made it possible for genetic information to be taken from totally different species and combined. By developing the means of cutting information from one organism and pasting it into the genes of another, scientists have unlocked the potential to manipulate radically the web of life.

This process of genetic modification (GM) has opened the door to the creation of a new kind of agriculture which its proponents say will provide benefits such as improved yields with reduced use of pesticides; the ability to grow crops in previously inhospitable environments leading to an improved ability to feed an increasing world population at a reduced environmental cost; improved sensory attributes of food (for example, flavour and texture); improved nutritional attributes (for example, combating anti-nutritive and allergenic factors and increased Vitamin A content in rice helping to prevent blindness in Southeast Asia); improved processing characteristics leading to reduced waste and lower food costs to the consumer (Institute of Food Science and Technology, 1999).

There has, however, been a growing tide of opinion against the use of genetically modified organisms in agriculture and indeed the European Union has actually legislated against the use of genetically modified crops. Campaigners against genetically modified crops have predicted the following consequences.

Damage to plants, insects, birds and soil organisms

There are worries that a move from selective pesticides to more general types will lead to adverse effects on wildlife. Also at issue are the effects that the frequent use of these pesticides will have on soilborne organisms which are prolific in healthy soils. The loss of these organisms could have wider consequences on ecosystems as they are known to aid nutrient uptake in some plants.

Herbicide-tolerant genes escaping into weeds and other crops

This would cause difficulties for farmers. It is claimed that, through cross-pollination or seed dispersal, new genes could escape and mix with non-genetically modified crops or their weedy relatives. If herbicide-resistant genes pass from genetically modified crops to other plant life it could result in weeds which are difficult to control. This could result in seeds from a previous year's crop emerging in a new and different crop.

Gene stacking

Where different genetically modified crops are grown together in close proximity there is the potential for a large number of pesticide-resistant genes to be accumulated in a small area. It is argued that these could stack up to make super-resistant weeds if they escaped into wild species.

Escapes of insect resistant genes

There are concerns that insect-resistant genes incorporated into the genetic make-up of genetically modified crops could escape into wild plant species giving them a similar resistance against insects. These wild plants would then have an advantage in their natural environment enabling them to out-compete other wild plants allowing them to become artificially dominant.

Possible loss of beneficial insects

It has been claimed that the toxins produced by insect-resistant genetically modified crops could pass through the food chain killing other 'beneficial' insects. Also, if crops are bred which are more effective at killing target insects this could have a deleterious effect on those insects' natural predators.

Pollution of non-genetically modified crops

Campaigners argue that once genetically modified crops become commonplace, the transfer of genetic material from them to non-genetically modified crops through pollination will mean that there will no longer be such a thing as genetically modified free foods. Indeed, the Soil Association argues that 'British organic food must stay completely genetically modified free, even if this makes the commercial growing of genetically modified crops impossible' (Soil Association website).

Pesticide-resistant weeds

Farmers have traditionally used a number of selective weed killers to control weed growth. With the introduction of herbicide tolerant crops farmers will come to rely upon a single non-selective weed killer. In the same way that bacteria have become resistant to antibiotics through over exposure, it is argued that 'weeds' will eventually become resistant to these herbicides making them more difficult to control within and outside agricultural systems.

Loss of biodiversity

It is claimed that the use of broad-spectrum weed killers on herbicide tolerant crops will cause the death of a wider range of 'weed' plants and therefore result in a reduction in biodiversity. Also, where single species of successful genetically modified crops take the place of the various crops which were once grown biodiversity will also be reduced leaving large swathes of monoculture crops.

Concerns have also been raised by critics of genetically modified crops over the means through which multinational companies are 'promoting' their genetically modified products, particularly in the world's poorer countries. Although there are obvious potential benefits which genetically modified crops can provide in environments which are hostile and where conventional crops are difficult to grow, to cite genetically modified crops as the antidote to world famine is misleading. Of particular concern are technologies such as terminator crops which are designed to produce sterile seeds. This eliminates the opportunity for farmers to conserve grain to plant in the next season which results in those farmers being tied into an agricultural system which forces them to buy their seeds from a supplier who also happens to provide the chemicals needed to maintain that system!

McNeill (2000) points out that, whereas in 1900 agriculture was labour intensive employing something like 70–90 per cent of the world's population, intensive farming methods have in some places resulted in less than 10 per cent of that country's population working on the land. Furthermore, the example of the Green Revolution shows that intensive farming methods 'promoted income inequality among farmers' (McNeill, 2000). In India, this situation has led to the movement of land-living people into cities, like Kolkata (Calcutta) which now suffers from serious social stresses.

In her book *Stolen Harvest* (2000) Vandana Shiva documents the plight of the people of Bengal as they farmed under colonial rule. In 1943, while the British forcefully took two-thirds (80,000 tons) of food grain grown in Bengal to feed their war effort, 3.5 million of the people of Bengal starved to death. Shiva goes on to decry the 'hijacking of the global food supply' by multinational companies as follows.

It is being experienced in every culture as small farms and small farmers are pushed to extinction, as monocultures replace biodiverse crops, as farming is transformed from the production of nourishing and diverse foods into the creation of markets for genetically engineered seeds, herbicides and pesticides. (Shiva, 2000: 7)

The Soil Association recently published a report highlighting the dangers of relying on genetically modified crops. In it they chart the economic impact genetically modified crops have had in North America. The report argues as follows.

Within a few years of the introduction of genetically modified crops, almost the entire \$300 million annual United States maize exports to the European Union and the \$300 million annual Canadian rape exports to the European Union had disappeared, and the United States share of the world soya market had decreased. (Soil Association, 2002)

They also point out that profitability from genetically modified crops is less than that of traditional crops due to increased seed prices and decreased retail prices for genetically modified products. Claims that farmers growing genetically modified crops are having to use more, not less, pesticide to control weeds in their crops, and that rogue genetically modified oilseed rape plants have become a problem in Canada, are also included in this document (Soil Association, 2002).

In the United Kingdom there has been criticism as to the impartiality of the information used to inform the public and ministers during the debate on genetically modified products. The claims that the research, which has heavily influenced the debate, originated from sources with a vested interest in the adoption of genetically modified organisms in British agriculture has raised a fundamental moral question. How do scientists who are funded by a particular company react when they see their conclusions begin to move in a direction which doesn't serve the interests of that company? The need for independent scientific research is paramount to ensure the confidence of the general public.

The Food Standards Agency (FSA) is a body that was set up to assess independently health and safety issues surrounding the food we eat. Part of their remit is to ensure that food is thoroughly assessed for safety and that consumers are given as much information and choice as possible.

The Food Standards Agency co-ordinated a national debate on the use of genetically modified foods in Britain. In their information leaflet the Food Standards Agency claimed to provide the basic knowledge needed to enter into the debate on genetically modified products. They provided arguments for and against the use of genetically modified foods and gave statistics as to the impact genetically modified food has already had on world agriculture. According to their information, in 2002 a staggering 58.7 million hectares of the worlds agricultural land (18 per cent of all crop land) was already farmed using genetically modified crops. In 2002 countries growing genetically modified crops included Argentina, Australia, Bulgaria, Canada, China, Columbia, Germany, Honduras, India, Indonesia, Mexico, Romania, South Africa, Spain, Uruguay and the United States of America. People eating processed foods in any of these countries were likely to be eating genetically modified foods (Food Standards Agency, 2004c).

Genetically modified products are not, however, restricted to those countries in which they are grown. Although no fresh genetically modified foods have as yet been cleared for sale here in the United Kingdom, genetically modified soya, genetically modified tomatoes (in purée form only) and genetically modified maize are all available. In fact, due to the large proportion of the world's maize and soya produced on farms growing genetically modified crops, many of our processed foods already contain genetically modified (or genetically modified derived) ingredients. Although European Union labelling laws stipulate that genetically modified products used as an ingredient should be identified on packaging, it is possible that in some foods, where the quantity of a genetically modified additive represents less than 1 per cent of the total ingredients, genetically modified ingredients can be eaten without the knowledge of the consumer. Here lies an obvious cause for concern if the Food Standards Agency is to achieve its remit of ensuring consumer choice.

On top of all these issues, many claim that feeding the world is not a valid argument for employing genetically modified products in agriculture as enough food is already produced to achieve this aim. The real problem lies in distribution (Ford, 2000) and the real challenge lies in securing just and fair means of international trade.

The Distribution Dilemma

Concern for the environment is one of the main arguments for choosing to eat organic produce. On the face of it buying organic might seem to be the 'right' thing to do. Yet only 20 per cent of the organic food consumed in Britain is supplied by British farmers. The rest is imported from abroad. So where does this leave the consumer?

The term 'food miles' is used to describe the distance our food travels to reach us. It embraces all the associated impacts that the transportation of a food product has on our lives. Currently, globalization of the food industry has resulted in a situation whereby food distributors fly apples 4,700 miles from the United States of America, onions over 12,000 miles from Australia and New Zealand, carrots from South Africa (5,100 miles) and beans from Kenya (3,600 miles) into the United Kingdom while British farmers are being forced to give up their fertile land. The environmental costs of these epic voyages make the wisdom and the sustainability of present trends in food distribution questionable.

For many, far from shrinking the world, global food markets appear to have distanced people from their food source. International trade, with tariffs and barriers consistently favouring the rich nations and discriminating against the poor, has resulted in the accumulation of wealth and resources by a small minority while the majority remain malnourished and destitute. According to Atkinson (2002: 20) in today's world 50 of the world's top 100 economies are multinational companies and not countries. In the current political climate is this situation likely to change? Does the political will exist to secure justice for the poor?

The consequences of decisions being made today reach far into the future and place a heavy burden on the shoulders of world leaders to make the right decisions for the right reasons. A burden also lies on the shoulders of scientists and research bodies to relay their findings willingly and transparently to companies and governments. Debates such as those surrounding genetically modified organisms and global warming are simply too important to be distorted through the application of 'spin'. Non-governmental-organizations (NGOs) and independent bodies such as the Food Standards Agency, have a vital role to play in ensuring that the necessary information is relayed accurately, and without prejudice, to ensure maximum and informed choice for the consumer. It is also up to consumers to make the most of the available information and to employ discernment when deciding which goods to buy.

Using Your LOAF

To this end Christian Ecology Link have devised an easy to remember acronym to help guide people through the complexities of becoming a discerning consumer. The breaking and eating of bread is of great significance to Christians and now, by focusing on the loaf itself, Christians can combine their convictions and their power as consumers to help bring about a more just and sustainable world. 'Using your loaf' simply means taking the time to study the labels and packaging of goods prior to purchasing them to ensure that the following criteria are met.

Locally grown

When it comes to food, the old slogan 'Buy British' has never been more relevant than today. In fact it could easily be replaced with 'Buy Local'. In the light of the environmental and social costs of intensive farming globally, and in the shadow of recent agricultural crisis here in the United Kingdom, supporting local farmers will prove essential to the sustainability of this timeless profession. Locally grown produce means less 'food miles' and less travelling for livestock which in turn mean reduction in pollution and improvements in animal welfare. Buying locally grown produce also secures the future of the local farmers who grow it.

Of course, the majority of farmers have a great natural affinity for the land they farm and the animals that live on it. After all, that is why most farmers take to the land in the first place. Given the opportunity, provided to them through consumer support, farmers gladly work to ensure a rich and diverse landscape. As is true of any profession, only when bound by the pressures of the global economy are farmers forced to lower their standards of stewardship and husbandry in order to survive.

Organically grown

There is no doubt that an overdependence on chemicals in agriculture has had adverse effects on the environment. Modern intensive farming methods have also resulted in a reduction in the number of people employed on the land. Any move away from this situation is to be welcomed. Furthermore, the need for genetically modified crops in a country with an abundance of top-grade agricultural land is doubtful. Chemical-dependent conventional agriculture at least avoids the need to set loose unnecessarily a technology that is not yet fully understood. Organic farming provides an opportunity to address all the above issues while also being beneficial to wildlife.

Recent improvements in labelling will ensure that consumers have the choice of purchasing locally grown organic produce. This should help provide the United Kingdom's organic farming movement with the boost it needs.

Animal friendly

Animal welfare must remain at the centre of the livestock industry. The 'animal's essence' (Gatward, 2000: 279) must be respected. Consumers can help ensure this by eating only meat raised in agricultural systems where livestock production is characterized by stockmanship and stewardship. By boycotting meat produced through methods that are not 'animal friendly' the more insidious side of meat production will eventually be left to wither on the vine. The market, informed and educated, can exercise its own discipline!

Fairly traded

It is not only British farmers who suffer under current market conditions. All over the world 'small' farmers are being pushed out of business through the inequities of international trade. Although the World Trade Organization (WTO) and its members cite free trade as being beneficial in the fight to eradicate poverty, non-governmental-organizations such as Christian Aid are critical of so-called free trade believing that poor countries must be able to protect and support their own vulnerable producers and infant industries. Developed countries all employ a range of policies, subsidies and tariffs to aid their own economic development, while current trade rules deny poor countries this same right.

Consumers can support the fair trade campaign by purchasing goods that carry the Fair Trade emblem. In doing so purchasers can ensure that producers are paid a fair wage for their efforts, wherever they may live in the world. As a result 'small' farmers can remove themselves from the grips of multinationals, who often otherwise bind them into unsustainable contracts. This will give the world's 'small' landowners the opportunity to lift themselves and their local communities out of poverty.

Although it may mean paying a little more for our food, if through reading the label, a product cannot be identified as being Locally produced, Organically grown, Animal friendly or Fairly traded, and preferably a mixture of the four, then the secret to eating well is simply to leave it on the shelf. That way we can support those working to produce our food. That way we can enable our farmers to continue in their role as stewards of God's earth. That way the key to a healthier future within the kingdom of God is left in the door unturned and unlocked!

References

Aiello, L. C. and Wheeler, P. (1995), 'Current Anthropology: The Expensive-Tissue Hypothesis', *Current Anthropology*, 36, 2 April 1995.

Anglican Society for the Welfare of Animals (2002), *Introducing Welfare Sunday*, Hook, ASWA.

Atkinson, S. (2002), *The Money Go Round, Globalisation and the Destruction of Farming*, Universities and Colleges Christian Fellowship Professional Groups.

Azeez, G. (2000), *The Biodiversity Benefits of Organic Farming*, Bristol, Soil Association.

BBC News (2000), 'Where there's muck there's . . .', [online], available from: http://news.bbc.co.uk/1/hi/uk/874456.stm [accessed 11 Jun 2004].

Benyus, J. M. (2002), Conservation with Janine Benyus, [online], Forum for the Future, available from: http://www.forumforthefuture.org.uk/news/ConversationwithJanine_page658.aspx [accessed 1 July 2004].

Carson, R. L. (1962), *Silent Spring*, New York, Mariner Books.

Food Standards Agency (2004a), 'Fifty Years of Food', [online], available from: http://www.foodstandards.gov.uk/healthiereating/66549/ [accessed 11 Jun 2004].

Food Standards Agency (2004b), 'Heart Disease', [online], available from: http://www.foodstandards.gov.uk/healthiereating/foodrelatedconditions/heartdisease/ [accessed 11 June 2004].

Food Standards Agency (2004c), 'GM: The Global Picture', [online], available from: http://www.foodstandards.gov.uk/gmdebate/aboutgm/108374?view= GM per cent20Microsite [accessed 11 June 2004].

Ford, B. J. (2000), *The Future of Food*, London, Thames and Hudson Ltd.

Garcés, L. (2002), *The Detrimental Impacts of Industrial Animal Agriculture: A Case for Humane and Sustainable Agriculture*, Compassion in World Farming Trust.

Gatward, G. (2000), *Livestock Ethics*, Canterbury, Chalcombe Publications

Institute of Food Science and Technology (1996), website: http://www.ifst.org [accessed 11 June 2004].

Institute of Food Science and Technology (1999), 'Genetic Modification and food', [online], available from: http://www.ifst.org/hottop10.htm [accessed 11 June 2004].

Linzey, A. (1994), *Animal Theology*, SCM Press.

McNeill, J. (2000), *Something New Under the Sun*, Harmondsworth, Penguin Books.

Schwartz, R. H. (1998), 'Are Jews Obligated to Be Vegetarians?' *The Jewish Vegetarian*, 124, March.

Shiva, V. (2000), *Stolen Harvest: The Highjacking of the Global Food Supply*, London, Zed Books.

Soil Association (2002), 'Seeds of Doubt Executive Summary', [online], available from: http: //www.soilassociation.org/web/sa/saweb.nsf/librarytitles/1924e. html [accessed 11 June 2004].

Soil Association (2004), http://www.soilassociation.org/web/sa/saweb.nsf/7bf3 d2dffe2556 d580256a680039de19/beff3211b63ab8.

The Economist (1996), 'Editorial', 20 April, pp. 93–5.

10. Ethnicity and Diversity

JOHN S. DAVIES

Summary

Large-scale population movements during the post-war period have increased Britain's profile as a multicultural society. Demographic changes have had a particular effect on Wales and its heartlands where inward and outward migration has led to economic, social, cultural and linguistic changes. Such changes are variously perceived as beneficial, harmful, inevitable or controllable. The Christian narrative is broadly affirming of diversity, but diversity, if its complexities are not managed, can lead to serious relational tensions and injustices. The Christian Church has a critical role to play in bridging the gap between affirming the values of difference in a multicultural and global world and recognizing where diversity is perceived as a threat. As Britain seeks to respond to the challenge to rethink the national story and for nations to reimagine themselves, the smaller nation of Wales is a fascinating context where this is being worked out. A new government, a new city and an expanding capital, alongside a commitment to economic and social regeneration, a revitalized bilingualism, a sense of national identity and a pledge to develop Wales' contribution as a region within Europe, all point to a new confidence at the beginning of the twenty-first century. The story of the survival of Welsh culture and identity is an offering of hope to other emerging communities, and as the nation plans for the future its very diversity has to be a source of its strength.

Introduction

It is sensible to speak of what we know and from a context that is familiar. I, therefore, make no apology for addressing the issues raised by the title of this chapter from the perspective of Wales, past and present, on the understanding that there are common experiences and factors within the particular situation of every region of Britain.

Christian Principles Concerning Diversity

One of the key themes and challenges of the New Testament narrative regarding the development of Christianity is its extension into diverse cultural situations. This led to its own tensions, not least those between Paul and the Christian community in Jerusalem, but also growth in the breadth, depth and reach of ideas, understanding and experience. Many significant texts about Christian community and, by implication, the nature of the Church, if not the whole of society, reflect early theological questions presented by the challenge of diversity.

The key scriptural passages, particularly in the Pauline literature, offer a range of metaphors and images. They all have a common concern to bridge the gap between what can be held together on the one hand and what can be affirmed as different on the other hand.

The image of the body (Romans 1.4; 1 Corinthians 12.12) must have been evoked by real disputes. It is used to demonstrate that in Christ every member has a different, but valuable, part to play in the whole. This is a particularly compelling and inspiring part of the New Testament vision, but it may not convince or compel so easily in the post-enlightenment atomization of modern western societies and individual attitudes. We are not, self-evidently, a 'one body' society or Church, except in some abstract, aspirational or mystical sense. The Christian image of the body is practical as well as visionary. It enables us to affirm and develop different roles and functions as all being of value and contributive to the whole. Chief executives and human resources directors, headteachers, bishops and prime ministers, all know the importance of this and of the difficulties of facilitating and inspiring its reality. Indeed such an image is of profound practical relevance wherever there is a conscious attempt to reconstruct the effectiveness and values of any organization or group from the family to the United Nations.

Other parts of the New Testament do not start with a vision of the single body and its different parts, but with a more realistic statement of diversity in first-century society. The lists given include most notably: slaves and free people, Jews and gentiles, male and female.

In the Acts of the Apostles 2, there is also a reminder of the real tensions around diversity of culture and language; Pentecost is not to be understood as an internal church transition point alone. It points to the reality of cultural diversity and the possibility of communication, if not communion, across ethnicity, language and geographical context. Our mass media, global transport and communications world create a virtual, if not a real, sense of being 'gathered in one place' and expose us to a wider variety of ethnic and cultural backgrounds than was possible even in this vivid and compelling picture of the early Church. So how has this paradigm been worked out in relation to the cultural and economic barriers that block such a vision?

In the Acts of the Apostles, individuals may not have understood the contextual and cultural backgrounds carried by different languages. Substituting contemporary equivalents in any part of the globe make the point more forcibly. For no cultural, social, ethnic, economic or linguistic background and identity is envisaged as a block to participation or stakeholding in the new order created by Christianity, either within the Church or within its vision of a redeemed society. This new order is not just intended for believers, let alone congregations, but for the whole of society.

A further key principle for Christians is the status of the stranger or the 'alien'. In Exodus 22.21 to serve God is to serve the world, therefore Israel is not to wrong or to oppress the resident alien, 'for you were aliens in the land of Egypt'. Strangers are not to be thrust aside but to be made welcome, and their rights respected (Ruth 2.10; Psalms 94.6, 146.9; Deuteronomy 10.18–19). And in Matthew 25.35–40 Jesus made care for the stranger an imperative of the Christian life, for 'just as you did it to one of the least of these who are members of my family, you did it to me'.

We might, therefore, ask what Christian principle lies behind the view or policy that only certain kinds of immigrants are, or should be, welcome. How does the theology of the incarnation, of a God who chose to come among humanity in poverty, weakness and vulnerability, speak to a society where we demand that others prove their value to society before we will extend a welcome to them? Does the gospel imperative to welcome the stranger distinguish between good and bad aliens? Is it not sometimes the case that God draws out what is best in people through vulnerability and fragility?

These are critical issues for the development of a Christian view of migration. It is true for Wales as, indeed, it is at this time true for Britain and the whole of Europe, so much so that it was a major subject for discussion at the Conference of European Churches in Trondheim, Norway in 2003.

While the Christian narrative is broadly affirming of diversity and emphasizes the importance of welcome, it is too simple, in any situation, to imply that any opposition to diversity and change is unchristian. There may be forms of diversity that are unjust or threaten violence. In the highly charged issue of immigration to Wales, for example, the kind of diversity which results in rising house prices for local people, let alone community tensions, is not a diversity to be welcomed, at least, not at first sight. This is where the issues of diversity become more complex. There are examples throughout the world of situations where rich incomers have brought economic disadvantage to 'indigenous' communities. There is also evidence that, occasionally, rich incomers have benefited communities economically and socially. 'Indigenous' communities in Wales report different and sometimes ambivalent experience and perceptions of incomers. Anecdotal evidence on this subject abounds but it is difficult to evaluate.

Managing diversity in Wales is complex. It is one thing for Christians and others to affirm the values of diversity in a multicultural and global world; it is quite another to face the realities, where diversity is perceived to bring its own economic and social threats.

The Impact of Immigration on Welsh Life

Emma James's research on the perceived effects of in-migration in Welsh rural communities (James, 2003) focuses on inward migratory patterns, quoting significant parts of the literature. She describes inward migration as a continual onslaught of foreigners that has significantly contributed not only to demographic, economic and social changes within Wales, but also to cultural and linguistic changes. Many areas of rural Wales have witnessed dramatic processes of restructuring in their local economies in the post-war period. Changes include a decline in agriculture and other primary industries, the increased dominance of service sector employment, and the reversal of depopulation trends that have previously characterized Welsh rural life prior to the 1970s. James insists that the impact of such changes has led to the existence of rural deprivation, poverty, employment problems and competition for housing which, in turn, have contributed to the continued out-migration of the younger generation from many of these areas in search of enhanced education and employment opportunities. This migration has significantly taken place within the Welsh heartlands, and therefore within core areas of the Welsh culture and language (Balsom, 1985), to the extent that rural Wales faces a possible crisis as a direct result of large-scale population movements of culturally dissimilar people (Day, 1989).

Independently of the impact of incomers, the structural basis of Welsh rural society has been changing because of other causes. Not least among these are the demographic, family and society patterns found throughout the United Kingdom, including especially the attitude of young people and issues of employment. It is possible that enduring kinship patterns would have been affected by these issues as well as by the impact of incomers *per se*. It would seem that the concerns expressed by Emma James, and the authors she quotes, make assumptions about the positive values of enduring kinship patterns and stability. But these assumptions also underestimate the need for, and ability of, people to become more flexible and adaptable to social and economic changes of other kinds. There is, therefore, no guarantee that enduring kinship patterns will be enough to protect small rural communities in Wales, as elsewhere, against larger scale economic and social change. In some cases it can be argued that enduring kinship patterns militate against this. Anecdotal evidence from other European countries, where there has been significant inward migration to rural areas, notably France, Spain and Portugal, suggests that the results are often more positive and that the benefits they have brought to the regeneration of those rural areas have been considerable. However, the cultural motives of incomers to Wales are also a factor. Many come with a desire to benefit from rurality, but at the same time from other cultural factors. Some arrive with a romanticized view of Welsh-speaking or Welsh-cultural rural living and cannot adjust to its realities. Others come with no knowledge at all of rural life anywhere and are clearly disappointed by its fixed reference points. In Emma James's studies many incomers were surprised at the lack of social class or distinction within villages such as might have been more prevalent in some English rural areas. They therefore perceived local people to be mixing outside the boundaries of normal social class ('We're not bothered about "who you are" around here. Money's not important . . .') and yet perhaps not being as willing to mix with them (James, 2003: 64).

At this deeper level of analysis it would seem that serious theological and pastoral issues arise. When this happens, has the local church been able to articulate them in ways that facilitate reconciliation and atonement? It is a demanding, but rewarding, role for traditional Christian ministry to discern, for example, scapegoating and its causes, which has a tendency to caricature ('They always speak Welsh when I come into the shop/pub . . .') and lead to an accumulation of suspicion. While scapegoating is the bread and butter of soap operas, the challenge is to look beyond the obvious, discover what is actually unsettling people and then try to draw out the right behavioural adjustments that will make a difference. While most people manage to live with a level of unresolved conflict and tolerance to diversity, there is a courageous ministry of reconciliation that constantly faces the churches.

It seems that one of the major dimensions of diversity in Wales is not of ethnicity as such but of locals and incomers. In fact, in most parts of Wales, the percentage of people born outside the United Kingdom and European Union is very small, as is the number of Welsh-born people from other ethnic backgrounds. Locals seem to invest everything in social stability as the way of ensuring the longevity of the community. Enduring kinship and other relationships are seen as crucial to that. Therefore, in Wales, incomers can present a real threat. It seems that the evidence points to a real and continuing problem. It may not always lead to overt conflict and violence, but certainly to relational tensions of a serious kind. These produce their own negative perceptions, which in turn perpetuate and contribute to future boundaries.

The Church, with its larger vision of community spirit and one that is committed to inclusion of strangers and outcasts, is bound to act counter-culturally within these situations. It is interesting to note how different denominations have responded differently. Theoretically those churches, like the Church in Wales, with a sense of global as well as of local presence, might be well placed to bridge the diversity, heal the conflict, challenge the models, and broker the gap between stability and flexibility as a definition of community spirit.

According to other research quoted by James (2003) people only

become aware of their culture when they stand at its boundaries. In
this sense incomers may serve to highlight a useful perspective. James
argues that where communities perceive themselves to be peripheral or
marginal in economic and social terms, the locality can view itself as
misunderstood, powerless, misrepresented, exploited, ignored or
patronized in ways that contribute to negative cultural capital. Again,
the churches have a useful ministry based on their knowledge of the
factors that contribute to this sense of marginality. They are, or should
be, well placed to understand boundaries and barrier issues as major
aspects of conflict concerning diversity.

It is legitimate for locals and incomers alike to expect to find the
local church and church life a place and source of brokering and healing across conflictual codes of behaviour. Church-based activities
indeed are often the most useful places for reconstructing community
spirit in ways that help both sides of a conflict to understand and
respect the needs and contribution of the other and to learn how to
behave flexibly and creatively across the boundaries. It may be appropriate for churches to invest in appropriate training to increase their
understanding of conflictual diversity issues, particularly in rural
areas, and to provide priests and lay people with new skills and
strategies for managing the implications of this diversity.

Identity and Confidence in the New Wales

A new government, an expanding capital city, commitment to economic and social regeneration, a revitalized bilingualism, a pledge to
develop and support a sense of national identity and develop Wales's
contribution as a region within Europe, all point to a new confidence
at the beginning of the twenty-first century.

Recent reports on the future of multicultural Britain asked us to
rethink the national story and for nations to reimagine themselves.
This implies that certain parts of the inherited cultural fabric should be
jettisoned or revised.

The issue is highlighted by the dilemma facing the Board of the
Welsh Millennium Centre: should this new arts facility in Wales be
branded as primarily a Welsh institution or an international one?
Clearly there are arguments and pressures on both sides, but the issue
is how to combine them. The Millennium Stadium, for its part, has
achieved much for sport in combining all that is best about Wales's

self-image in football and rugby along with its wider role and significance within the United Kingdom as a branded centre of excellence. When, however, it comes to the non-sporting components of culture in Wales, as focused in the new Welsh Millennium Centre, what should be the approach? Who has the authority to refashion the cultural fabric of Wales and who are the influential bodies in the rebranding process?

Rebranding is a mainstream part of the Welsh Tourist Board's function, but if its marketing material is to balance the traditional heritage images of Wales with more forward-looking dimensions of urban development, entrepreneurial opportunity and internationalism, it will have to reflect substantive change. Such change will depend upon the role of other national organizations, including the Welsh Assembly Government (WAG), the Welsh Development Agency (WDA) and Early Learning Wales (ELWa) in genuinely increasing the capacity of Wales to become an effective performer on a United Kingdom and European, if not world class, stage.

Diversity, National Identity and the Future

Again, we are faced with different narratives of perception and reality. There are those, including the historian Gwyn A. Williams, who argue strongly that the heritage and history image is full of mythologies:

> Wales is impossible. A country called Wales exists only because the Welsh invented it. The Welsh exist only because they invented themselves. . . . They survived by making and re-making themselves and their Wales over and over again. (Williams, 1991: 13–15)

This is sometimes called the 'St Fagan's myth'. In other words, the history and heritage image is a construct, which sells a certain perception of Wales that can be both positive and negative depending on the situation. The point is, however, that such a construct nourishes certain brand images within Wales (and its internal consumers) that may not be the best platform for progress in the future. Hence the dilemma of the Wales Millennium Centre. There are important choices being made in these discussions and it is not obvious that the Church in Wales is contributing significantly to the debate. The Church in Wales has its own spiritual and cultural influence and investment in the history of Wales, as well as in its future, and for organizational and gospel reasons it faces similar dilemmas: how should it use the rich treasury of spiritual history, with all its ups and downs, to further the gospel's contribution to new thinking about the future needs of the communities of Wales? One thing is certain: the Church in Wales cares passionately about individuals in those communities. Yet, unless there is real content to the language of regeneration and other strategies, those communities are at risk of further degrading.

Economic development must be earthed in the indigenous skills and the experience of people in the communities of Wales. But it has to find a new way forward through economic diversification and multi-skilling which will require a flexibility of spiritual and cultural attitudes. This will not be helped by always looking backwards or appealing to a sense of identity and purpose that may be atavistic, 'not hurrying on to a receding future, nor hankering after an imagined past' (see 'The Bright Field' in Thomas, 1993). The Church in Wales, along with every denomination, has its own contribution to make to the new thinking about diversity and development in Wales, and the publication of *Ar Daith/On a Journey* (Church in Wales, 2002) has been a formative consultative document in inviting local churches to grapple with key changes in Welsh society as they recognize God who is active in all human endeavour.

The appointment of a Welsh Assembly Government liaison officer by Cytun/Churches Together in Wales has also made a significant contribution to establishing a shared narrative (see Edwards, 2003).

Here is a sound basis for the churches to move forward in flexible and inclusive ways, welcoming and celebrating the challenges of new demands, broader horizons and even future insecurities, instead of holding on tight to what little sense of fixed identity our image of the past gives us.

Other Kinds of Exclusion

Sensitivity is crucial, but the national agencies of Wales know they will be doing greater harm if they are not honest about the problems and not seeking to empower people to face the future with more hope and passion. An aspect of the profile of diversity in Wales is the mismatch between, on the one hand, policy-makers, funders, regenerators, educators and developers, all of whom are totally committed to making life better for the communities of Wales and, on the other hand, those in local communities who feel isolated or excluded from what is available. Health funding, policing, environmental projects, wind farms and the aftermath of the Foot and Mouth Disease crisis with its long-term effects on traditional farming are just some of the issues which attract feelings of powerlessness. Access is about education, information, spirituality and perception. The Church is, perhaps, more aware than many other agencies of the variety and value of local activity, volunteering, entrepreneurship, ideas and activism. It is also informed and cares about the extent of real economic and community problems and the effect of generational poverty and unemployment, isolation and exclusion which has caused so much spiritual depression, physical illness, melancholia and helplessness.

Multiculturalism

In the new Wales, issues of ethnic minorities are a focus of public policy. However, this public position sits uncomfortably with growing evidence of marginalization, widening inequality and widespread racism. Unemployment among some African groups in Cardiff runs at 90 per cent. Increased awareness reveals a legacy of neglect. A growing concern on the part of policy-makers for the way we treat minorities has been whether the high value we place on minority groups has embedded itself into behavioural realities. The paradox seems to be that the more we talk about a multicultural society as a value, the harder it is to achieve in practice. The problem with multiculturalism as a value is that it positions minorities in such a way that makes it difficult for them to comply with the simplistic categories into which they are placed.

Welsh Assembly Government policies are rightly, but controversially, raising expectations about identity and the capacity and motivation for addressing issues of diversity. This may drive positive change in terms of changing attitudes but, of course, it will always also be undermined in localities, not least by the tabloid press and the implicit racism that seems endemic in much of contemporary society, where there is perceived economic and social threat.

However, the main challenge for policy-makers is that of reconstructing Welsh identity, and not just that of dealing with minority

ethnic groups. What is at issue is the positioning of a whole post-
devolution nation, first, in relationship to its former 'colonial' masters,
and second, in relationship to the wider world. In asserting the values
of traditional self-image in Wales, to which the Church has contributed considerably, the question remains to what extent are we
creating a situation of value conflict and complexity? The classic
dilemma arises of how to assert local identity without turning this into
an exclusive attitude toward the rest of the world or, put another way,
how to prosper in a post-modernist, multicultural, global world and
still retain the genuine and positive values of indigenous local culture.
It seems that the only way out of this dilemma is to face facts and
manage the complexity of it.

Welsh Language

This is why Wales has formally adopted a bilingual policy. Much is at
stake, not only for the handling of diversity, but for constructing an
inclusive framework for the future.

The 'two language' culture of Wales is an integral part of the
nation's culturally diverse heritage and also a spur to the outward-
looking agenda of those who are striving with an inclusive vision
for the future of the nation. The Welsh-speaking Welsh and the
non Welsh-speaking Welsh have co-existed for centuries and the
boundaries between them are becoming increasingly permeable. The
survival of the Welsh language has been remarkable and has happened
despite a culture of discouragement and repression that formally
began with the Act of Union in 1536.

Christianity has played a critical role in the survival of the Welsh
language. The Methodist reformations and the development of non-
conformist culture in Wales provided a safe space in which the
language could be treasured and continue to evolve. The translation of
the Bible into Welsh in 1588 by Bishop William Morgan and other
notable Welsh scholars ensured that the people of Wales were able to
worship in their mother tongue. The great traditions of hymnwriting
and poetry also played their part in keeping the language alive.

By the twentieth century there was still a vigorous Welsh language
culture. This has been helped by the development of Welsh medium
education and Welsh television and radio broadcasts. 'The Welsh as a
people have lived by making and re-making themselves in generation

after generation, usually against the odds' (Williams, 1991: 304), and in the twentieth century, writes Jane Aaron (2003), they were doing so in two languages.

R. S. Thomas saw the Welsh language as a key to understanding Wales's contribution to the emerging global culture of the twenty-first century. In his poem 'Afallon', Thomas (1995: 25) wrote of the currency of a small nation's language in a world 'oscillating between dollar and yen'. Thomas was able to speak powerfully about the opportunities and the dilemmas of the two language cultures of Wales. He was a Welshman who learned Welsh and therefore wrote his poetry in English, and there is a prophetic edge in what he writes about how the history of the Welsh language informs the cultural contribution of the nation.

At the beginning of the twenty-first century the Church in Wales, as a bilingual church, is uniquely placed to continue to be a bridge and a reconciling force between the two languages of our nation. The creative tension between holding the tradition and yet still being welcoming and open to the 'other' is a valuable one and is a gift that the Anglican Church can contribute in the emerging new Wales.

Christianity is uniquely realistic about the range and depth of the issues involved. Its classical texts, as found in the New Testament and in the early period, are the result of the churches wrestling with real issues of the relationships of diverse communities and people in a real world. The Church is often well placed to engage constructively and creatively with diversity.

Church members' behaviours can reflect the failures and successes of local communities' attitudes to diversity, but Christianity retains its public commitment: to be a source of healing and reconciliation, communication and communion across, between and within different diversities, offering not only a safe place and a welcome, but also indeed a vision lived, which makes possible a valuing of strangers, of variety and of difference.

The Future of Liberal Democracies as a Protection of Diversity

Disturbances surrounding the placement of asylum seekers in North Wales's largest town, Wrexham, as well as in northern English cities, hint at the limits of liberalism to solve its own problems of diversity. Multiculturalism, as a model for dealing with diversity, is central to the rhetoric of liberal societies, but liberal societies find it hard to manage the breakdown of such rhetoric in the practical attitudes of racism, exclusion and violence that characterize many parts of our society. Liberal society rhetoric about tolerance as the basis for the handling of pluralism and political order breaks down in the face of internal fundamentalisms. The European Union human rights discourse, based on European liberalism, uses fundamental human rights to protect individuals within liberal societies, but then has to face the negative reaction of different faith communities to equality agendas and legislation (for example, the Employment Act's implications for gender and sexual orientation). Faith communities increasingly make the case that they wish to be excluded from the general 'fundamental human rights' based legislation. An obvious example is the Act of Synod, which allows Church of England parishes to practise discrimination legally against women priests because they are exempt from the 1975 Sexual Discrimination Act (see Furlong, 1998). Another example is a proposed 'opt-out' clause which would give bishops and clergy the right to refuse to ordain or marry transsexual people in certain circumstances.

Thus, when religion wishes to re-enter the liberal project over other aspects of diversity (for example, to defend the rights of asylum seekers in order to preserve genuine diversity), it may be perceived as in an already discredited position because it is partial about human rights and diversity. How can faith groups or any other partisan group in a liberal society argue for the common good when it takes up a defensive position regarding certain partial goods?

Other Factors Influencing Diversity

As with other parts of the United Kingdom, the obvious distinctions, based on ethnicity or culture, language or religion, are sometimes obscured by lateral class divisions.

Ethnicity within the white community of Wales has its own distinctive problems that should not be underestimated. These include geographical divisions caused by poor transport or infrastructure, a division emphasized by the economic corridors that have developed around the M4 access in South Wales (a particularly vibrant economic area) and the A55 corridor in North Wales.

The success of Cardiff has alienated some in North Wales and this has been exacerbated with the geographical location of the Welsh Assembly Government, which is also in the capital. The recent status given to Newport as a third city in the south where, arguably, it might have been given to Wrexham in the north, has not helped feelings of alienation. The key challenges of diversity, as they present in the specific context of Wales, seem to be the management of different kinds of identity tension.

Young People and Diversity of Expectations

While it is difficult to construct an identity on the basis of an unknown future, or on the basis of economic challenge alone, it is also clear that identity will continue to be fractured and at risk unless the transition from the past, at least to the present, is managed in a creative and forward-looking way. If identity is constructed primarily on the stories and histories of the past, this may alienate a younger generation where neither education nor peer group nor parents have been effective in passing on a credible or compelling narrative. Wide pastoral experience leads to the conclusion that, in some cases, young people are rejecting even those stories and myths of the past that encourage a positive image of Wales. They may see them as dysfunctional and divisive. They may view them as lacking in the capacity to manage a transition into the present, let alone the future. This is not unique to Wales; it is more a comment about the nature of growing up, particularly in teenage years. It can be a particular problem in Wales where young people perceive a backward-looking attitude to correlate with traditional ways which no longer deliver access into present needs and opportunities. This is particularly prevalent in traditional agricultural families and areas, to the extent that employment opportunities are perceived by young people as a key route out of social isolation. They are prepared to travel for the sake of accessing opportunities. At this point neither kinship ties nor community and administrative, let alone national, boundaries apply.

There is, therefore, a close relationship between the experience of participation in society and questions of identity.

Rural and Urban Diversity

An obvious issue of diversity in Wales is that between rural and urban. In the self-image of Wales, there is a clear sense of rurality and its ways. This functions as a strong perception of identity and difference even though in economic terms agriculture itself provides only 2 per cent of GDP. Central civil occasions such as the Royal Welsh Show and the National Eisteddfod illustrate in different ways the sense of identity which has been constructed around both cultural heritage and rural landscape and ways of life. Rural identity is under considerable threat, not least from the implications of BSE and Foot and Mouth Disease, but also from the implications of future changes to the Common Agricultural Policy and European enlargement. Traditional agricultural communities may no longer be sustainable without subsidies.

From a Christian point of view, important questions concerning the morality of western rural communities relying upon protectionism and subsidy at the expense of agricultural communities in developing countries can be asked. From one point of view, the problems of rurality are specific and part of the difference that is intrinsic to Welsh identity. From another point of view, however, the problems of rurality should not be isolated as uniquely different, and should be perceived as part of a larger economic and social challenge of regeneration across the whole of Wales. Many of the socially isolating problems in rural areas such as transport, including access to retail, leisure, education and hospital facilities, are challenges for small towns as well as for villages. Many people living in villages closer to towns and cities, with better access to economic and cultural opportunities, do not see themselves as sharing the problems of rural Wales, particularly agricultural rural Wales.

What at first looks like a significant social divide between urban and rural areas is in fact more complicated with oscillating similarities and differences and unexpected clusters of attitudes and needs. New regeneration policies are committed to reducing the differences that traditional divides have implied and to treating economic and social need as a strategic as well as a local issue. Locally, new partnerships around community strategies and Communities First projects are beginning to explore new ways of addressing common or divergent problems by bringing local people closer to the decision-making structures. Representative democracy is only one way of increasing participation.

Conclusion

Cultural diversity in Wales can be both underestimated and exaggerated. Wales is a richly diverse nation, although the differences between the various cultures and communities are often much more subtle and complex than the stereotypes and surface perceptions reveal. This presents the major agencies and decision-makers of Wales with a difficult set of strategic options. The dilemma can be seen very clearly in the single issue of the Welsh language: in the very choice that has to be made about which language to use even to describe the problems of diversity in Wales, policy-makers are aware of how this will influence not just the perception of the problem, but the reality as well.

In all of this the Christian Church is well placed to listen and to participate in conversations at every level in Wales. At a recent conference on rural issues, it was apparent that the Christian Church is the most widely represented and staffed voluntary organization active throughout Wales, with representatives in every community.

In her National Eisteddfod lecture, Jane Aaron described how the story of the survival of Welsh culture and identity is an important offering of hope to other emerging communities. What characterizes Welsh identity in all its diverse forms is the way in which it has grown, and sometimes flourished against the odds. The Welsh exist 'to disseminate the hope that it is possible to withstand colonising effects for hundreds of years and to support a minority culture in a world of global capitalism' (Aaron, 2003: 16). The diversity of Wales is one source of its strength; its vulnerabilities are another.

REFERENCES

Aaron, J. (2003), *The Welsh Survival Gene*, Cardiff, Institute of Welsh Affairs.
Balsom, D. (1985), 'The Three Wales Model', in J. Osmond (ed.), *The National Question Again: Welsh Political Identity in the 1980s*, Llandysul, Gomer Press, pp. 1–13.
Church in Wales (2002), *Ar Daith/On a Journey*, Cardiff, Church in Wales Publications.

Day, G. (1989), 'A Million on the Move? Population Change and Rural Wales', *Contemporary Wales,* 3, 137–60.

Edwards, A. (2003), *From Protest to Process: Stories from the National Assembly for Wales,* Bangor, Cyhoeddiadau'r Gair.

Furlong, M. (1998), *Act of Synod: Act of Folly,* London, SCM Press.

James, E. (2003), 'Research on Your Doorstep: Welsh Rural Communities and the Perceived Effects of In-migration', in C. A. Davies and S. Jones (eds), *Welsh Communities: New Ethnographic Perspectives,* Cardiff, University of Wales Press, pp. 49–79.

Thomas, R. S. (1993), *Collected Poems,* London, Phoenix.

Thomas, R. S. (1995), *No Truce with the Furies,* Newcastle upon Tyne, Bloodaxe.

Williams, G. A. (1991), *When was Wales?* Harmondsworth, Penguin.

11. Listening to the People

ALAN SMITH

Summary

In this chapter I argue that there is an urgent need for sociologists, church leaders and theologians to take the discipline of empirical theology more seriously. I offer a description of empirical theology and the tools that it uses. I note the relation of empirical theology with sociology and how both disciplines can be used to shed light on 'social capital'. Then the tools of empirical theology are employed in a case study of the contribution that churchgoers make to social capital in the rural areas of North Shropshire. Data supplied by 502 parochial church councillors are set alongside national figures provided by the British Social Attitudes Survey. The findings add to the growing body of research that demonstrates how belonging to a church is associated with a distinctive set of values and attitudes, which result in practical caring and community involvement, and which builds social capital in rural areas.

Introduction

'Listen to the patient: she is telling you the diagnosis.' This advice came from the lips of a professor of medicine to her clinical students as they began their training as doctors. The same advice is applicable to the Church. For example, in shaping the priorities and policies for rural ministry it is easy for church leaders to fall into the trap of assuming that they know what people in rural areas are like, or what they want, without ever checking out their assumptions. Such assumptions, if based on false premises or half-digested experience, can then achieve a life of their own and are passed from generation to generation.

Rackham (1994: 14), in his fascinating study of the formation of the English landscape, coined the word 'factoid' to describe the propagation of half-truths into accepted facts, which are universally held to be true. He cites as an example the 'fact' that once England was covered with forests. If fallacies about the history and evolution of the landscape can distort our understanding of the countryside and current ecological priorities, the same potential for self-deceit is true for the spiritual and communal landscape that the Church inhabits and addresses in forming its priorities. There is an urgent need for sociologists, church leaders and theologians to reflect on the contribution that empirical theology can make to our understanding of rural life and ministry, by using tools that can enable us to listen more accurately to what is actually going on, as opposed to what we suppose is going on.

Empirical Theology

Theologians have traditionally employed the disciplines of history, language and philosophy to reflect on the foundational source documents of the Christian faith (such as the Old Testament, the New Testament and the Early Church Fathers) in order to understand and to interpret them afresh for each generation. Although a relatively new discipline, empirical theology is already making a new and distinctive contribution to the theological task. It uses the tools of the sociologist, psychologist, anthropologist and statistician to describe or measure objectively people's religious allegiances, experiences, practices, attitudes or beliefs. These data are then used to reflect theologically on the influence of religion in the life of an individual, community or nation, which can be used to develop policies or strategies.

Some have questioned the value of empirical theology (see, for example, the letter from the Revd Dr G. E. Marrison in the *Church Times*, 17 April 2003), sometimes because of questions of methodology, but also because of concern that it may detract from the theologians' primary task of understanding and interpreting the tradition. However, proponents of the discipline claim, I believe rightly, that there is an urgent need for theologians to take the insights of empirical theology more seriously, otherwise there is a danger that their work may not engage with the world as it actually is. For example, Gill has argued:

theologians should pay careful attention to things as they are and could be before pronouncing upon things as they ought to be. A concern for theological issues which simply ignores the empirical, or projections based upon empirical data, is finally unhelpful. (Gill, 2002: xii)

Gill is critical of church leaders (especially Anglican) for refusing to listen to the insights and findings of empirical theology and in particular the nature and extent of the decline in churchgoing. As a result of this, he believes, they are handicapped in formulating appropriate and creative responses, which in turn exacerbates the decline. Jackson (2002: 70–8) makes the same point when he notes that the Church of England spends a considerable amount of time collecting and publishing statistics and yet makes little effort to learn from them and build strategies in the light of them. This chapter seeks to describe empirical theology and its methodologies, and then employs the tools of empirical theology to investigate a group of Anglican Christians who worship in one rural area today, North Shropshire.

What is the Subject Matter of Empirical Theology?

The scope of empirical theology can be illustrated by four main examples. The first example concerns the exploration of religious *experience* (or more accurately, experiences which people choose to identify as religious), such as the sense of the transcendent, the experience of being guided, or religious dreams or visions. This is the area in which foundations for the study of empirical theology were first developed by scholars such as Starbuck (1899), James (1902), Hall (1904) and Leuba (1916). It has grown into a discrete discipline and, for example, is the focus of much of the work of the Alister Hardy Research Centre in Oxford (Beardsworth, 1977; Robinson and Jackson, 1987; Hay, 1990). It is closely associated with the allied discipline of psychology.

Second, there is research based upon declared religious or denominational *allegiance* ('I am a Muslim' or 'I am a Methodist'). For example, the 2001 British Census collected and published this type of data. This was the first British census to ask about religious affiliation and it revealed that 71.6 per cent of the population were Christians, 0.3 per cent were Buddhists, 1.0 per cent were Hindus, 0.5 per cent were Jews, 2.7 per cent were Muslims, and 0.6 per cent were Sikhs. Just under one person in six (15.5 per cent) stated that they had no religion and 7.3 per cent chose not to answer the question. This research is closely linked with the work of sociologists and is often used by those responsible for developing social policy.

Third, there is research into religious *practice*, such as attendance at public worship, personal prayer, fasting, baptism or confirmation. The earliest major example of this foundation of empirical theology is the 1851 Religious Census of Great Britain (Mann, 1852–3). Since then, others have used this approach, for example, Wilson (1966: 1–18), Currie, Gilbert and Horsley (1977), Gill (1993), MARC Europe Surveys (Brierley, 1980, 1991), De Graff and Need (2000) and Jackson (2002). This area has much in common with the study of anthropology.

Fourth, there is research into religious *beliefs, values and attitudes*, where the subjects are questioned about their beliefs and the extent to which those beliefs affect their attitudes and behaviour ('I believe in life after death' or 'I think that going to church makes me a more caring person'). Examples of this approach are found in Cox (1967), Francis and Kay (1995), Kay and Francis (1996) and Gill (1999).

What Tools Does Empirical Theology Employ?

Empirical theology uses the tools of the social scientist. Hammersley and Atkinson (1994: 3–14) described the two different methodological approaches. The first they called 'positivism', which is based on the methods used by the natural sciences where the researcher seeks to observe and measure, say by means of standardized surveys or interviews. A good example is provided by the *British Social Attitudes Surveys* (BSA), which have been running since 1983 and are 'designed to chart movements in a wide range of social attitudes in Britain, including attitudes toward politics, the economy, the workplace, and other social and moral issues' (Brook, Taylor and Prior, 1990: 1). Stress is placed upon the role of the researcher as observer. The advantage of this approach is that there is a relatively high level of objectivity and a large number of subjects can be consulted easily. One of the major drawbacks is that a limited number of categories have to be chosen in advance which consequently restricts the range of responses that can be made. For example, some of the subjects may not be happy with any of the categories from which they have to choose. In order to minimize such problems it is necessary to use the questionnaire in a pilot study so it can be discussed with the respondents and refined in order to allow the subjects to define the categories.

The second approach Hammersley and Atkinson named 'naturalism'. In this approach the researcher, using the tools of the ethnographer, enters into the world of the subject and tries to understand the social meanings that lie behind various forms of behaviour. The researcher's task is to describe what is found in that particular culture and any attempts to posit universal laws are generally resisted. Such research may use a variety of tools such as formal and informal interviews, focused interviews, group discussions and diaries. While this method allows the researcher to make a detailed account of the views of each subject, it can run into the danger of the subject being influenced by the researcher. Furthermore, it can be difficult for the researcher to draw general conclusions and to make meaningful comparisons of changes or trends over time. Nevertheless, it is an approach which has been widely used by those studying religion in the United Kingdom and it has yielded a rich seam of insights that have contributed to our knowledge.

Religion and Sociology

Ironically, it is the empirical approach to the study of religion that has been one of the main factors in producing the widely held view, current in our society, that Christianity has little or no effect on people's attitudes or behaviour. This 'factoid' is now being questioned by academics. Gill (1999: 32–4) traced the origin of this assumption back to three pieces of research, namely the work undertaken by Mass-Observation (1947) and published under the title *Puzzled People*, Gorer's *Exploring English Character* (1955) and some of the early Gallup Polls, which were used by Wilson (1966). Gill is critical of the definitions of churchgoing use by *Puzzled People* and the way that Gorer confused empirical and moral statements which may have 'blurred moral differences between churchgoers and non-churchgoers' (1999: 38).

Gill noted that many theologians and sociologists have worked on the assumption that being a member of a congregation which meets for worship has 'little (beneficial) moral effect upon churchgoers'

(1999: 2), that 'a review of literature within the sociology of religion over the last few decades does seem to confirm a widespread conviction that the beliefs and behaviour of churchgoers are little different from those of non-churchgoers' (1999: 31) and that 'churchgoing is seldom thought to be an activity that has an appreciable effect upon moral/social attitudes or behaviour' (1999: 31). Gill questioned the way that some scholars have interpreted the data and also pointed out that other polls, such as the 1954 BBC survey (BBC, 1955) and the 1964 ABC Television survey (ABC, 1965), showed a clear correlation between churchgoing and a distinctive set of attitudes (Gill, 1999: 38–40). These findings have been backed up by a European Values Systems Study Group survey (Abrams, Gerard and Timms, 1985: 50–92), Francis (1982) and Francis and Kay (1995). A correlation has also been established in research undertaken by Bouma and Dixon (1986) in Australia.

Gill examined data from the British Household Panel Surveys and the British Social Attitudes Surveys and concluded as follows:

The mass of new data shows that churchgoers are indeed distinctive in their attitudes and behaviour. Some of their attitudes do change over time, especially on issues such as sexuality, and there are obvious moral disagreements between different groups of churchgoers in a number of areas. Nevertheless, there are broad patterns of Christian beliefs, teleology and altruism which distinguish churchgoers as a whole from non-churchgoers. It has been seen that churchgoers have, in addition to their distinctive theistic and christocentric beliefs, a strong sense of moral order and concern for other people. They are, for example, more likely than others to be involved in voluntary service and to see overseas charitable giving as important. They are more hesitant about euthanasia and capital punishment and more concerned about the family and civic order than other people. None of these differences is absolute. The values, virtues, moral attitudes and behaviour of churchgoers are shared by other people as well. The distinctiveness of churchgoers is real but relative. (Gill, 1999: 197)

Religion and Social Capital

Gill's conclusions have a direct bearing on an area of interest for many social scientists, social commentators and western governments: namely, the extent to which civil society is thriving, with its citizens actively involved in their local communities, and exercising their democratic right to participate in the political process. The well-documented decline of voting in elections (Bromley and Curtice, 2002: 161–2) creating a vacuum, which is sometimes filled by such groups as the British National Party, the increasing distrust of politicians and the political system (Bromley, Curtice and Seyd, 2001: 204–8), and the decrease in the number of donors to charitable causes (Report from the National Council for Voluntary Organisations and the Charities' Aid Foundation, reported in *The Times*, 20 August 2003) have raised questions about people's commitment to the communities in which they live. These concerns are fuelled by the regular diet of newspaper stories about 'no-go areas' in inner cities, about increases in road rage attacks, and about violent crimes. At a more mundane level, commentators have also noted some significant ways in which communities are changing. Until quite recently communities were rooted in (and to some extent circumscribed by) the immediate locality. Today many people may not even know the names of their neighbours, and instead relate to a network of people who share common interests or leisure pursuits, and who may live a considerable distance away from each other. It is claimed that the use of the internet and mobile phones is accelerating the emergence of 'virtual communities'. At a deeper level, some people have expressed concern about the level of trust in our society, including, for example, the Reith Lectures, given by Baroness Onora O'Neill (2002) and the Archbishop of Canterbury's New Year message (Williams, 2003).

Most of these concerns about the fabric and quality of society are brought together under the widely used umbrella-term 'social capital', a phrase which was first coined by Hanifan in 1916 (Rae, 2002: xi). Various scholars have attempted to define social capital. Bourdieu (1985: 248) suggested 'the aggregate of the actual or potential resources which are linked to possession of a durable network of more or less institutionalised relationships of mutual acquaintance or recognition'. Hall (1999: 417) defined it as 'the propensity of individuals to associate together on a regular basis, to trust one another, and to engage in community affairs'. Putnam has offered several different definitions, such as 'features of social organization, such as trust, norms, and networks, that can improve the efficiency of society by facilitating coordinated actions' (1993: 167), 'features of social life, networks, norms, and trust, that enable participants to act more effectively to pursue shared objectives' (1996: 34), and 'connections among individuals, social networks and the norms of reciprocity and trustworthiness that arise from them' (2000: 19).

Much research has been undertaken in order to understand the nature of social capital, how it is changing and the factors that influence it. It has now been established that there is a clear correlation between involvement in organizations and social trust. For example, in their research on social capital, Johnston and Jowell (2001) compared membership of organizations (such as community, countryside, sports, cultural, religion and church attendance) with the proportion of people who think that 'most people can be trusted'. The results are striking. For example, only 42 per cent of those who did not belong to a community organization agreed with the proposition, compared with 57 per cent of those who belonged to two or more community organizations. There was also a marked difference between those who did not belong to a religion, or rarely attended public worship, with those who were regular attenders. For example, only 45 per cent of those who did not belong to a religion agreed that 'most people can be trusted', compared with 50 per cent of those who belonged to a religion and attended church once a week or more frequently (Johnston and Jowell, 2001: 183).

At this stage two points need to be noted. First, what exactly is meant by membership? Johnston and Jowell use the term, but do not define it. It is likely, for example, that the commitment in belonging to the National Trust (which involves the leisure pursuit of visiting buildings and gardens of historical interest) is qualitatively different from belonging to Greenpeace (in which members are activists involved in campaigning). In turn both are different from being an elected parochial church councillor in a Church of England parish, which involves regular meetings to make decisions.

Second, it should not be presumed that all forms of social capital are intrinsically good for society. Putnam has made a distinction between 'bridging' forms of social capital (which are associated with a greater level of social involvement) and 'bonding' forms (which may be used to benefit some people, while at the same time excluding others). As an example of 'bonding' social capital, Johnston and Jowell write: 'We only have to look at Northern Ireland, one of the most intensely "organised" societies in the world, to see these "dark" and exclusive forms of social capital at work over the years' (2001: 193).

A Local Study: The Rural Church and Social Capital

It was against this backcloth that Johnston and Jowell's (2001) study of social capital in Britain, with its wealth of statistics, raised the question of whether a more detailed study of rural churchgoing and social capital might yield interesting results. At the early stages of writing this chapter, a series of about 70 meetings with the members of the Anglican parochial church councils in the Shrewsbury episcopal area of the Diocese of Lichfield was being planned to take place in 2002 and 2003. These meetings could provide the ideal opportunity to ask all those present to fill in a questionnaire, which would provide a great deal of information about their attitudes toward their communities and the different ways in which they were involved in them.

Methodology

Since Johnston and Jowell had already developed and used a questionnaire in order to measure social capital and had published the results, it was decided to use many of the same questions. This meant that there was a ready-made control group against which the contribution that Shropshire Christians were making to social capital could be examined. Despite the questionnaire already having been used extensively, a pilot study was still desirable and this involved 20 churchgoers in two groups. Having filled in the questionnaire the respondents were questioned to ensure that they understood the instructions and the questions. The pilot study resulted in a few minor adjustments to some of the wording and the layout.

Sample

The respondents cited in this chapter were all involved in the life of their local church, not just by attending worship but also by holding elected positions as parochial church councillors. They were, therefore, not a typical cross-section of churchgoers. A total of 502 people filled in the questionnaire, of which 39 per cent were male and 61 per cent were female. They were predominantly middle-aged and older (3.0 per cent were under 39, 8.2 per cent were 40–49, 24.7 per cent were 50–59; 37.5 per cent were 60–69, and 26.7 per cent were over 70).

The responses set out below are from those who worship in rural parishes, defined as having a population of less than 2,000 people. It is important to note that this sample may include some churchgoers who live in an urban area, but who travel to worship in a rural church.

Analysis

In the following tables the responses of the general population reported in the British Social Attitudes Survey (BSA) are compared with the responses reported by the parochial church councillors (PCC). The statistical chi-square test of χ^2 has been used to check whether the differences between the two groups are statistically significant or not. Statistical significance has been checked against the three conventional levels of .05, .01 and .001. The level .05 means that the difference could have occurred by chance only five times in a hundred, while the level of .001 means that the difference could have occurred by chance only once in a thousand times. The letters NS mean non-significant and indicate that any apparent difference between the two groups represents only chance fluctuations.

Listening to the Findings

Organizational involvement

As I have indicated above, in order to identify and reflect upon the different dimensions of social capital, a number of surveys have asked questions about membership of organizations, on the basis that this indicates a level of commitment to and involvement with the local community. The first part, therefore, of the questionnaire sought information about membership of various community groups (Table 1), 'green' or countryside groups (Table 2) and work groups (Table 3).

Table 1 shows that a higher proportion of the parochial church council members belonged to community organizations, apart from

Table 1: Membership of community organizations

	BSA %	PCC %	χ^2	$p<$
Neighbourhood watch scheme	11	21	34.2	.001
Tenants' or residents' association	6	4	4.8	.05
Political party	3	14	89.0	.001
Parent-teacher association	2	4	3.9	.05
Parish or town council	1	8	87.5	.001
Neighbourhood council	1	2	2.7	NS

Note: BSA data based on N = 2293.

tenants' or residents' associations. The reason for this may be that these are more likely to be found in urban and suburban areas, rather than rural areas. Particularly striking is the higher level of membership of neighbourhood watch schemes (21 per cent compared with 11 per cent), political parties (14 per cent compared with 3 per cent) and parish or town councils (8 per cent compared with 1 per cent). These statistics reveal that parochial church councillors were much more likely to hold elected positions in their local community and to have civic or community responsibilities.

A different picture emerges when we examine the membership of green or countryside organizations (Table 2). In the first seven categories a larger proportion of the parochial church councillors belonged to these groups than the respondents in the British Social Attitudes Survey. In some cases the differences are particularly stark, such as membership of the National Trust and countryside organizations. Part of the reason for this may be that some of these groups are specifically concerned with rural matters and are, therefore, more likely to be of interest to people who live in rural areas, whereas the British Social Attitudes Survey sample included those from urban backgrounds as well as rural.

However, in the last four categories, which are more concerned with urban issues or radical campaigning groups (such as CND, Friends of the Earth and Greenpeace) there was no statistical difference in the responses of the two groups. Thus it appears that the parochial church councillors are more likely to be committed to

Table 2: Membership of 'green' or countryside organizations

	BSA %	PCC %	χ2	p<
National Trust	9	46	279.2	.001
Royal Society for the Protection of Birds	5	17	61.7	.001
Other countryside sport or recreation group	2	16	186.1	.001
World Wildlife Fund	4	7	8.5	.01
Other wildlife or countryside protection group	2	12	67.1	.001
Council for the Protection of Rural England/Scotland/Wales	0	4	40.7	.001
Ramblers' Association	1	4	11.3	.001
Urban Conservation Group	1	1	0.1	NS
Campaign for Nuclear Disarmament	1	1	0.1	NS
Friends of the Earth	1	2	1.8	NS
Greenpeace	1	2	2.7	NS

Note: BSA data based on N = 1075.

groups that protect the countryside and support conservation, but there is no difference in the level of involvement in campaigning groups.

Turning to Table 3, it is clear that compared with the British Social Attitudes Survey sample, a smaller proportion of the parochial church councillors belonged to a trade union and a larger proportion had membership of a staff association. The general picture that emerges from the statistics in these three tables is that the Shropshire parochial church councillors were much more likely to belong to organizations and to be involved in them, than the people in the British Social Attitudes Survey.

Table 3: Work

	BSA %	PCC %	$\chi2$	$p<$
Membership of a trade union	19	12	14.4	.001
Membership of a staff association	3	6	11.6	.001

Note: BSA data based on N = 3335.

Social trust

Although membership of organizations gives some indication of involvement and participation in the life of the community, most human encounters take place on a one-to-one basis during the routine events of daily life. Human encounter and engagement invariably include an element of trust, except when we are relating to one another at the most superficial levels. A number of surveys have tried to measure these levels of trust by asking people to respond to such statements as, 'Most people can be trusted' and 'You can't be too careful in dealing with people'.

Table 4: Social trust

	BSA %	PCC %	$\chi2$	$p<$
Most people can be trusted	45	92	347.9	.001
You can't be too careful in dealing with people	54	54	0.0	NS

Note: BSA data based on N = 2293.

Table 4 shows that, compared with the British Social Attitudes Survey, the parochial church councillors claimed to be more trusting. More than twice the proportion of those questioned felt that most people can be trusted (92 per cent compared with 45 per cent). There was no statistical significance in the responses of the two groups to the statement that one cannot be too careful in dealing with people.

Following this initial enquiry three scenarios were described in order to find out how comfortable the respondents would be in seeking help from a neighbour, and two scenarios about asking help from a passer-by:

> Suppose that you were in bed ill and needed someone to go to the chemist to collect your prescription while they were doing their shopping. How comfortable would you be asking a neighbour to do this?

> Now suppose you found your sink was blocked, but you did not have a plunger to unblock it. How comfortable would you be asking a neighbour to borrow a plunger?

> Now suppose the milkman called for payment. The bill was £5 but you had no cash. How comfortable would you be asking a neighbour if you could borrow £5?

> Suppose you are in the middle of a town you do not know very well. You are trying to find a particular street and have got a bit lost. How comfortable would you be asking any passer-by for directions?

> Again suppose you are in the middle of a town you do not know very well. You need to make an urgent phone call from a phone box but you only have a £5 note. How comfortable would you be in asking any passer-by for the right change?

Table 5 gives the responses to these statements from the British Social Attitudes Survey sample and the parochial church councillors. In response to four of the five scenarios, a higher proportion of the parochial church councillors indicated that they were comfortable about asking for help from a neighbour or even from someone they did not know.

Table 5: Feelings about asking for help

	BSA comfortable %	PCC comfortable %	χ2	*p*<
Asking a neighbour:				
to collect a prescription	80	95	60.3	.001
to borrow a sink plunger	86	94	21.8	.001
to pay the milkman	38	37	0.1	NS
Asking passer-by for:				
directions	89	95	16.5	.001
change for the phone	57	66	13.7	.001

Note: BSA data based on N = 2293.

A further scenario was described to find out how likely people would be to help a vulnerable stranger in need:

Suppose you were walking down a local street. Ahead of you there is a group of teenagers blocking the pavement, forcing an elderly woman to walk out into a busy road. How likely is it that you would help the woman by asking the young people to move?

Table 6: Assisting a vulnerable stranger

	BSA %	PCC %	χ2	*p*<
Definitely help her myself	54	50	2.3	NS
Probably help her myself	37	44	7.8	.01
Probably not help her, but hope someone else would	6	2	12.9	.001
Definitely not help her, but hope someone else would	2	<1	3.7	NS
Don't know	1	4	17.1	.001

Note: BSA data based on N = 2293.

The responses to the scenario of helping a vulnerable stranger were mixed. There was no statistical difference in the responses of the two groups that they would 'definitely help her myself', but 7 per cent more of the parochial church councillors said that they would 'probably help her myself'. Fewer of the parochial church councillors said that they would 'probably not help her, but hope that someone else would', but a higher proportion were not sure how they would respond. Thus, overall the parochial church councillors indicated that they were more likely to help a vulnerable stranger.

Trust in institutions

Four questions were put to the respondents in order to assess their level of trust in a range of democratic institutions and to seek their views about those who are in positions of authority:

How much do you trust British governments of any party to place the needs of the nation above the interest of their own political party?

How much do you trust British police not to bend the rules in trying to get a conviction?

How much do you trust top civil servants to stand firm against a minister who wants to provide false information to Parliament?

How much do you trust politicians of any party in Britain to tell the truth when they are in a tight corner?

Table 7: Groups which can be trusted 'just about always' or 'most of the time'

	BSA %	PCC %	$\chi 2$	$p<$
Government	20	16	3.1	NS
Police	68	67	0.2	NS
Civil servants	39	37	0.4	NS
MPs	12	12	0.0	NS

Note: BSA data based on N = 998.

In response to the statements about trusting those in authority, Table 7 shows that there was no statistical significance in the responses of the two groups.

Conclusion

In order to illustrate the contribution of empirical theology to understanding rural church life, this chapter posed the question 'What do we know about the contribution of rural churchgoers to social capital?' When compared with the research undertaken by the British Social Attitudes Survey, it was shown that parochial church councillors in Shropshire were more likely to be members of community organizations (Table 1) and to be members of 'green' or countryside organizations. However, there was no clear difference between the two cohorts in the level of membership of campaigning groups (Table 2). This latter point is further strengthened by the lower level of membership of trade unions among the parochial church councillors. At the same time, a larger proportion of parochial church councillors belonged to staff associations (Table 3). A far higher proportion of the parochial church councillors claimed to be trusting (Table 4) and in response to various scenarios they exhibited far higher levels of trust toward neighbours and passers-by (Table 5). Their reactions to a vulnerable stranger in need of help were not very dissimilar from those in the British Social Attitudes Survey, although there was a slightly higher proportion who indicated that they were likely to assist (Table 6). There were no significant differences in the attitudes toward authority figures between the two groups (Table 7).

These findings support those of Johnston and Jowell (2001), which identified a direct connection between group membership (which in this case was expressed by serving on an elected body of the local church) and social capital. However, one should be cautious before jumping to conclusions about causality (Schultz, 2002: 81). As Johnston and Jowell concluded:

> To the extent that the connection between social trust and social participation is causally linked, it is likely to be a reciprocal link: so, the more trusting people are, the more likely they are to be joiners, and vice versa. (Johnston and Javell, 2001: 182)

Nevertheless, this research shows that the parochial church councillors in this study were more likely to contribute toward social capital than people in general, and as such they were making a tangible and significant contribution to the life of their communities. This is an important finding for the churches, since it demonstrates the importance of churchgoing as a strong socializing force. Traditionally, Christians have taught that churchgoing (and thereby worship) is important because human beings have been made to know and love God. What has not been measured previously is the way in which attending a church also affects the behaviour of churchgoers, and in particular, means that they are more likely to get involved with others and in their local community. Churchgoing should not be under-estimated in its power to motivate people to contribute to the common good of society.

These findings are also significant for those responsible for formulating public policy. It is generally considered to be important to encourage people's commitment to and involvement in society and the British government has expressed its desire to increase active citizenship. Some research has already taken place in an attempt to understand 'faith-based volunteering' and has shown that 'a large number of members volunteer regularly and an even larger number occasionally' (Lukka and Locke with Soteri-Procter, 2003: 11). In the light of their considerable contribution, they conclude that 'public agencies . . . should do more to inform faith communities about the sources of external support available' (2003: 11). By their very nature, it is unlikely that faith communities could be used to deliver public services in any systematic way. Nevertheless, governments may wish to consider ways in which they can offer additional support to churches and other faith communities that can demonstrate that they are increasing the level of 'bridging' social capital by their social involvement and community service.

In conclusion, this study of Christians in rural Shropshire adds to the growing body of research that demonstrates that belonging to a church is associated with a distinctive set of values and attitudes, which result in practical caring and community involvement, and which builds social capital.

REFERENCES

ABC Television (1965), *Television and Religion*, London, London University.

Abrams, M., Gerard, D. and Timms, N. (eds) (1985), *Values and Social Change in Britain*, Basingstoke, Macmillan.

Beardsworth, T. (1977), *A Sense of Presence: The Phenomonology of Certain Kinds of Visionary and Ecstatic Experience Based on a Thousand Contemporary First-hand Accounts*, Oxford, The Religious Experience Research Unit.

Bourdieu, P. (1985), 'The Forms of Capital', in J. G. Richardson (ed.), *Handbook of Theory and Research for the Sociology of Religion*, New York, Greenwood, pp. 241–58.

Bouma, G. D. and Dixon, B. R. (1986), *The Religious Factor in Australian Life*, Melbourne, South Australia, MARC Australia.

Brierley, P. (ed.) (1980), *Prospects for the Eighties*, London, Bible Society.

Brierley, P. (1991), *Prospects for the Nineties: Trends and Tables from the English Church Census*, London, MARC Europe.

British Broadcasting Corporation (1955), *Religious Broadcasts and the Public*, London, Audience Research Department, BBC.

Brook, L., Taylor, B. and Prior, G. (1990), *British Social Attitudes 1989 Survey: Technical Report*, London, Social and Community Planning Research.

Bromley, C. and Curtice, J. (2002), 'Where Have All the Voters Gone?' in A. Park, J. Curtice, K. Thomson, L. Jarvis and C. Bromley (eds), *British Social Attitudes: The Nineteenth Report*, London, Sage Publications, pp. 141–67.

Bromley, C., Curtice, J. and Seyd, B. (2001), 'Political Engagement, Trust and Constitutional Reform', in A. Park, J. Curtice, K. Thomson, L. Jarvis and C. Bromley (eds), *British Social Attitudes: The Eighteenth Report*, London, Sage Publications, pp. 199–225.

Cox, E. (1967), *Sixth Form Religion*, London, SCM Press.

Currie, R., Gilbert, A. and Horsley, L. (1977), *Churches and Churchgoers: Patterns of Church Growth in the British Isles since 1700*, Oxford, Clarendon Press.

De Graff, N. D. and Need, A. (2000), 'Losing Faith: Is Britain Alone?' in R. Jowell, J. Curtice, A. Park, K. Thomson, L. Jarvis, C. Bromley and N. Stratford (eds), *British Social Attitudes: The Seventeenth Report: Focusing on Diversity*, London, Sage Publications, pp. 119–36.

Francis, L. J. (1982), *Youth in Transit: A Profile of 16–25 Year Olds*, Aldershot, Gower.

Francis, L. J. and Kay, W. (1995), *Teenage Religion and Values*, Leominster, Gracewing.

Gill, R. (1993), *The Myth of the Empty Church*, London, SPCK.

Gill, R. (1999), *Churchgoing and Christian Ethics*, Cambridge, Cambridge University Press.

Gill, R. (2002), *Changing Worlds: Can the Church Respond?* Edinburgh, T. and T. Clark.

Gorer, G. (1955), *Exploring English Character*, London, Cresset Press.

Hall, G. S. (1904), *Adolescence: Its Psychology, and its Relations to Physiology,*

Anthropology, Sociology, Sex, Crime, Religion, and Education, New York, Appleton (two volumes).

Hall, P. A. (1999), 'Social Capital in Britain', *The British Journal of Political Science*, 29, 417–61.

Hammersley, M. and Atkinson, P. (1994), *Ethnography: Principles in Practice*, London, Tavistock Publications.

Hay, D. (1990), *Religious Experience Today: Studying the Facts*, London, Mowbray.

Jackson, B. (2002), *Hope for the Church: Contemporary Strategies for Growth*, London, Church House Publishing.

James, W. (1902), *The Varieties of Religious Experience*, London, Longman, Green and Company.

Johnston, M. and Jowell, R. (2001), 'How Robust Is British Civil Society?' in A. Park, J. Curtice, K. Thomson, L. Jarvis and C. Bromley (eds), *British Social Attitudes: The Eighteenth Report*, London, Sage Publications, pp. 175–97.

Kay, W. K. and Francis, L. J. (1996), *Drift from the Churches: Attitude toward Christianity During Childhood and Adolescence*, Cardiff, University of Wales Press.

Leuba, J. H. (1916), *The Belief in God and Immortality: A Psychological, Anthropological and Statistical Study*, Chicago, Open Court.

Lukka, P. and Locke, M. with Soteri-Procter, A. (2003), *Faith and Voluntary Action: Community, Values and Resources*, London, Institute for Volunteering Research and Centre for Institutional Studies, School of Social Sciences, University of East London.

Mann, H. (1852–1853), *1851 Census Great Britain: Report and Tables on Religious Worship, England and Wales*, London, British Parliamentary Papers.

Mass-Observation (1947), *Puzzled People: A Study in Popular Attitudes to Religion, Ethics, Progress and Politics in a London Borough*, London, Gollancz.

O'Neill, O. (2002), 'Reith Lectures: A Question of Trust', [online], available from: http://www.bbc.co.uk/radio4/reith2002/ [accessed 11 June 2004].

Putnam, R. D. (1993), *Making Democracy Work*, Princeton, Princeton University Press.

Putnam, R. D. (1996), 'The Strange Disappearance of Civil America', *The American Prospect* (Winter), 34–49.

Putnam, R. D. (2000), *Bowling Alone: The Collapse and Revival of American Community*, New York, Simon and Schuster.

Rackham, O. (1994), *The Illustrated History of the Countryside*, London, Weidenfeld and Nicholson.

Rae, D. (2002), 'Foreword', in S. L. McLean, D. A. Schultz and M. B. Steger (eds), *Social Capital: Critical Perspectives on Community and 'Bowling Alone'*, New York, New York University Press.

Robinson, E. and Jackson, M. (1987), *Religion and Values at Sixteen Plus*, Oxford, Alister Hardy Research Centre and Christian Education Movement.

Schultz, D. A. (2002), 'The Phenomenology of Democracy: Putnam, Pluralism, and Voluntary Associations', in S. L. McClean, D. A. Schultz and M. B. Steger (eds), *Social Capital: Critical Perspectives on Community and 'Bowling Alone'*, New York, New York University Press, pp. 74–98.

Starbuck, E. (1899), *The Psychology of Religion: An Empirical Study of the Growth of Religious Consciousness*, London, Walter Scott.

Williams, R. (2003), 'Archbishop of Canterbury's New Year's Message', reported in *The Times*, 1 January 2004.

Wilson, B. R. (1966), *Religion in Secular Society: A Sociological Comment*, London, Watts.

12. Listening to the Scriptures

JOHN S. WENT

Summary

There is a rich variety of images or models about the Church in the New Testament; historically, some images have been particularly significant. At a time of rapid cultural change, a crisis of images can occur. Alongside changes in the wider society, the Church has faced major changes in recent years; there are very different expectations of clergy today. At every stage of church history the gospel and the Church embodying that gospel have been influenced by cultural factors. Can New Testament insights about the Church inform current debate about the rural Church? In the New Testament the key factor is community, even though historically the institutional model of the Church tended to dominate.

Avery Dulles (1976) examines various models and looks at criteria for evaluating them, especially homing in on their capacity to give church members a corporate sense of identity and mission. The image of the pilgrim people of God has value in helping the contemporary Church to sit light to aspects of its inherited past that may no longer further its mission and in helping it respond to fresh mission challenges.

While recognizing the comparative strength of the Church in rural areas and the consequent need for change not to undermine that strength, there is a need to ensure that the rural Church is in good heart well into the twenty-first century; for this to happen, a sense of the Church as community needs to be recovered, a community where Christians have a mature and informed understanding of their faith, where dependence on God is expressed through the life of prayer, where meaningful fellowship is nurtured, where the gifts of the whole people of God are fostered, and where there is serious engagement in mission, sharing the good news of Christ in word and action. There will need to be a proper balance between what is best expressed in the local context (a parish church for a potentially tiny community) and what is best expressed across a wider area, a multi-parish benefice or deanery.

Introduction

Paul S. Minear (1961) identified approximately 100 images of the Church in the pages of the New Testament. His book, commissioned by the World Council of Churches Faith and Order, was concerned with issues of Christian unity. The World Council of Churches has in recent times majored on three models in relation to the nature of the Church: *sign, instrument* and *communion. Sign* serves to remind us that the Church always needs to point to a reality greater than itself and serves to prevent the Church from being too preoccupied with its self-importance; it reminds us of the provisional nature of the Church and its structures. *Instrument* underwrites the significance of the Church as an instrument to further the purposes of God, which are much wider than the Church, embracing the whole of creation. *Communion* points to the central reality of community at the heart of the life of the Church, sharing a common life in God, Father, Son and Holy Spirit, in spite of the divisions that historically have separated Christians from one another.

Avery Dulles (1976), again writing out of ecumenical concerns, worked with a small set of models. He argued that to be fully effective models must be deeply rooted in our corporate experience as Christians. He pointed out that in times of rapid cultural change a crisis of models is to be expected. Many traditional models lose their former hold on people, while new models have not yet had time to gain their full power. Biblical models are largely pastoral and may lose their power for city dwellers, while retaining some significance for the rural scene.

It is commonplace when dealing with theological images or models to distinguish between those used for explanation and those used for exploration. The former tend to be much more fixed; the latter more flexible. If they fail to help us in our journey of exploration, it is easier to jettison them in order to find new models that work more effectively for us.

Rapid Change in Society and Church

I am writing this chapter on the day that an aunt of mine celebrated her ninety-first birthday. During her lifetime she has witnessed enormous social changes. Today's world could not be more different from the world into which she was born just prior to the outbreak of the First World War. Technology, transportation, the world of work, the consumer world, social and moral values, all these areas and many more have undergone and continue to undergo major changes.

The Church has often been looked to, especially by traditionalists, as an unchanging bastion, a safe haven, at a time when wider society is changing at an alarming rate. Yet the Church cannot be immune from changes in the wider society. As a bishop in a rural, fairly traditional diocese I am aware that the Church I now serve is significantly different from the Church into which I was ordained in 1969. As an archdeacon for six years in the Diocese of Guildford, pastoral reorganization was hardly ever on my agenda. For seven years as a suffragan bishop in the Diocese of Gloucester, pastoral reorganization has hardly ever been off my agenda. My predecessor two years before I arrived had drawn up a pastoral plan; I was asked to draw up a new plan within six months because his plan was already out of date; my plan was out of date within a short space of time. Indeed we find the goalposts are constantly changing and the message we seek to get across, especially to our many small communities, is the need for flexibility.

The implication of change for the life of the Church is helpfully mapped out by Gordon Kuhrt (2001). The number of stipendiary clergy has reduced from a peak of 23,670 in 1901 (though of that number 4,150 were over the age of 65; there was no compulsory retirement age then) to approximately 9,500 today. Inevitably that has resulted in the need for a very different style of ministry (increasingly seen in episcopal terms, overseeing the gifts and ministries of lay Christians as well as leading a team that may include NSMs, OLMs, readers, a youth worker, and so on) in the urban and suburban context, but especially in the rural context where the multi-parish benefice has become the norm and increasingly in many dioceses runs to five, six, seven or more parishes in a united benefice. Though the number of full-time paid clergy reduced dramatically during the twentieth century, the overall number of clergy (when non-stipendiary and locally ordained clergy are added) is not significantly less and it is often pointed out that during that same period of time the number of readers in the Church has increased dramatically. All of this underlines the changing role of the reduced number of full-time paid clergy. Stephen Croft (1999), Warden of Cranmer Hall, helpfully reflects on the episcopal dimension of the parish priest.

Bishop Michael Turnbull (2001), in a chapter on the parish system, believes that it is right to continue to emphasize the value of locality, while recognizing that for most people this is no longer the parish as we have known it and that we need to establish locality ministries rather than parish ministries. He paints a picture of a Church for the twenty-first century: collaborative rather than isolationist, prayerful rather than hyperactive, ready to use all people's gifts, enabling them to take responsibility, sacrificial in giving out of a confidence in what is being supported, deeply conscious of the missionary challenge in an alien and secular society.

A Contextualized Church Embodying a Contextualized Gospel

The word 'contextualization' was first used as recently as 1973 by Shoki Coe of the Theological Education Fund of the WCC (see Thomas, 1995: 175); however, the doctrine of the incarnation, God becoming a human being in a particular cultural, time-specific context, provides the theological rationale for a contextual approach to theology and mission; furthermore, a study of the history of the Church shows how the gospel has been adapted to different cultural contexts (for example, an Alexandrian form of Christian faith in the early period, Robert de Nobili in the early seventeenth century among high caste Hindus in Madurai in Tamil Nadu, India) and the Church that gives expression to the gospel has also found different cultural forms in different cultural contexts. Within the New Testament itself, in Acts 15, a key cultural mission issue is raised about an appropriate lifestyle for Gentile Christians as opposed to Jewish Christians.

Charles H. Kraft's *Christianity in Culture* (1981) is one of many books that from the 1980s onwards examined the cultural dimensions of mission, exploring anthropological and social issues in a missionary context. There is no such thing as a culture-free expression of Christianity; however, rather than imposing our cultural form of Christian faith in mission, we introduce individuals, communities, to a living relationship with Christ and allow their faith in Christ to become authentically theirs, contextualized in their own culture. That process does not happen overnight. It was several centuries before western civilization rejected slavery as incompatible with Christian values. We trust the power of the gospel to transform culture and cultural values over generations. The form Christian faith takes in different parts of Africa or Asia or Latin America is likely to differ significantly from the form Christian faith takes in our western world. Even in our western world the form in which Christianity is expressed is likely to differ according to whether those being evangelized are all white people over 50, or white people in their teens and twenties, or black people in an inner-city area. Christian faith challenges values in a culture as well as finding expression in and through the values of that culture. As Christianity takes different forms of expression in different parts of the world each must value and respect how Christians elsewhere are applying the faith and its values in their own culture. There should however be a willingness to engage in mutual assessment, criticism and evaluation, for it is likely that the pressure to conform to non-Christian values can compromise the essentials of the faith. In scholarly circles it has been recognized that self-interest often significantly shapes the way we choose to interpret evidence or situations. This has led to an emphasis on the importance of being 'suspicious' about such underlying self-interest. This so-called 'hermeneutic of suspicion' needs to operate freely, exposing through 'suspicion' those areas of self-interest that significantly shape our views.

Andrew Walls (2002) remarks on the significant transition in the history of mission from a crusade mentality where the gospel was imposed as part of territorial conquest to a healthy concept of entering someone else's world on their terms to live alongside them, living out Christian values. Such an approach potentially allows for the gospel to be genuinely inculturated.

Key New Testament Insights

The cultural settings of the New Testament and twenty-first-century Britain are poles apart, yet there may be underlying principles about the Church that can helpfully apply to two very different cultural contexts. *Ecclesia*, the New Testament word for Church, can refer to the Church meeting in someone's home (local), to the Church in a particular city or region or to the universal Church. It never refers to a building. It is always a community. There were no special church buildings until the third century. In the earliest period Christians met in a home; most homes would only have been able to accommodate a group of about 30. Cities like Rome or Corinth would have had several Christian groups meeting in different homes across the city.

It is likely that there was a link between 'city churches' and Christians in outlying villages. St Paul reflecting on his missionary strategy in Romans, chapter 15 speaks of having completed the preaching of the gospel from Jerusalem to Illyricum; he could not possibly have gone as a missionary to all the villages; it appears that his strategy was to plant churches in cities and then to encourage those city churches to share the gospel with outlying rural communities. Writing to Christians in Thessalonica he speaks of the word of the Lord ringing out from them in Macedonia, Achaia and farther afield. In the post-New Testament period bishops look after city churches, sharing their ministry with a group of presbyters who, among other responsibilities, take care of outlying rural communities.

The Central Image of the Church as Community

The Church above all is seen in community terms. The Greek Old Testament usage of *ecclesia* stands for the community of God's people gathered in God's presence for worship, to receive instruction, to be equipped to live as God's distinctive people and to shine as a light for God among non-Jews (Isaiah 42.6; Psalms 96.3; Genesis 12.3). In New Testament terms it is the people of God gathered for worship, to share in the Eucharist (the early chapters of Acts), to listen to God's word, pray, enjoy fellowship and be equipped to live as God's distinctive people sharing in God's continuing mission in and through Jesus Christ, in the power of the Spirit. Different New Testament writers offer different perspectives, but the sense of the Church as primarily and fundamentally community is a common strand running through the whole New Testament. It is found in John's writings, in the high priestly prayer of Jesus and in the opening of 1 John; in both passages there is a sense of the Church as a fellowship of Christians, bound together in the love of God, Father, Son and Holy Spirit. It is in Paul's writings, for example through the imagery of the body of Christ in 1 Corinthians 12. It is in 1 Peter 2 where links are traced between the

Old and the New Testament people of God. We see it in the letter to
the Hebrews where we are given a picture of the people of God standing on the edge of eternity, with a vision of a God of awe-inspiring
glory and holiness held before them. They have been called to live as a
pilgrim people, bearing costly discipleship. This picture of the Church
as community, rooted in the trinitarian life of God, has been majored
on in ecumenical discussions in recent years, offering a uniting theme
for Christians of very different theological outlooks.

An Institutional Model in the History of the Church

The first model offered by Dulles (1976) is that of the Church as institution. In spite of the strong New Testament emphasis on community,
an institutional model dominated the Church in the West for
centuries; the Church was defined with reference to its visible structures and the rights and powers of its officers. This model found its
fullest expression in the Dogmatic Constitution on the Church prepared for Vatican I. In contrast the Vatican II documents (see Abbott,
1966) a century later reflected a marked change in Roman Catholic
thinking, with a significant shift to a more communal understanding
of the Church, though the full implications of that have yet to be fully
worked out.

Though the primary emphasis in the pages of the New Testament is
on community, within the later New Testament documents (for
example, the Pastoral letters) there is evidence that, as the Church
grows, it needs to acquire appropriate structures and these structures
are related to secular structures of the time. The New Testament
Church becomes increasingly a structured Church, a process further
developed within the history of the Church. However, structures serve
and nurture community and in that sense are always secondary. It is
vital for today's Church to find new structures, appropriate to
our society, that will serve and nurture the life of the Church as community rather than stifle that community life.

Other Models of the Church

The second model offered by Dulles (1976) is that of the Church as
mystical communion, the New Testament image of the body of Christ.
Emil Brunner (1952), he points out, drew radical conclusions from

this understanding of the Church, rejecting all law, sacrament and priestly office as incompatible with the true nature of Church. Dietrich Bonhoeffer (1954), without drawing Brunner's radical negative conclusions, explored this understanding of the Church in his short, but theologically significant, book *Life Together*. Within Roman Catholic circles Yves Congar (1984) has sought to hold together the twin polarities of the Church as institution and communion by means of a particular emphasis on the work of the Spirit.

The third model offered by Dulles (1976) is that of the Church as sacrament, the Church that dispenses the sacraments, but is also a sign or sacrament itself of the presence of Christ. In Catholic circles and more recently also in Charismatic circles, the Church has been seen as the continuing presence in the world of the incarnate Christ. That still begs the question of what kind of Church serves as a sacrament: is it the institutional Church or the Church as the community of the people of God?

The fourth and fifth models offered by Dulles (1976) are respectively the Church as herald and as servant. The image of herald lays emphasis on the central place of the word preached; in the New Testament this is the emphasis of Luke, where the Church is brought into existence and grows through the proclamation of the word. It was a major insight of the Reformation. Article 19 sees the pure preaching of the word and the right administration of the sacraments (gospel sacraments) as constitutive of the Church. Paul Avis (1981: 215) summarizes the view of the Reformers as seeing the gospel preached as constituting the christological centre of the Church. In the twentieth century P. T. Forsyth (1917) hammered home his conviction that the gospel constitutes and creates the Church. Karl Barth's famous saying from his commentary on Romans is often quoted: the Church is 'no more than a crater formed by the explosion of a shell' (see Barth, 1963³: 36). The later Barth in his *Church Dogmatics* (1936–81) showed rather more interest in the visible structure of the Church while remaining as emphatic about its true heart and centre.

The image of servant speaks for itself; it reminds the Church of its calling to be a channel of God's compassionate, caring, servant love seen supremely in the life and ministry of Jesus Christ. Dietrich Bonhoeffer (1981) described Jesus as 'the man for others' and on the basis of that christological insight described the Church as 'only church when it exists for others'. This was a major emphasis for many writers in the 1960s when there was a concern to make the Church 'more relevant' in a rapidly changing society. This was true of J. A. T. Robinson's writings (1965). Similarly Harvey Cox (1965) spoke of the Church in the secular city being called to be *diakonos*, the servant struggling for the wholeness and health of the city. This emphasis on the Church as servant inspired liberation theology in the 1960s with a particular focus on the Church existing in base communities in places such as Latin America almost as a protest over against a Roman Catholic emphasis on Church as institution.

Within this focus on the Church as servant, different approaches have characterized different writers and theological perspectives. John Robinson argued for jettisoning the Church's structures, which he saw often more as an obstacle than a help to mission; he had a vision, as many did in the 1960s, for the Church working through the world's structures rather than generating separate structures. In Charismatic circles there has often been an equally strong emphasis on a servant Church, but this theological tradition places the emphasis on the Church's own distinctive ministry.

After exploring different models, Dulles (1976: 180–1) introduces seven criteria for evaluating the models. The third of his criteria speaks of the capacity of a particular model to give church members a sense of their corporate identity and mission. The seventh of his criteria refers to the fruitfulness of a particular model in enabling church members to relate successfully to those outside the Church. I would add the ability of a model to relate across denominational divisions, working effectively ecumenically; the emphasis on Church as community has been a theme that has proved increasingly unifying within the ecumenical scene, with a particular emphasis on *koinonia*, the life in common that Christians share (the trinitarian life of God, their fellowship together within the body of Christ).

Reflections on the Rural Church Scene

There is evidence to suggest that people in contemporary Britain are not enamoured with institutions. The Church as institution may be a significant 'switch-off' for many in our society, especially younger people. Equally, there is evidence that in a society where there is an increasing experience of isolation and fragmentation, many are hungry for an experience of authentic community and spirituality.

When we focus specifically on the Church in rural areas there is still among existing church members and among occasional churchgoers a strong sense of the Church as institution. The loss of the local parish priest is often viewed with considerable disquiet. There is a very strong will to keep the local church building at all costs, even if that church is serving a tiny community. In the Diocese of Gloucester interesting discussions recently took place with the churchwardens and parochial church council members of a church serving a community of 97 people. The Pastoral Committee recommended linking it with a market-town already linked with a neighbouring village of 700 people. The vicar was prepared to take on the extra village on the understanding that it would have only a fortnightly service. The villagers had felt unchurched for many years. Having at long last 'received their village church back' they were determined to have it open for public worship weekly. In the hope of an eventual resolution to this problem, the diocese agreed to wait before implementing pastoral reorganization. *Faith in the Countryside* (Archbishops' Commission on Rural Areas, 1990) recommended weekly worship wherever possible at the same time in each local settlement. The Bishop of Gloucester's original mission statement had as it first aim: 'to encourage in every community lively weekly worship, accessible and outward looking'. However, a revised format omitted 'weekly' as small communities increasingly appear to see value in a fortnightly pattern as more realistic for a parish priest looking after as many as seven, eight or nine villages, even though others are leading worship.

In a largely rural diocese there is a reluctance to take decisions that might undermine the strength of our village churches. A considerably higher proportion of the population attend church than in the more urban and suburban parts of the diocese. At major festivals (in the Diocese of Gloucester they include Christmas, Easter, Remembrance Sunday, Harvest and Mothering Sunday) there can be an incredibly high proportion of villagers in church. At one village church during an interregnum I presided at a service on Christmas morning at which 35 per cent of the villagers were in church, and there have been even higher percentages recorded on such special occasions.

There is a natural reluctance to 'rock the boat' and a recognition of the danger of alienating strong-minded and often traditional people for whom churchgoing (even if not weekly) is still part of their tradition. However, at the same time there is an awareness that we have a duty to prepare people in the rural setting for a very different long-term future if the Church is to survive well into the twenty-first century.

One model that features a great deal in contemporary ecumenical discussions, though not specifically mentioned by Dulles (1976), is that of the pilgrim people of God. It is more an Old Testament than a New Testament model, though the Old Testament image is picked up on several occasions in the writings of the New Testament (for example, 2 Corinthians 6.16; Romans 9.25; 1 Peter 2.9–10). This model has considerable strengths in enabling congregations to sit light to structures and to be open to the ever-new future to which the living God may call them. It readily conveys a challenging call to live as God's distinctive people, as salt and light. It can helpfully hold before a local congregation the challenge to move out of the building to share in God's work of mission in the wider world.

A traditional Anglican ecclesiology, especially in the village, has wanted to be very careful not to draw clear lines between 'insiders' and 'outsiders'. Electoral roll numbers are often higher for a village church, because village people see themselves as church members even if rarely attending. Potentially, such an open relationship with the local church can be used to draw people from the edge into the centre, from nominalism to committed discipleship. Realistically, such an understanding of the Church fosters complacency which may undermine effective evangelism. A 'people of God' ecclesiology may help to recapture the cutting edge of mission. By encouraging others to 'journey with us' as the people of God it may be possible to draw people into more committed involvement without alienating them. In several of our Cotswold villages we have to our pleasant surprise found Alpha courses effective in drawing people on the edge more into the centre without creating a divisive sense of 'them and us'.

I have suggested that, though in the rural context an institutional model of the Church is still in favour, we need to rediscover the New Testament focus on the Church as community. One issue in the rural scene is that the primary form of community is the village itself, even though many of our villages contain a potential division between 'genuine old village people' and 'newcomers' (who in turn often divide between those totally involved in village life and those who see it simply as an idyllic, away-from-it-all base from which to work). It is quite a challenge to work out how the Church can be a distinctive community; yet it is an issue that must be wrestled with for the sake of mission.

A Distinctive Community Responding to the Scriptures

The Church as a community in the New Testament is a community gathered around the scriptures. The New Testament Church had the Old Testament scriptures; from early on the letters of Paul, though it was only later that a decision was made to include some of those within the canon of scripture; the words and works of Jesus at least in an oral form. The shape and emphases that Matthew gives to his account of Jesus' ministry indicates that in his community and in the community for which he writes, teaching plays an important part. The letters of Paul combine clear theological and ethical teaching, again an indication that these played an important part in the shaping of communities of faith in New Testament times. All of this coheres with the picture Luke chooses to paint of the early Christian community in Jerusalem, constantly gathering to listen to the apostles' teaching.

An area where the Church has failed historically, especially in the rural scene, has been that of grounding Christians in solid teaching. Generally speaking the sermon has not proved an effective means of helping Christians to grow into a mature faith that shapes values and lifestyle. Programmes such as Emmaus or the more ambitious Methodist programme *Disciple* (see Methodist Church, 1993) have more recently been used effectively even in village churches, but often most effectively across a benefice or even a deanery rather than in an isolated village setting. I have recently been impressed by a benefice Lent course (seven churches) which attracted 70 to a series of teaching evenings with visiting speakers and a deanery Lent course attracting up to 90 for a course on spirituality.

A Praying Community

Another characteristic mark of the first Christian communities was their life of prayer, again noted in Luke's thumbnail sketch of the early Jerusalem church. Luke takes a particular interest in the prayer life of Jesus and in the prayer life of the early Church. St Paul in his letters prays regularly for the life of the Christian communities that he has planted and those for which he has come to have a pastoral concern, even though not planted by him; in turn, he expects the local churches to uphold him in prayer. The Pastoral letters envisage prayer being regularly offered, as does the letter of James specifically in the context of prayer for healing, reconciliation and thanksgiving. The letter to the Hebrews gives a picture of a Christian community with its back up against the wall, facing persecution, encouraged by a vision of the heavenly Jerusalem, myriads of angels and the spirits of good men made perfect; they are invited to worship God with reverence and awe.

The Diocese of Gloucester has a link with two dioceses in the Church of South India, Dornakal and Karnataka Central. Through our partnership many of us have been deeply impressed by the quality of prayer life of the Indian Church, especially in rural areas; there is a strong sense of local communities of Christians making prayer their lifeline, praying with a keen expectation that God will answer their prayers in significant ways. In some of our rural benefices members of local ministry teams take responsibility for ensuring regular times of prayer in each of the churches across the benefice; in some of our rural areas prayer partnership schemes for lay Christians prove to be an effective way of putting prayer on the agenda and enabling Christians to grow in their prayer life.

The prayer life of the local Christian community is centred especially on the Eucharist. That is true again of Luke's thumbnail sketch of the Christian community in Jerusalem; it is true of the Christian communities in Corinth with which Paul corresponds; eucharistic imagery appears to run through the letter to the Church in Laodicea in Revelation. There is an issue about where the primary eucharistic community is to be located. In Anglican ecclesiology there is a strong strand that sees the primary eucharistic community as the diocese gathered round the bishop. Whether or not we see that as the primary focus, it is an important perspective to hold on to, especially at a time when many simply want to tread an independent path with no concern for the wider vision of the people of God. In the New Testament the local expression of Church (the church in the home) is never in isolation, but always part of something greater, the church in the city, the church in a region, the Church universal. However important the life of the local church is, especially in terms of its local mission, it must never lose sight of being part of something much larger. The Anglican Church is not congregational in its self-understanding; the local congregation is part of a deanery, a diocese, a national Church, a worldwide Anglican communion. Every Sunday in the creed we publicly affirm our faith in a Church that is 'one, holy, catholic and apostolic'. The catholic nature of the Church is about its universality; the local is always part of something larger.

An issue in a multi-parish benefice is where and how often the Eucharist is to be celebrated. Is there a case for only one Eucharist in a benefice on a Sunday, with a variety of other forms of worship across the benefice, some specifically designed to attract the unchurched? Recently, some dioceses have experimented with 'communion by extension'; a reader or other appropriately authorized lay person takes the consecrated elements from a service within a multi-parish benefice to another church within the benefice and leads an appropriate act of worship, distributing the previously consecrated elements. In Monmouth diocese at the time of Archbishop Rowan Williams's departure there were 80 authorized 'ministers of the Eucharist' officiating regularly at such services.

The Church of England village church (on occasions this may also be true of a local Methodist church) often serves a wide cross-section of Christians from different denominational backgrounds who choose to worship in their local church rather than travel several miles to their own denominational church. There is great strength in such a cross-denominational community of Christians serving the needs of their local community in the name of Christ.

Sharing a Common Life

Luke's cameo portrait of the early Church in Jerusalem includes a reference to 'sharing the common life'. That included a very practical sharing of material possessions. There was a sense of belonging to a family. St Paul's Corinthian correspondence makes it clear that local churches did not always operate at their best; there is no such thing as an 'ideal' or 'perfect' New Testament Church from which the later Church departed; yet, at its best, a sense of fellowship broke down barriers commonly erected in the wider society, barriers between men and women, Jew and non-Jew, rich and poor, slaves and free people. At its best, as Tertullian later noted, the Church was a community bound together in the love of God, immensely attractive to outsiders. Again, we are back to the question of a distinctive lifestyle for the local church. One of the joys of the village church, unlike more eclectic suburban churches, is the inclusiveness of the local church; in one of our Cotswold churches I recently witnessed a Lord and Lady kneeling at the altar rail next to the village blacksmith; old and young worship side by side.

Is a medieval building the best setting for fostering fellowship? Does a Grade 1 listed building allow sufficient flexibility? These issues are also explored by John Saxbee in Chapter 1 and Alastair Redfern in Chapter 13 of the present volume. Church growth practitioners have argued that every Christian needs to relate to other Christians at three different levels for the sake of a healthy Christian life: we need to relate to others within a cell group, at the level of congregation (30–50 people), and at the level of celebration event. In the rural setting, you will usually need a deanery-wide event in order to attract sufficient numbers for a celebration; for a congregational event of 50 to 90 people you will often need more than one benefice. The local church operates at cell level often in numerical terms; but would a cell group be more effective in a home than in a medieval building?

The Ministry of the Whole People of God

The concept of the Church as a fellowship includes the idea of a fellowship of gifts. It is not only in the Pauline letters that the idea of the Holy Spirit giving gifts to all members of the local church is found, it is in 1 Peter alongside a clear reference to duly appointed church leaders. The ministry of the whole people of God was a truth tragically lost sight of in the course of church history, with a growing emphasis on a special priesthood that at times seemed to have more in common with an Old Testament model of priesthood than any New Testament teaching. The Reformation challenged the inherited priestly model of the medieval Catholic Church and yet failed generally to release the gifts of the whole people of God. It simply replaced one kind of full-time professional, a cultic priestly figure standing behind the altar, with another full-time professional, standing six feet above criticism in a pulpit. It was to be another 400 years before the liberation of the whole people of God in ministry and mission began at last to get underway.

The ministry of the whole people of God has found its way on to the agenda in recent years in part due to the shortage of full-time stipendiary priests. However, there have also been theological factors at work, a recovery of important New Testament insights and Charismatic renewal with its emphasis on the work of the Holy Spirit in gifting individual Christians in unique ways. Many dioceses have introduced a variety of forms of lay ministry. The Diocese of Rochester has a variety of authorized ministries, pastoral assistants and lay evangelists alongside readers. In the Diocese of Gloucester, along with several other dioceses, we have in recent years developed local ministry teams. Such teams, consisting of lay and ordained members, are commissioned locally at the start of their training and mandated at a diocesan service. The commissioning and mandating make it crystal clear that the members of the local ministry teams are not there to undertake all the work of ministry and mission, but rather are a sign and a model of the ministry and mission to which God calls every member of the Church. The clergy are not set over against the teams, but are themselves members of the team. Once the team has been in existence for a time, it is hoped that the members of the team will identify one or more of their number as a suitable candidate for Ordained Local Ministry.

Part of the ethos of Local Ministry teams in the Diocese of Gloucester is that they might take the place of the local incumbent in multi-parish benefices which have been particularly hard hit by the reduction in the number of full-time clergy. In some cases a local ministry team operates at parish level, while in other cases across a benefice. In the future we envisage a team operating across a whole deanery. We are looking to introduce a team ministry, for example, in the former Winchcombe deanery (an area comprising a population of 8,500 with 5,500 based in Winchcombe and with 16 churches) and in Fairford deanery (with 23 churches, 2 small market towns, many small villages and a total population of 11,000). We envisage such team ministries being 'serviced' by a team rector, one or more team vicars, a curate in training, some house-for-duty clergy, readers, possibly a deanery youth worker, part-time administrator and a local ministry team serving the whole area or subdivided into several smaller, more local teams.

Along with the Diocese of Oxford (Dorchester area) and aware of the national government initiative relating to market towns as resource centres for outlying villages, we are exploring ways in which we can make better use of our market town churches as resource centres for multi-parish benefices. Helpful work in this area has also been undertaken by the Arthur Rank Centre.

Mission and Evangelism

Any engagement in mission and evangelism needs to be from a sufficiently broad understanding of mission. Here the five marks of mission developed by the Anglican Consultative Council and warmly affirmed by other Churches provide a helpfully full definition (see Warren, 1996: 7):

- to proclaim the good news of the kingdom;
- to teach, baptize, and nurture new believers;
- to respond to human need by loving service;
- to seek to transform the unjust structures of society;
- to strive to safeguard the integrity of creation and sustain and renew the life of the earth.

The picture Acts 2 offers of evangelism is what might be referred to as spontaneous church growth. Luke writes of a Church with such an attractive lifestyle that every day new people were drawn in, added to the Church by the Lord of the Church. Whether or not that is an idealized picture, certainly elsewhere the New Testament assumes lay Christians will live out the good news and will be prepared to be articulate about their faith, about the distinctive hope they have as Christians, a hope rooted in the death and resurrection of Jesus Christ. Alongside a picture of evangelism as a natural spontaneous outworking of faith, we have noted a clear evangelistic strategy on the part of St Paul, a strategy based on planting churches in cities and then encouraging those churches to reach out into surrounding rural areas with the good news. Roland Allen (1912) was undoubtedly right to argue that the primary agent for evangelism in an area is the local church, entrusted with responsibility by God to share the good news of Jesus Christ with its particular locality.

Bishop Michael Nazir-Ali (1990), while General Secretary of the Church Mission Society, argued similarly for the primary responsibility of the local church for its own local mission, but then in addition he finds an important place for partnerships in mission. Although in the past those tended to be one-way between the West and countries in

Africa, for example, fostering an unhelpful dependence of African churches on missionaries and mission agencies, today there is a more helpful biblically based sense of partnership in the gospel, with Christians from parts of Africa coming to stand alongside us in some of our toughest mission contexts.

For our rural communities it is the local church that has the primary responsibility for evangelism and mission in its own context. Yet, often that missionary enterprise will be facilitated best by a sense of partnership, certainly across a benefice, often across a deanery. For example, one of the deaneries in Gloucester Diocese with 23 churches, including two small market towns and many small villages, runs a deanery Alpha course producing adult confirmation candidates each year; a small village church attempting to run something similar could never be as effective. It is vital wherever possible to work ecumenically. There is an important role for the diocese, providing resources, for example, to train and support youth workers, to provide youth camps to help young people grow in their Christian discipleship, encouraged by meeting with other young Christians from across the diocese, and to provide resources for youth congregations in the local deanery.

One advantage of developing a deanery missionary strategy is that in addition to a focus on the local parish, the traditional Church of England mission unit, it is possible to focus too on a variety of networks across a wider area. There is considerable evidence that in twenty-first-century Britain any effective missionary strategy must take networks as well as more geographical contexts seriously. Any such deanery mission strategy needs to take seriously the five marks of mission agreed ecumenically.

Stephen Croft (2002) argues that it is not enough simply to engage in pastoral reorganization, giving more and more parishes to a single parish priest. We have to look at mission strategies which reimagine (to use his language) the Church for the twenty-first century. He lays out theological foundations and gives many practical examples; such experiments must be worked out in the rural context where the challenge is particularly great to ensure that the Church does not just continue to exist for the next ten or twenty years (though that in itself is a considerable challenge), but proves to be vibrant and growing, an effective missionary agent in our contemporary world.

REFERENCES

Abbott, W. M. (ed.) (1966), *The Documents of Vatican II*, London, Geoffrey Champman.

Allen, R. (1912), *Missionary Methods: St Paul's or Ours?* London, Robert Scott.

Archbishops' Commission on Rural Areas (1990), *Faith in the Countryside*, Worthing, Churchman.

Avis, P. (1981), *The Church in the Theology of the Reformers*, London, Marshalls.

Barth, K. (1933), *The Epistle to the Romans*, Oxford, Oxford University Press.

Barth, K. (1936–81), *Church Dogmatics*, Edinburgh, T. and T. Clark.

Bonhoeffer, D. (1954), *Life Together*, London, SCM Press.

Bonhoeffer, D. (1981), *Letters and Papers from Prison Abridged Edition*, London, SCM Press.

Brunner, E. (1952), *The Misunderstanding of the Church*, London, Lutterworth.

Congar, Y. (1984), *Diversity and Communion*, London, SCM Press.

Cox, H. (1965), *The Secular City*, London, SCM Press.

Croft, S. (1999), *Ministry in Three Dimensions*, London, Darton Longman and Todd.

Croft, S. (2002), *Transforming Communities*, London, Darton Longman and Todd.

Dulles, A. (1976), *Models of the Church*, Dublin, Gill and Macmillan.

Forsyth, P. T. (1917), *The Church and Sacraments*, London, Hodder and Stoughton.

Kraft, C. H. (1981), *Christianity in Culture*, New York, Orbis.

Kuhrt, G. (ed.) (2001), *Ministry Issues*, London, Church House Publishing.

Methodist Church (1993), *Disciple: Becoming Disciples through Bible Study*, Nashville, Tennessee, Abingdon.

Minear, P. S. (1961), *Images of the Church in the New Testament*, London, Lutterworth.

Nazir-Ali, M. (1990), *From Everywhere to Everywhere: A World View of Christian Mission*, General Rapids, Michigan, Zondervan.

Robinson, J. A. T. (1965), *The New Reformation*, Philadelphia, Westminster.

Thomas, N. (ed.) (1995), *Readings in World Mission*, London, SPCK.

Turnbull, M. (2001), 'The Parish System', in G. Kuhrt (ed.) *Ministry Issues*, London, Church House Publishing, pp. 213–15.

Walls, A. (2002), *The Cross-Cultural Process in Christian History*, New York, Orbis.

Warren. R. (1996), *Signs of Life: How Goes the Decade of Evangelism*, London, Church House Publishing.

13. Listening to the Anglican Tradition

ALASTAIR L. J. REDFERN

Summary

What can the Anglican tradition, in a rural context, highlight in terms of proclaiming and enacting the gospel of Jesus Christ for the twenty-first century? This chapter will offer an outline answer to that question, using a case study of a benefice in Fenland Lincolnshire. The basic premise is that the uniqueness of the Anglican tradition is focused upon the parochial system, and our chief challenge is to re-form this gift to be a continuing tool for God's invitation to all his people to embrace the path to salvation more firmly.

Parish and Place

The parish depends for its identity upon a proper sense of 'place': not simply upon the provision of priesthood or other forms of ministry. These are often subsequent to, and dependent upon, a sense of placedness which is the bedrock of the inclusive, incarnational strand in Anglican theology, most powerfully articulated by the all embracing notion of laws in the work of Richard Hooker (Hooker, 1907). God's purposes, human potential and choices, and the working of creation are all encompassed in a single system, wherein the notions of correspondence and appropriateness provide common measuring rods and guides (Redfern, 2000: 14–24).

In the parish system this quintessential Anglican (and Aristotelian) theology is quite literally earthed. Thus in the development of a Christian culture in the British Isles, the presence of monastic communities and holy saints in the Celtic tradition met with Roman organization of dioceses from Augustine of Canterbury, working through those who controlled the land, to form a Church of England that was located in places (Brooke, 1999: 3–6).

This sense of place was initially 'incarnated' by bishops, and by monastic communities which acted as 'minsters', servicing a wide area of hinterland (Godfrey, 1969: 13–21). More locally, Christians set up stone crosses to be a focus of presence and for meeting together (Godfrey, 1969: 27–9). Eventually these crosses were succeeded by church buildings, which were initially resourced from minsters, but by the twelfth century the parish system had been more widely established in Europe, and ministry was provided locally through endowment of a living and the licensing of an incumbent by the bishop (Addleshaw, 1953: 10–15).

In the context of the argument of this chapter, it is important to notice the sequence. First, as the faith is spread, Christians find focus and identity in a local area around a stone cross: apostolic, representative ministry is provided from minster/monastic centres. Second, Christians find focus and identity in a local area in a church building established by private initiative, while more formal ministry is still provided from minster/monastic centres (Godfrey, 1969: 30–1; Wright, 1988: 9–10). Third, Christians find focus and identity in a local area in a church building and a local ministry.

Thus the provision of a focus in terms of place, precedes the provision of a focus in terms of formal ministry and a representative 'persona' who is locally based. This sequence indicates something profoundly important about Anglican theology: the experience of God's grace is always earthed in a particular context, to which formal representative public ministry provides resource. In this sense, place comes before parson or 'persona'. (See also the point made by John Saxbee in Chapter 1 of the present volume.) This chapter will explore the significance of this bedrock of Anglican tradition for the twenty-first century.

Being a Parish in a Plural World

The case study to be used in this chapter involves a millennium project in a group of three villages in Fenland Lincolnshire. Each community was very different, as was each congregation. One congregation focused on children and young families, with a wide range of regular workshops, activities and special services. One congregation was more concerned to preserve its traditional pattern and ethos of worship. One congregation was a small group of mainly elderly people.

At one level this scenario illustrates the collapse of the parochial system. Large but incompatible demands from each congregation could put enormous pressure upon the one person trying to be 'vicar' to each of them. The variety of approaches to worship and mission could be seen as indicative of the incoherence of the Church of England, particularly in terms of offering any kind of 'common' worship and witness to those outside.

Here was not an untypical recipe for clergy stress, lay frustration and widespread community indifference. How could there be a way of upholding the 'parish' system of a church in every community, while recognizing the inevitable variety of tastes, needs and aspirations in these places, let alone among members of each congregation? Such a situation might make it seem almost inevitable that the minister should be drawn even more deeply into servicing the complex needs of the church membership, while the wider notion of 'parish' therefore appears to be increasingly irrelevant.

www.thedisappearanceofplace.com

I spend a great deal of my time in rural Lincolnshire driving behind huge lorries, as the nation's food is ferried out on a daily basis. When I arrived in 1997, I would sometimes follow a large vehicle, being able to read on the back 'Marshall-Butterwick' with an address and telephone number. I had visited Marshall's farm and factory, and thus I could interpret this information to 'place' that vehicle, its role and purpose. Here is something fundamental to human culture for millennia: the central importance of 'place' to role and identity. In the twenty-first century, as I drive behind these awesome trucks, all I can see on the back is www.freshfoods.com. I do not have a clue if the lorry is local, or from Portugal or Spain, or anywhere else. Place is unimportant. The key is function and efficient communication. That is a mark of the 'global' world in which we all live.

In this 'global' context, with its accent upon mobility, people relate to a whole host of 'places'. To be rich is no longer expressed by means of a 'stately' home: today the accent is upon owning a number of homes in different locations. Identity and function are rooted in the liberal project which invites everyone to construct their own space and lifestyle, with the minimum of constraints and the maximum of opportunities for new experiences and money-making possibilities (Grasso, Bradley and Hunt, 1995: 2; Himmelfarb, 1994: 74–107). The paradox is that this model of entrepreneurial freedom is the germ of enormous conflicts, competition and stress (Giddens, 1991: 2–7).

This 'model' of human being, the www.model, is characteristic of the 'urban' culture we all inhabit, even in the depths of south Lincolnshire. Brueggemann argues that as 'urban' people we are displaced: instead we move in 'space' which can be a weekend, a holiday, an experience, a task, a relationship (Brueggemann, 1978: 5). All of these 'spaces' are designed to enable our freedom and have a necessary future orientation sustained by our faith in progress, growth and development. By contrast, rural culture has been focused in the centrality of place, which brings roots, restrictions, commitments and an obligation to the past as formational of that locality.

The parish is quintessentially a 'place'. Its demise is increasingly predicted by a generation encouraged by our all-pervasive urban culture, desiring to live in the freedom given by 'spaces'. The reality of this choice, being made so widely at the beginning of the twenty-first century, is the stress of being dislocated and displaced, a refugee populace abandoning parish and the responsibilities it brings.

This background underpins the separated, 'voluntary' nature of the Christian congregations in the three churches of our case study, and the apparent distance between the local church and the local community.

The 'Parish' Project

In 1999 the vicar of the three parishes gathered a small group to plan a project which would try to give the Christian congregations a sense of common purpose and practice in terms of their missionary outreach, and also aim to invite all those resident in each community to own and celebrate their particular placedness, with all its limitations and responsibilities. The project was to put on a series of mystery plays. This idea sprang from the success of an adult nativity play in which the vicar played a donkey! A local teacher was recruited to write the plays, loosely based upon the stories of Noah (creation, flood and a covenant of new life), the nativity (the birth of Jesus of Nazareth), and Easter (the crucifixion and resurrection).

Publicity, meetings and auditions recruited a cast and a whole host of back-up people for each of the three plays. The primary school supported the project, children made masks and many participated as animals. A large-scale enterprise was the making of the costumes. Local farmers agreed to provide a long trailer, plus a tractor for each play.

Months of preparation drew a large number of people, church and non-church, into this common enterprise and into the discipline, commitment and corporate vision required to produce such an ambitious project. The scale of the project was matched by the degree of support and investment offered from each community. A sense of being together in a 'place' was being enfleshed around three foundational stories from scripture. Rehearsals and meetings always began and ended with prayer, to emphasize that all these activities were marks of a desire to be a Christian community, rather than to be a more narrowly 'church' community. Covenant to make a common community project around the gospel story was the key, rather than conformity to particular liturgical or ecclesial practices.

On the great day, the casts assembled. There was much excitement as costumes were given a finishing touch and makeup applied. The first play was performed in the centre of one of the villages, with suitable local references. It was enthusiastically received by a crowd which had gathered around the trailer. The first play was then towed on to the next village for a repeat performance before another audience, and then to the third village. Back at base, the second play was performed, before moving on, and then the third. In each place people had gathered around the Christian stories, ministered to them by this travelling co-operative of church members and associated supporters. By the time that the third play reached the final village, there was a vast crowd, including all the other performers. This story was a localized version of the resurrection of Jesus Christ from the dead, the kernel of the Christian gospel. It was followed by a wonderful party uniting all ages and all comers.

The gospel story had been enacted and owned in each 'place', gathering a wide cross-section of each community to tell this story, to hold it up for public inspection, and to be the focus of a joy and richness in being thus located, across all the usual divisions and differences. Around these 'ministerial teams' had gathered local residents to share this moment of interaction between 'being together in that particular place' and elements of the gospel message. The memory and the impetus thus achieved have long continued to bear fruit and energize networks, friendships and resources for the well-being of each 'parish', both for Christians gathering for worship, and for neighbours connecting more fruitfully in a common place. Examples of 'placed' activities arising from the project include the establishment of a men's group and of a sewing group.

Good News Placement

Beneath the welter of freedom-bringing self-concerned opportunities which characterize modern culture, people actually find their identities and appreciation of 'truth' by gossiping in small groups, in particular places. Even those who form relationships via internet chat rooms have to confront the fact that for any such connection to come to proper fruition, those concerned need to leave the self-serving security of their screens and stand on common ground, face to face. Human being and human relationship has to be placed, located in particularity. Brueggemann calls this necessity 'storied space' (Brueggemann, 1978: 5–7): it requires commitment, and a willingness to risk engaging in what is therefore, quite literally, a shared perspective on the world. This shared perspective is inevitably parochial: a local, common placedness. Yet this sharing of a common perspective, even if interpreted in radically different ways, is the key building block of that greater harmony and more positive connection that human beings so desperately seek.

This is not just a convenient pastoral remedy to the loneliness and isolation brought to us by our urban, freedom-seeking world. More important, joining our stories with those of others, around the greater, and potentially common narratives of creation, salvation and resurrection to new life, provides the germ of faith, hope and love whereby meaning and truth are focused. To be 'placed' can be good news, as this project made so clear, irrespective of whether or not this includes involvement in the Church as an organization.

The Pressures of Placement

However, the project was not without its tensions and its heartaches. There were plenty of struggles, disagreements (even rows!) and disappointments. There was the usual fare of gossip, backbiting and clique forming which accompanies human enterprise. This reality about fallen humanity is somehow more appreciable in the rural context. Our urban world calls for struggle and victory, with evaluation in terms of success or failure, and the measure is made in terms of competency and performance. Life is seen as linear, in terms of progress and development. Backsliding and backbiting are both discerned as dysfunctional. Impatience and frustration come from any falling short.

In a rural environment, the predominant reality is the rhythm of the seasons, the ongoing tension between darkness and light, sowing and harvesting. (For a similar suggestion see John Saxbee in Chapter 1 of the present volume.) There is an inevitable element of waiting and watching, feeling the vagaries of the weather. Humanity is much more clearly boundaried, fallible, dependent. Life is cyclical and not simply linear. Human prayerfulness is not just about progressing, but also about waiting, watching, wondering and walking in the wilderness in anticipation of a greater blessing.

Urbanization was originally an attempt by human beings to protect themselves from the mysterious powers of nature: the unknown elements in not just climate, but in those other than kin. Religion provided rituals and stories to illuminate these boundaries and give clues as to how they might be handled. But from the earliest of times a more direct 'solution' was for people to band together in larger settlements, surround themselves with walls, and trust in their own powers and ingenuity to feed and protect themselves. Urban culture has always contained the germ of a defiant human independence (that is, the biblical story of Jerusalem); religion has tended to be useful for the ultimate boundary issues of birth, love and death. Rurality has been the stronger ground for a less anthropomorphic religious fervour in the western world, embracing inclusive, mysterious gatherings around tradition and buildings, which provide a determinative, and protective framework for the unfolding of human living. Rurality has fostered a spirituality of essential dependence, rather than one of confident and progressive creativity.

But a major feature for the twenty-first century in the western world is that the self-confident all-pervasive urban world is itself threatening rural life and the entire planet. Urban population and aggression threatens to overwhelm the 'natural' world with contamination if not downright destruction. The religion of this urban world is anthropo-logical, plural, future-orientated and displaced. The key factors are quality and service for consumers, provided by competent staff and sensitive leadership. The Divine has lost authority and relevance, by failing to provide these positive systems deemed so necessary for modern well-being and human flourishing. Thus the language and concerns of so much religion (including urban Anglicanism, our general way of being Anglican in today's world) is that of structures, organization, and relevance to context. The agendas are dominated by maintaining clerical numbers and presence, accessibility and account-ability. Lay involvement in church life must be increasingly accredited, with benchmarks and competencies undermining local autonomies (Roberts, 2001: 162–4). Little is heard of sin, repentance, crucifixion and resurrection: the agenda of the supernatural.

By contrast, the Anglican tradition is focused upon a rural notion of placedness, interconnection, dependency upon the otherness of God, a counter-cultural critique of contemporary capitalism. The keys are stories of creation, salvation and resurrection from the dead: not by human achievement, but by the gracious gift of God to those who can face up to the reality of the wilderness, and who can learn to wait and watch and pray. Rhythms are as important as progressive plans. Darkness, death and the gloom of the 1662 *Book of Common Prayer* are as constant ingredients to the spiritual life as light, love and new life.

Placement brings pressures: the crucial question is how are these pressures to be handled?

The Promise of Place

When Michael Ramsey was grappling with these tensions, which have long dominated church life, he argued that Anglicanism 'is sent not to commend itself as "the best type of Christianity", but by its brokenness to point to the universal Church wherein all have died' (Ramsey, 1936: 220). He recognized the basic truth which Paul and Augustine strove to safeguard, 'that the Church will always be a *corpus permixtum*: a mixed body' (Augustine, 1996: 189). Hooker made this notion a bedrock of his understanding of the Anglican tradition: 'for lack of diligence observing the difference, first between the Church of God mystical and visible, then between the visible sound and corrupted, sometimes more, sometimes less' (Hooker, 1907: 289). Anglican tradition has always been all-embracing. This is at the heart of the legal definition of the parish. Every resident is treated as a member, with the freedom to come and claim the marks of membership as and when they choose, and on their terms. This models something fundamental and amazing about the grace of God in Jesus Christ.

While some gather to form committed worshipping congregations, raised up to hold this gospel in each place, most will come on their own terms and in their own way. The 'common' ground, though clearly located in the great stories of creation, salvation and resurrection, is best introduced and offered by inviting this large diaspora to connect with the church community and with each other in terms of their most basic human need. Hence the tradition of offering appropriate 'moments' which give focus to placedness, in terms of both relationships and geography.

Yet, beyond these well-tried, and still well-used, 'occasional' offices, there is an urgent task to offer 'moments' which invite people to leave their personal screens, and engage with others in common commitments and visions, focused on the human need to be 'placed', and in that context to be noticed. The gathering element is not specific assent to any doctrines, nor to a code of behaviour, but rather it is participation on an occasion commonly observed, around which stories and perspectives are shared.

People come together for this 'common-ness' and are then free to 'use' their experience as they choose. But the discipline and commitment of place has been acknowledged. In this sense much of the practice of Anglicanism is always hidden, beyond the purview of the institution, simply the activity of grace amid the mixed bunch of humanity. The rural Church has always lived with this frustrating mystery: the danger of our current urbanization is a narrowing of concerns to that of the performance and well-being of the institutional Church and its public image. According to Cranmer in the *Book of Common Prayer*, we gather for these occasions of worship and communion, 'for all such good works as thou hast prepared for us to walk in'.

The project in these Lincolnshire parishes was one way of producing this opportunity. It would work equally well in an urban environment, but its essence is a hallmark of an Anglican rural tradition which holds a precious key to handling the gospel in a new century by acknowledging the foundational importance of being together in a particular place for identity, commitment and common life.

Place and People

There is a tendency to proclaim that 'the Church' is the people, not the building or the clergy. Although this is true in the New Testament accounts, such an analysis becomes dangerous and simplistic when it is proclaimed uncritically in an age which puts people first, and is concerned with human rights. Karl Lowith, a German philosopher in the twentieth century, highlighted this issue by distinguishing between 'the human world' and 'the world' (Wolin, 2001: 76–7). The former is existence observed and measured from a human standpoint: it summarizes an increasing tendency in western culture. However, to operate within the 'human world' is to ignore the reality of a much greater and more mysterious 'world', the cosmos itself, the context which makes humankind a small and very dependent part of a more extensive whole. Lowith insists that this humbling perspective is the truth which religion safeguards (an argument also advanced by William Temple, 1940: 66–8) and for Christians such an insight raises serious questions about the relative priority and importance of the Church as building or people/clergy.

Jesus was always quick to put the mystery of human being (the human world) into a bigger context (the world), using material reference points such as the temple and its disciplines, bread, wine, sunset and sunrise, oil and spittle, all aspects of materialism charged with something of the supernatural. This wider emphasis gives an important clue, fundamental to the Anglican tradition, about the importance of buildings and the *Prayer Book*, both signs of the world which is common to all human beings: tangibility as a carrier of transcendence.

In one of the villages in our case study benefice the church was attended by only four people. The church building was in poor repair. The vicar visited every home in the village to seek support for restoration work. We held consultative meetings. Apart from the four regular worshippers, each of whom also attended services in the other villages, there was no interest in saving this building. Reluctantly and with the advice and support of the diocese, the decision was taken to explore the possibility of declaring the church building redundant. Suddenly, all hell seemed to break loose! The vicar was accosted in the churchyard by a person wielding a shotgun, her car was damaged, rotten eggs were pushed through her letter box. A very raw nerve had been touched.

At present the process regarding redundancy is still underway, but there is a clear lesson. The church building is more important in a rural community than the (non-resident) vicar, and more significant for local people than the presence and activities of the small congregation. This is not simply superstition, or the undoubted power of the profound combination of stone, glass and wood which clearly does connect with spiritual feelings. Rather, in a reality which has steadily contracted to the 'human world', with the clergy as a professionally trained 'human' face of the Church, there is a growing realization that such representatives are not at all dependable. The clergy are often no longer resident in the community, their availability and their skills are both limited, their human foibles are more honestly owned, and sometimes cruelly exposed. Clergy tend to move after five or six years. The 'human world' is fallible, sometimes unreliable and often focused upon its own concerns.

By contrast, the church building stands for the dependability of God, and for God's power and presence as located, permanent and enduring. No wonder people in rural communities give priority to the Church as building rather than as clergy or people. And in a sense, this instinct is right. Urban churches, too, need to consider the importance of place in terms of a holy building: something which can speak with eloquence of the greater glory, power and dependability of God, of the 'world' as God's cosmos, literally transcending the human world with its transitoriness and fallibilities. The building is dependable, holy, and transcendent of the normal human world in a way which a professionalized clergy and a struggling congregation cannot hope to incarnate.

And yet, in the countryside, a major concern with church buildings is the focus on installing toilets. Such projects are certainly important, but on their own they concentrate upon matters practical, utilitarian and anthropocentric. Henry Scott Holland famously stated that the incarnation demanded a proper concern with drains, but only as a prologue to far greater realities.

Thus, if the church building is to be nurtured and honoured as a place which gives focus to the world, and not just to the convenience of the human world, then it might be more important to encourage investment in beautifying the holy space, and promoting those occasional moments whereby busy secular people can confront each other and the transcending dependability of God.

The church building, under the stewardship of an outward-looking congregation, can be an agent of associational religion as well as a focus for gathered worship, providing a place that enables a variety of responses, including the inarticulate and that of participating by mental association and spiritual aspiration, while apparently maintaining a distance and a detachment. The 'humanization' of clerical roles has tended to undermine the potential for the vicar to fulfil this more mystical representative role, and it may be that the future of the gospel as a call to transcendence in our material human world will depend more than ever upon the maintenance of such a holy place in the midst of each community. A place separated and yet connected, utilitarian and yet mysterious, a focus for the groaning of the whole of creation (Romans 8.22–23). Every community needs such a sign of presence, purpose and participation, a place which is public, accessible and open, a representative place, local and located. Local Christians need to gather in such places, rehearse the stories of the gospel and invite their neighbours to participate. Sometimes the first move may involve providing something more transient and engaging to highlight this connection between the faith and people's placedness, such as a trailer carrying a mystery play.

The Church was not established at Pentecost by a word which drew a congregation. The Church was established, as Hooker (1907: 229) makes clear, out of the bleeding side of Jesus Christ where the limitation and mortality of the human world seeks salvation in a greater world. Our heritage of church buildings and faithful congregations provides a focus and a place for recalling and re-enacting this mystery. Rural Britain still nurtures the germ of this fundamental truth about the workings of the Christian gospel.

Place Before Parson/Persona?

The strategy of the benefice project highlighted in the case study, recognized the importance of the sequence from which the Anglican tradition of parish and place developed.

The mystery plays were equivalent to setting up a stone cross, inviting Christians and others to gather at a particular place in the midst of the community, to explore a common commitment and perspective around the great stories of creation, salvation and resurrection. Any 'place' needs a reference point, whereby a covenant of common endeavour and exploration can be offered resources from the formal ministry of the Church: in this case the vicar, a non-stipendiary minister, and recognized lay leaders.

Subsequent developments have led to an increased focus upon both church-based activities (men's group, sewing group, children's workshop days) and the church building. In the most lively village the sense of placedness has continued through a regular coffee morning held in the church, where general neighbourliness and conversation unfold alongside a prayer corner and the opportunity to light candles, both of which have become increasingly valued, especially by those not involved in Sunday worship. This coffee morning in the church building is the occasion most used by those who want to cash the inclusivity of the Anglican tradition in terms of coming to seek out the vicar or other local representative ministers to make arrangements for occasional offices, the blessing of homes or rings, and other moments of encounter.

The classical sequence is being re-enacted and re-established. First, the stone cross/the mystery plays provide a place for focus in the community, around acknowledgement of the gospel stories, a place open to all, resourced by the formal ministry of the Church. Second, the church building, open and accessible, provides connection with the formal ministry, and incarnates something of the transcendence and dependability of God. Third, an organized, public 'representative' ministry develops a locally based and owned role, operating in pubs and halls, as well as in the church building. This localized ministry rests upon connection and credibility established by, and dependent upon, this process rooted in the reality and power of acknowledging the human need for 'placedness'.

The Parish Is more than one Place

An obvious danger of lauding the importance of place, is the fact that the nature of this boundariedness and limitation too easily becomes

monochrome and restrictive in a destructive way. Sadly Anglican
parochialism has often operated in this narrowing sense (for example
see Morris, 1992), and in the contemporary Church with its carefully
chosen liturgical preferences, this becomes the seed of a gathered club
with its own exclusive ethos and membership.

But the parish does not have to be monochrome and excluding in
this way. In the thirteenth century, as urbanization first developed in
Europe, and as the original minster models of churches gave way to a
series of local autonomous parish churches, each separately endowed
and staffed, there was always a flexibility and pluralism about the
sense of place.

For example, in south Lincolnshire, in 1284 Castle Bytham ceased
to be part of a group of some 20 churches serviced on a minster model,
and was finally endowed and established as a parish in its own right
(Brooke, 1999: 14–15, 33–4). Yet 100 years later, in 1389 in the nearby parish of All Saints, Holbeach, a guild of shepherds was established, to provide a structure of worship, including candles being lit
and the elevation of the host at the mass, for those whose lifestyles
prevented them from making the normal regular commitment to
church attendance (Wright, 1988: 34). Thus a dual system was being
developed in terms of the parish as place. On the one hand it provided
a place for the traditional gathered worship and witness of the local
people; while on the other hand, provision was made for a separate
system of loose association, focused in occasional provision of
worship, candles being lit and the activities of guilds and chantries,
often organized and controlled by lay people (including the employment of clergy for particular tasks) to provide opportunities for
worship and pastoral care (Wright, 1988: 30–3).

Guilds were increasingly important after the solidification of the
parish system by the end of the twelfth century. New and shifting communities which grew as the result of developing urbanization required
a more flexible framework for placedness and connection. Guilds and
chantries provided networks of interest, based upon the conscious
commitment of participants, and depended upon the contribution of
members: thus they lacked the inclusivity of the parish and were not
organized to help the poor or other non-members. However, their
'placedness' in terms of the parish, its church building, and an overlap
in the use of the resources of formal representative ministry, ensured a
duality of systems which allowed rural rootedness and urban flexible

mobility to remain earthed in a common sense of place and its supportive ministerial systems (Brigden, 2001: 78–84).

The 'parish', in its developed Anglican form, never claimed to have a monopoly of the spiritual life and its attendant pastoral and pedagogical systems. There was scope for lay initiatives to establish networks of commitment and common concern, nourishing spiritual life as appropriate, and offering separate schemes for pastoral engagement. The interaction between the all-inclusive parish and any guilds and chantries servicing particular interests and concerns is the true basis of the Anglican tradition of the outworking and exploration of gospel agenda being 'placed' within specific locations and their resident communities.

This flexible and plural approach to place is characteristic of our case study parishes too. Alongside the gathered regular committed congregation in each community, endeavours such as the mystery plays, the regular children's workshops and a whole host of occasional activities, including services in pubs but often centred upon the church building, all serve to provide a web of opportunities for association in a myriad of ways. Each of these ways is highlighted by worship, and the blessing of networks for sharing and caring, thereby catering for those whose lifestyle and priorities preclude a regular commitment in the conventional way.

This plural use of place has a long pedigree, and is something that rural and urban churches need to rekindle if the properly inclusive tradition of Anglicanism is to be honoured in our time. It is a tradition peculiarly suited to a century beginning its life with the label 'postmodern'. A number of systems and ecclesiologies coinhere in a place: that is to say in a geographic localness, a particular building, and a common life founded upon the proximity of neighbourliness and the resources of a public representative ministry.

The Parish as Place: Refocused

We face a moment when there are strong temptations to abandon the parish system and its focus on placedness, in favour of modes of operation which would appear to be more flexible, more amenable to particular constituencies, and more targeted and efficient in terms of performance, use of resources and results. The outcome would be a retreat into a sect-like security and the canons of mere self-satisfaction.

The Anglican tradition seeks to honour a gospel that is radically inclusive in invitation and in operation. It was well-summarized by Archdeacon Dealtry. In *A Charge Delivered at the Visitation in Hampshire in 1838*, he argued that the parish system is designed to:

> afford the means of religious instruction and of public worship to the entire population . . . not, however, interfering with any man's conscience, but taking care that everyone who wishes for these benefits shall have the opportunity to possess them . . . The obligations of the Church are co-extensive with the spiritual wants of the people. (Dealtry, 1838: 3)

In our all-pervasive urban culture, which has been characterized as consisting of individuals adrift in a universe without fixed bearings, with self-fulfilment as the chief aim, and any sense of meaning being dependent upon the subjective unification of fragmented experience (Hervieu-Leger, 2000: 165), there is an urgent need to recognize anew the treasures of our Anglican rural tradition. The notion of place and parish offers a number of stable, transcendent reference points and a clear meta-narrative, earthed most clearly in church buildings, faithful congregations, the holy scriptures, the creeds and liturgies of common worship, and a unified apostolic system of public ministry. These resources for new life coinhere in the tradition of the parish and provide a foundation from which a wide range of gospel responses to the mysteries of this life can be made in a connected, focused and earthed manner. Moreover, this model of 'parish' as placedness provides scope for lay ownership of the local church and offers a healthy undermining of the centrifugal forces of institutionalized Christianity which so easily coagulates around a clerical, professional organization. To be human is to be placed. That is the fundamental reality about the gift of life embodied by Jesus of Nazareth.

In our case study, the initial, and therefore crucial impetus which brought people into connection with the local church was not the gospel story, nor the existence of the regular worshipping congregation, rather it was recognition of a significant event (the mystery play, involving neighbours) happening in the midst of their particular place, and thus inviting their attention and participation. Once the contact had been established, the common sense of placedness provided a foundation for further interaction, a renewed appreciation of the church building and a greater readiness to engage with public representative ministers and with the local congregation. Being-together-in-a-particular-place became the means of stimulating conversation, co-operative working to meet local needs, and the development of that shared perspective which opens people's eyes to the greater agenda of the kingdom.

To engage with biodiversity, diet, globalism, agriculture, community, culture and any other issues of rurality requires this kind of underpinning. There can be great debate about the more easily identifiable resources of Anglican theology: the emphasis upon incarnation; the interplay between scripture, tradition, reason and experience; the dynamic between what is given and what might be; the system of authority which is focused, yet participative and consultative. However, all these resources rest on something more basic in terms of an Anglican tradition of theology: the notion of a common life, in a common place for common concerns and interests, moments of exploring the possibilities of a common perspective. Larger areas of catholicity and connection, for instance dioceses or provinces, or towns, regions and nation states, all depend for their effectiveness upon these qualities and opportunities being modelled and available at a more local and accessible level. If there is one connecting theme running throughout our Lord's own ministry, it is that he was always going on to the next village. Rural communities have always provided an important model of how the gospel works: the focus is upon the identity and connections made around a sense of parish and place.

REFERENCES

Addleshaw, G. W. O. (1953), *The Beginnings of the Parochial System*, London, St Anthony's Press.
Augustine (1996), *De Doctrina Christiana*, New York, New City Press.
Brigden, S. (2001), *New Worlds, Lost Worlds*, London, Penguin.
Brooke, C. N. L. (1999), *Churches and Churchmen in Medieval Europe*, London, The Hambledon Press.
Brueggemann, W. (1978), *The Land*, London, SPCK.
Dealtry, W. (1838), *A Charge Delivered at the Visitation in Hampshire: September 1838*, London, J. Hatchard & Son.
Giddens, A. (1991), *Modernity and Self-Identity*, Oxford, Polity Press.
Godfrey, J. (1969), *The English Parish 600–1300*, London, SPCK.

Grasso, K., Bradley, G. and Hunt, R. (1995), *Catholicism, Liberalism and Communitarianism,* London, Rowman and Littlefield.

Hervieu-Leger D. (2000), *Religion as a Chain of Memory,* Oxford, Polity Press.

Himmelfarb, G. (1994), *On Looking Into the Abyss,* New York, Knopf.

Hooker, R. (1907), *Of the Laws of Ecclesiastical Polity,* London, J. M. Dent.

Morris, J. N. (1992), *Religion and Urban Change,* Woodbridge, The Boydell Press.

Ramsey, A. M. (1936), *The Gospel and the Catholic Church,* London, Longmans Green.

Redfern, A. (2000), *Being Anglican,* London, Darton Longman and Todd.

Roberts, R. H. (2001), *Religion, Theology and the Human Sciences,* Cambridge, Cambridge University Press.

Temple, W. (1940), *The Hope of a New World,* London, SCM Press.

Wolin, R. (2001), *Heidegger's Children,* Princeton, New Jersey, Princeton University Press.

Wright, S. (ed.) (1988), *Parish, Church and People,* London, Hutchinson.

Theological Reflection

ROWAN WILLIAMS

The most basic question that has to be addressed by the Church in the countryside is how it is equipped both to hear and to communicate good news. This suggests that there can be no consideration of a rural theology that does not at the same time reflect on the relation between the rural and the urban. Good news is what we share in the Church. That is to say, no bit of the Church is going to know everything about the gift of God in Christ: the challenge is to manage the variety of human context and experience in the Church in such a way that it becomes a sharing of Christ with one another and so with the wider world. Mutual isolation and mutual confrontation between rural and urban are not options for the Christian. Like all Christian communities, they need each other.

But the relation is undoubtedly very complicated. For much of the Church's history, there was still an assumption somewhere around that the town–country connection was essentially that of market and producer. As towns acquired new identities by way of the concentrated development of both financial services and non-agrarian production, that is, through capitalism and industrialization, the assumption became increasingly unreal. But it is (surprisingly?) not true that the Church was wedded to agrarian styles and patterns, except in the lives of some monastic communities. Its early European development was regularly a story of movement from town to country; it was a major shaper of the urban life of the early Middle Ages as bishops emerged as protectors of the concentration of commerce in towns (and so ultimately protectors of incipient financial services) and cathedral schools, and later universities, attracted large transient populations of young adults.

Historically, then, it is not that the Church was bound in with a rural economy and timetable, rather that it was regularly on the town side of the relationship, so that its leadership and administration focused on urban locations, 'exporting' the faith to an imperfectly Christianized and rather threatening countryside. Thus, in spite of the powerful mythology of a religious countryside over against a godless town, the fact is that the Church, for all its eventually pervasive presence in the country, retained a model of moving *out* from town to country, with the attendant problems of decision-making being centred in towns. As the classical relations between town and country changed in the West, with the mutual dependence of producer and market practically vanishing as industrialization advanced, the focus of the Church's life remained in towns; what active mission, sharing good news *from* the country, might look like was seldom fully thought through.

So one aspect of trying to construct a theology for and of the rural Church is asking what is distinctive about rural Christian and human experience so that it can form an offering of Christ's good news to other kinds of community within the Church. I want to outline very briefly two aspects of this which may help focus discussion. They could summarily be described as having to do with a theology of *land* and a theology of *limit*.

Land

Rural life often involves anxiety and conflict over questions of land ownership and appropriate land use; yet the claim to 'own' land is a complex one, and its complexity is recognized by many in the countryside. There is a strong sense of something like trusteeship, an awareness that to own land is to be a steward and manager of long-term processes rather than simply the proprietor of a piece of disposable material territory. Those who treat it more in this latter way are often the object of disapproval or even incomprehension.

And the Christian might well want to connect this with the vision set out in Leviticus 25 (the 'jubilee' passage). The land is God's; it is not to be alienated in perpetuity from the families who originally occupy it because it is held in trust for God, so to speak. The sale or exchange of land is the sale of a certain number of harvests (v. 16), a matter of the specific use of the land for a period. And because it is God's, it must be granted a 'sabbath' every seventh year, so that the occupier may be reminded of the need to trust the giver; just as in the fiftieth year, the year of jubilee, all claims are cancelled, and there is a 'sabbath' for all activities involving profit, ownership, power over others as well as power over the soil.

The land given by God is more accurately *lent* to the human occupier for the particular purpose of cultivation; but that cultivation must not be carried out in a way that obscures the ultimate ownership of God. Land cannot be a commodity to be traded (hence the jubilee principle of redemption and return of land that has been leased, along with the remission of slavery in the fiftieth year; the principle is the same); its inalienability is not a matter of guaranteeing unchallengeable human ownership but rather the exact opposite, a testimony to the fact that it is not simply at the disposal of an occupier. So far from confirming some imagined Judaeo-Christian principle that puts the earth, the material environment, in a position of absolute subordination to humanity, this passage reserves to God the 'rights' over the processes of nature and commands practices that recall this to mind. God gives the land, but only as part of a gift that is mobile, developing, the gift of a system of life in whose processes human beings have a hugely significant but not isolated role. The trusteeship of land is only intelligible in connection with the injunctions to let the land enjoy its sabbath and to rectify the imbalances, including slavery, which emerge from our economic practice.

This is not simply a (potentially sentimental) exhortation for human beings to feel themselves part of a greater organic whole. It establishes something central about the nature of God's gifts, that they are never in any circumstance, rural or otherwise, given as dead objects to be hoarded. Land is given for harvests, harvests are given for just distribution; our human social activity has to continue the action of God in shaping an environment whose processes nurture life. The rural experience, interpreted in the light of this significant scriptural passage, begins to set the scene for understanding the supreme gift of God in Christ, why this is pre-eminently a gift given for sharing, the incorporation of human beings into a cosmic pattern of life-yielding and life-bestowing.

Limit

This testimony that the nature of God's gift precludes absolute possession or hoarding leads into the second theological theme, that of limit. There is no way in which rural experience can be tidied and sanitized into a controlled affair. Matters which in urban settings are mostly minor shifts and contingencies (weather is the obvious example) are in the country serious challenges and obstacles or dangers for cultivation, for travel, for supplies. From time to time, devastating epidemics take a grip on the countryside and affect everything in sight for long periods. Who in the countryside can yet forget the horrors of the Foot and Mouth plague in 2001? The patterns of growth and rhythm in rural life may be experienced as reassuring or as enslaving or both at different times, but they are not fully escapable, however much technology allows us to force the pace and the market urges us to do so. Unseasonal lambing may now be possible and almost obligatory, but nothing can alter the winter temperatures that threaten newborn lives.

Rural life at what we may think its most characteristic is about making humanly habitable and usable a landscape that is deeply resistant to human management. Of course the countryside is a 'made' landscape (this is sometimes said nowadays as if it were a new discovery); that's what agriculture is about. And even when agriculture accounts for a relatively tiny part even of a rural economy, as is increasingly the case, the rural dweller, commuter as much as anyone else, is unavoidably aware of weather and seasons and the problems they pose. Indeed, some would say that the impulse of some town-dwellers to move into the countryside is something to do with a dissatisfaction with the overprotected atmosphere of urban life; almost as if an urge to be a bit more vulnerable were rooted in human beings, as if there were a sense of something significant lost in a protected environment. Country living, country pastimes, like the increasing popularity of 'wild' trekking holidays, show some feeling for what it is that atrophies in us if we are defended from the inexorable confronting of our physical limits. And some recent television programmes, extrapolating from present trends to the possible breakdown of our systems of protection (the collapse of the electricity grid or the water supply), have starkly reminded us that even the most apparently controlled physical environment is not infinitely exploitable and malleable.

Once again we are returned to a theology of our creaturehood, our location within processes given for our use but not our domination. Much in contemporary culture encourages a covert picture of human identity in terms of a sovereign will, only loosely connected with physical constraints. But, as St Augustine memorably put it, only when we come down to earth are we able to rise with Christ; the mind and will, so long as they entertain fictions about their isolation and sovereignty, cannot appropriate the good news that the material world itself is transfigured by the resurrection, and that the society of material and historical persons is transfigured by the communion of the Holy Spirit, through absolution by God and reconciliation with each other.

Is this part of the good news that rural experience, and the rural experience of Christian faith, offers to urban? If so, it may give one or two clues as to what the churches should be reflecting on in the rural context, even on that most difficult question of how the actual shape of rural church life maintains a distinct identity.

Conclusion

It will not do in our mission to assume that evangelism and the routine of worship in the countryside can or should be a straight transfer from urban, let alone suburban patterns; some of the malaise and frustration that are felt in rural churches have to do with this, with expectations brought from elsewhere, as well as expectations formed by a fantasy past. Part of what I have been suggesting, and part of the whole thrust of this book, is that so far from our living in the afterglow of a golden age of rural piety which has characterized the greater part of Christian history, it would be more accurate to say that rural faith is still finding its distinctive voice. And that cannot be resolved by importing styles and structures formed in other settings. The current economic and social challenges are enormous, as these essays show; but happily they also show that the response of the churches is increasingly serious and creative, conscious of the diversity of rural lives. We can reasonably hope that ahead of us lies a new level of engagement with mission in this environment.

Name Index

Subject Index